The Vietnam Veterans Memorial at Angel Fire

MODERN WAR STUDIES

William Thomas Allison
General Editor

Raymond Callahan
Jacob W. Kipp
Allan R. Millett
Carol Reardon
Dennis Showalter
David R. Stone
James H. Willbanks
Series Editors

Theodore A. Wilson
General Editor Emeritus

The Vietnam Veterans Memorial at Angel Fire
War, Remembrance, and an American Tragedy

Steven Trout

 University Press of Kansas

© 2020 by the University Press of Kansas
All rights reserved
Third Printing

Published by the University Press of Kansas (Lawrence, Kansas 66045), which was organized by the Kansas Board of Regents and is operated and funded by Emporia State University, Fort Hays State University, Kansas State University, Pittsburg State University, the University of Kansas, and Wichita State University.

Library of Congress Cataloging-in-Publication Data
Names: Trout, Steven, 1963– author.
Title: The Vietnam Veterans Memorial at Angel Fire : war, remembrance, and an American tragedy / Steven Trout.
Other titles: War, remembrance, and an American tragedy
Description: Lawrence, Kansas : University Press of Kansas, [2020] | Series: Modern war studies | Includes bibliographical references and index.
Identifiers: LCCN 2019042784
  ISBN 9780700629336 (cloth)
  ISBN 9780700629343 (paperback)
  ISBN 9780700629350 (epub)
Subjects: LCSH: Vietnam Veterans Memorial (Angel Fire, NM)—History.
Classification: LCC F804.A64 T76 2020 | DDC 978.9/22—dc23
LC record available at https://lccn.loc.gov/2019042784.

British Library Cataloguing-in-Publication Data is available.

EU Authorised Representative Details: Easy Access System Europe | Mustamäe tee 50, 10621 Tallinn, Estonia | gpsr.requests@easproject.com

In memory of my father,
Conrad N. Trout
(May 30, 1938–February 26, 2019)

Victor Westphall and the Vietnam Veterans Peace and Brotherhood Chapel, 1972. Courtesy of Getty Images.

Contents

List of Illustrations   ix

Acknowledgments   xi

Introduction   1

1. Father and Son   15

2. A Casualty of Vietnam   55

3. Terrible News in a Beautiful Place   87

4. Peace and Brotherhood   119

5. A National Memorial   147

Epilogue: Phantoms of Peace and War   181

Notes   199

Bibliography   217

Index   225

Illustrations

Victor Westphall and the Vietnam Veterans Peace and Brotherhood
    Chapel, 1972   vi
The Chapel at Angel Fire viewed from the southeast   3
The chapel from the northeast   8
The chapel's west wall with the Moreno Valley in the background   11
The Westphall family's home   16
The living room of the Westphalls' custom-built home   17
Victor in one of his strongman poses, holding David aloft   22
Jeanne Westphall, July 1944   23
Ensign Victor Westphall in 1943   24
David and his father prior to Victor's deployment in the Pacific   27
Wings for Per   29
Victor and his two sons in front of the family trailer   35
The Westphall family in 1949   37
David, number 35, playing for Highland High School   40
David studying in his house in Missoula   48
Map of northern Quang Tri Province   57
The last-known photograph of David Westphall   78
Map of Leatherneck Square   81
The National Veterans Cemetery in Santa Fe   92
Jeanne Westphall with David, circa mid-1940s   105
Victor outside his cabin near the chapel, circa early 1970s   108
The photograph of David displayed in the chapel   114
Walter Westphall during pilot training at Craig Air Force Base,
    1969   116
The chapel as it appeared in November 1970   126
The interior of the chapel, circa late 1970s–early 1980s   142
The chapel at night   149
Victor in front of the chapel, *Parade*, November 1979   168

Victor inside the chapel, *Parade*, November 1979   169
Sign at the base of the hill during the memorial's status as a New Mexico state park   183
Walter with his family in 2013   187
Walter and Victor near the ambush site   188
The Viking Surprise with the chapel garden in the foreground   191
Dear Mom and Dad by Doug Scott   193
Army of the Republic of Vietnam remembrance bricks at Angel Fire   196
The chapel at dawn   197

Acknowledgments

This book tells the story of a remarkable memorial to American Vietnam War veterans and the equally remarkable family that built it. It was not an easy story to tell, and without the help of many different people, I would not have persevered.

Among these, no one played a larger role than Walter Westphall, whose kindness, readiness to fact-check details, and, most of all, patience never flagged. Walter could have reacted, understandably enough, with suspicion and coldness when I first approached him with this project. Instead, he welcomed me and told me whatever I wanted to know. If this book earns any praise at all, the credit goes to Walter, who never tried to steer me in one direction or another, even when the narrative touched upon sensitive topics and deeply painful memories. Any factual errors or blunders in logic are, of course, my doing.

Three members of the board of directors for the David Westphall Veterans Foundation met with me for face-to-face interviews and offered invaluable assistance. To these gentlemen—Chuck Howe, Dick Dickerson (a talented photographer, as readers of this book will see), and Chuck Hasford—I am forever indebted. Kate German, the superintendent of Vietnam Veterans Memorial State Park, likewise gave generously of her time in order to answer my many questions. Lanny Tonning, whom I have yet to meet in person, cheerfully agreed to a phone interview, which proved a great pleasure. Frank Richardson provided his vivid impressions of Victor Westphall by email, and my friend Robert Adams presented me with a short essay chronicling his recent visit to the memorial. Jan Therkildsen, a master researcher, helped me track down a number of obscure newspaper articles.

I must also thank the wonderful staff at Texas Tech University's Vietnam Archive, especially Amy Kathleen Mondt; the ever-helpful librarians in the Interlibrary Loan Department of the Marx Library at the University of South Alabama, especially Rebecca Young; Kristina Polizzi and her colleagues in the Doy Leale McCall Rare Book and Manuscript Library; Lynne Chronister and Angela Jordan in the University of South Alabama Office of Research and Economic Development (this office generously helped cover the cost of indexing this volume); Milton Cohen, an accomplished scholar of American literature, and his lovely wife, Florence, who graciously opened their home to me while I stayed in Angel Fire conducting research; James P. Coan, who provided excellent maps of Northern Quang Tri Province and Leatherneck Square, as well as Dan Waterman of the University of Alabama Press, who facilitated my use of Mr. Coan's materials; Daniel Rogers, who photographed the Army of the Republic of Vietnam bricks at the memorial for me; Michael Satchell, who granted permission for the reproduction of photographs that originally formed part of his *Parade* article on the Westphalls' memorial; Jim Goss, who allowed me to include his wonderful photograph of Victor and Walter Westphall at the ambush site; John Slattery, a Marine Corps veteran of the Vietnam War who kindly read and critiqued my account of David Westphall's experiences overseas; and Mike Briggs, formerly the editor in chief at the University Press of Kansas, who understood immediately that this haunting memorial in New Mexico needed a book-length history. He understood because he had been there. Ted Wilson, the editor of the Modern War Studies series, and Joyce Harrison, who took Mike's place when he retired, could not have been more enthusiastic about the project or more understanding—especially as I missed one deadline after another. Other professionals at the University Press of Kansas—Kelly Chrisman Jacques, Andrea Laws, and Michael Kehoe—provided invaluable assistance throughout the publication process. And Amy Sherman, a superb copyeditor, improved the book considerably through her many corrections and queries.

Ron Milam, a history professor at Texas Tech and a member of the board of directors for the David Westphall Veterans Foundation, helped in many ways. I cannot thank him enough for his invitation to organize a panel on the Angel Fire memorial for "1968 and the Tet Offensive," a conference held at Texas Tech in 2018. Featuring Ron, Walter Westphall, and Carie Nguyen, that panel was simply electrifying. Moreover, Ron's excellent study *Not a Gentleman's War* gave me a better understanding of what David Westphall experienced as a marine junior officer in Vietnam in 1968.

Several scholars who know far more about the Vietnam War than I ever will—or about war remembrance in general—helped me write the best book I could. Bill Allison, David Anderson, Philip Beidler, John Bodnar, and Kyle Longley offered suggestions that improved the manuscript considerably. At the University of South Alabama, writer-in-residence Frye Gaillard, a good friend and a great prose stylist, offered continual encouragement. And so did my friends and colleagues Susan McCready, with whom I codirect the University of South Alabama's Center for the Study of War and Memory, and Ellen Harrington, Cris Hollingsworth, and Patrick Shaw, three of the English Department's finest. Jennifer Haytock, whose work on American war literature I so admire, also took a lively interest in the project. Andrzej Wierzbicki, dean of the College of Arts and Sciences at the University of South Alabama, provided important assistance by approving my sabbatical leave during the fall 2018 semester. Without this precious block of uninterrupted writing time, this book simply wouldn't exist. I deeply appreciate Dean Wierzbicki's understanding that department chairs must lead by example—by writing monographs, in my case. Three of my oldest and closest friends, Greg Farley, Daryl Palmer, and Bob Rook (whose magnificent photographs grace many of the pages in this book), never let me give up on the project. And neither did Martin Parsons, my dear friend in the United Kingdom.

Finally, I must thank my parents, Conrad and Lois Jean Trout, who read the original book proposal for this project and provided useful feedback (my father, alas, did not live to see the finished product), and my wife, Maniphone Sengsamouth-Trout, who was with me on the fateful day when I first visited Vietnam Veterans Memorial State Park in Angel Fire, New Mexico. After wandering through the chapel and the visitors center, Maniphone and I walked silently to our car, both feeling overwhelmed by the beauty and poignancy of this extraordinary memorial (about which we had previously known nothing). After all, as a Laotian American and a first-generation immigrant, Maniphone has her own complicated relationship with the Vietnam War. Before we had turned back onto the Enchanted Circle, I announced that my next book would tell the story of David Westphall and the remembrance he inspired. Maniphone instantly expressed her support, but she could hardly have suspected the length or complexity of this particular project. And so, I end these acknowledgments with yet another apology to my wife for having to arrange far too much of her life to fit the tyrannical demands of book authorship. I promise to wait—at least a year or two—before starting the next one.

Steven Trout

Introduction

> At the summit, 8500 feet above the daily routine,
> I was captivated by the purity of the Chapel's white
> steeple seemingly reaching for the clouds.
> —"*Reflections on the Angel Fire Memorial*," by Robert
> Adams, US Air Force, 1968–1972

> Your memorial has much more dignity than the
> one in Washington.
> —In a letter to Victor Westphall, December 18, 1982[1]

Northeast of Taos, New Mexico, a scenic drive known as the Enchanted Circle weaves its way through the Sangre de Cristo ("Blood of Christ") Mountains. If driven in a clockwise direction, this eighty-five-mile loop takes motorists north from Taos, through the high desert that is home to the nearby Rio Grande gorge, and up to the town of Questa, where the route turns east and climbs into the forested slopes of the Sangre de Cristo range. After ascending to Red River, a ski community located roughly at the circle's halfway point, the road drops south into the long, largely treeless Moreno Valley, flanked on one side by the massif that surrounds Wheeler Peak (the tallest mountain in New Mexico) and on the other by Eagle Nest Lake, a ribbon of gray, usually white-capped water. Just a few miles beyond the lake, shortly before the road bends westward to reconnect with Taos, a sign unexpectedly appears on the right: Vietnam Veterans Memorial.

Some of the drivers who turn off the Enchanted Circle and on to the small road that leads up to this out-of-way memorial have traveled thousands of miles with this specific destination in mind. Others are simply curious, perhaps wondering how a place connected with the Vietnam War came to be located amid a valley high in the Sangre de Cristos. But whether they are pilgrims or tourists simply passing through, visitors seldom leave the park without being profoundly moved, even shaken. To put it mildly, the place leaves an impression. Dramatically set on a hilltop overlooking the nearby resort community of Angel Fire, whose name it informally shares, the site consists of a collection of monuments and artifacts, all clustered around an unexpectedly large and dramatically designed chapel. Many of these commemorative objects seem familiar. Bricks engraved with the names of servicemen and servicewomen line the walkways, just as they do at many other American war memorials. Likewise, the bronze statue of a Vietnam-era infantryman, depicted writing a letter to his family, would look at home next to any Vietnam veterans memorial in the nation. And even Americans born long after 1973 will recognize the park's single military vehicle—a 1960s-vintage Bell UH-1 "Huey" helicopter, tilted forward on its concrete mooring as if lifting off from a hostile landing zone.

But the chapel that serves as the park's centerpiece—dazzlingly white, coated in stucco smoothed by hand, and reaching at its tallest end a height of nearly fifty feet—is unique. It is a beautiful but otherworldly structure that looks, at first sight, as if it might have been left behind by extraterrestrials. Visitors find it difficult to describe. To the writer Corinne Browne, who traveled to Angel Fire throughout the 1970s, the building rose out of the hill "like a wing." By day, it suggested "a ship's prow." At night, it reminded her of a "ghost's arm, pointing out to the stars."[2] To another visitor, the chapel resembled "a dove or a sea bird."[3] And to yet another, the building stood "at 8,500 feet like a great white angel spreading her wings across the Moreno Valley."[4] When viewed from the side, the chapel might also be likened to a gigantic thorn, an apt characterization, perhaps, given the pain that the building both symbolizes and seeks to assuage.

Originally known as the Vietnam Veterans Peace and Brotherhood Chapel, this enigmatic building predates everything else on the hilltop, and from 1971 to 1982 it served as America's only national memorial to veterans of the Vietnam War, a precursor to the Wall in Washington, DC.

The Chapel at Angel Fire viewed from the southeast. Photograph by Robert Rook.

Despite the best efforts of the memorial's founders and their allies, no governmental entity conferred or recognized this designation. However, the Chapel at Angel Fire was a national site just the same. Future presidential candidate John Kerry, then the spokesman for the Vietnam Veterans Against the War (VVAW), gave the main address at the memorial's dedication ceremony in 1971, and over the next decade tens of thousands of Vietnam veterans made pilgrimages to this remote corner of the American Southwest.

They came not only for the stunning mountain vistas and space for quiet reflection that the chapel offered but also for the opportunity to talk with its chief founder, Victor "Doc" Westphall, who personally greeted each and every veteran. As American involvement in Vietnam ended and the nation fell into a numbed silence regarding the conflict's meaning, the memorial at Angel Fire became one of the few places in the United States where veterans of the war in Southeast Asia could speak with someone who respected their service (even while condemning the policies that demanded it) and who understood their anguish, their guilt over having survived.

Victor understood all too well. Three years before the chapel opened its doors, he received word that his oldest son, a lieutenant in the Marine Corps, had been killed in Vietnam. Along with sixteen of his comrades, twenty-eight-year-old David Westphall died near the Marine stronghold at Con Thien (the "Hill of Angels"), the victim of an enemy ambush. Together with his surviving son, Walter, who would later serve in the Vietnam War as an Air Force pilot, and his wife, Jeanne, Victor set about creating a memorial to David and to all the other lives lost in the conflict that was still raging in Southeast Asia. The Westphalls would see that they were not forgotten. At the same time, through the chapel that honored their memory, the family would symbolize the urgent need to end war—all war—for good. New Mexico architect Ted Luna provided the blueprints for the memorial, envisioning an avant-garde structure that would, in Victor's words, leave none of its visitors with "quite the same attitude toward peace and war."[5] The grieving father provided the funding, which turned out to be nearly everything he had.

A highly successful homebuilder, who also held weightlifting records and who earned an interdisciplinary humanities doctorate from the University of New Mexico, the multitalented, ultra-energetic head of the Westphall household made a fortune during the post–World War II housing boom in Albuquerque. However, the ever-mounting cost of the chapel, which he continually improved, quickly consumed his resources. Victor launched the project with money from David's life insurance policy and then sold off the large ranch that he had acquired, for development purposes, in the Moreno Valley—all but the five hilltop acres upon which the memorial stood. Donations from veterans and their families also helped keep the venture afloat, but just barely.

In 1982, after years of financial struggle and fruitless attempts to interest federal authorities in the memorial, Victor persuaded the Disabled American Veterans (DAV) to assume financial responsibility for the site. However, his personal connection to the chapel and its mission of remembrance and peace only intensified—much to the detriment of his marriage, which David's death had already wounded. Eventually, Victor moved, without his wife, into a small apartment located at the back of a visitors center constructed adjacent to the chapel. He remained there, always delighting to shake the hands of Vietnam veterans and to talk with them (in some cases, transforming their lives through his suggestions and patient listening), until his death in 2003. Over the course of three decades, the memorial—its urgent message, its day-to-day upkeep, and, perhaps most importantly, the veterans it drew—had become his entire world. What follows is an account of extraordinary achievement, but also destructive obsession and governmental indifference. Few memorials in American history, either public or private, have demanded so much devotion from their founders or exacted such a terrible price.

A blend of biography, history, and memory scholarship, this book tells a story of annihilating grief and frenetic creation, followed by the sorts of unexpected twists and turns that so often make up the anything-but-static lives of public memorials. The narrative offers a history of a very specific site of memory, but also—and just as importantly—an intimate portrait of a troubled young man and the impact of his death on his parents and brother. David Westphall, as it turns out, is an interesting subject in his own right, a gifted wordsmith and lover of the humanities who—at least to an extent—discovered in military leadership and the adrenaline rush of combat a palliative for psychological demons that had plagued him since his childhood.

The first two chapters focus on the Westphalls, from Victor's brief but formative experience of homesteading in early twentieth-century Montana to David's final assignment in Vietnam. Chapter 1 begins with Victor's foundational experiences in the 1930s and 1940s. Who was this dynamic figure? And how did the Second World War, which he witnessed in the Pacific theater as an officer in the US Navy, help shape the values and convictions that he would later express through the memorial? At the very heart of the chapel's history are a father's love (along with a deep sense of guilt) and a loss so shattering that it transformed a successful entrepreneur and respected scholar into a self-appointed architect of public memory, a learned visionary to some, an obsessed crank to others. This section of the book locates the seeds of Victor's antiwar philosophy in his early life, long before family tragedy inspired him to enter the public arena as an unlikely apostle of world peace.

David moves to center stage in the chapter's second half, which covers his childhood and adolescence in Albuquerque, his disastrous marriage, and his decision to volunteer for a field assignment in Vietnam. Enhanced by the testimony contained in David's detailed and often beautifully written letters from Southeast Asia, chapter 2 chronicles Lieutenant Westphall's seven months of overseas service, from his arrival in Da Nang to his death on May 22, 1968.

The picture of David offered here is a complex one. Indeed, the details of his life, as recorded in his correspondence and in a biography (titled *David's Story*) penned by his father, complicate the narratives employed in his commemoration. As we will see, he thought little, for example, of the kind of antiwar ideology that Victor would later promote. Along with other political hawks at the time, David believed wholeheartedly in stopping the spread of communism one potential domino at a time. And although evidence suggests that he was frustrated by the US military's appallingly ineffective strategies and tactics in Vietnam, he remained a committed Cold Warrior to the end.

He was also, for many of his twenty-eight years, a profoundly unhappy young man. Part of that unhappiness came from his father. As one might expect, given Victor Westphall's volcanic energy and unflagging self-discipline, the relationship between parent and child was a stormy, often tortured one. A gifted high school athlete, David might have achieved renown as a football player were it not for his anxiety-induced clumsiness on the field, caused by his father's unrelenting expectations, and Victor's know-it-all attitude when dealing with his son's coaches. More than once, Victor's well-intentioned meddling robbed his son of opportunities. Convinced of his personal unattractiveness, David also found relationships with women difficult. In 1962, he married Mary Lynne Willmarth, a former classmate from Highland High School in Albuquerque. On the eve of their wedding he apparently suffered a nervous breakdown, and just three years later the couple divorced.

Thus, when he departed for Vietnam as a second lieutenant in 1967, David left behind a series of disappointments and half starts—frustrated athletic ambitions, a broken marriage, and an earlier, largely unsatisfactory four-year stint as an enlisted man in the Marine Corps. But not everything in his life had been so bleak. In order to qualify for officer's training, he enrolled at the University of Montana in 1965 and pursued a bachelor's degree in Spanish with subspecialties in Russian and history. It was his happiest time. Finally freed from the burdens of athletics and marriage, he impressed his professors with his intellect and challenged them with his conservative views.

And during a trip to Mexico, which he took to improve his language fluency, he met a young schoolteacher named Irene de la Rosa Fuentes, who seemed to understand him instantly. Happiness perhaps beckoned as never before in David's life. But then, all too quickly, came his deployment to a combat zone in Vietnam, which he welcomed, and that fateful encounter with enemy forces near the Hill of the Angels.

Focused primarily on the eleven-year period when the chapel served as a de facto national Vietnam veterans memorial, chapters 3 through 5 examine the intersection of personal loss and public remembrance. Chapter 3 offers a detailed account of the Westphall family's initial reaction to David's death, the decision to create a memorial in his honor (which started with Jeanne), and the planning and construction of the chapel. The memorial's rise to national prominence in the early 1970s receives consideration in chapter 4. Here Victor's personal appraisal of

The chapel from the northeast. Photograph by Robert Rook.

the American mission in Vietnam, as well as his hopes for a world without war (expressed through the memorial and through his peace scholarship), figure prominently, along with his controversial gestures of forgiveness toward the North Vietnamese government.

During its first decade, the Vietnam Veterans Peace and Brotherhood Chapel perhaps attracted upward of a hundred thousand visitors, mostly veterans and their families. However, by the late 1970s the torrent of pilgrims had become a proverbial trickle, and the memorial's founders, struggling to meet ever-increasing operating costs, confronted the bleak possibility of the memorial's imminent closure. Chapter 5 focuses on the Westphalls' quixotic efforts to secure federal recognition for the site, as a means of moving it to a secure financial footing, followed by their successful wooing of the DAV, an initially promising development that soon led to rancor. In particular, this chapter follows the legislative campaign led by New Mexico senator Pete Domenici, one of the memorial's most indefatigable advocates. Throughout the mid-to-late 1970s, Domenici repeatedly introduced bills in the US Congress calling for the recognition of the chapel as a national monument. But to no avail. And when he attempted to graft funding for Angel Fire onto legislation supporting a national Vietnam War memorial in Washington, DC—what would become eventually become the Wall—he again met with defeat. Among other things, this chapter offers a case study in the politics of remembrance, a subject in which the Westphalls (Walter in particular) became painfully well versed.

A brief epilogue brings the memorial's story up to the present day, chronicling both changes in ownership and modifications made to the Westphalls' original conception. The latter are extensive. Indeed, the memorial today might best be termed a memorial complex. The epilogue considers the implications of the multiple monuments—the engraved bricks, for example—that now sit alongside the chapel's avant-garde architecture.

Before embarking upon the complex history of the Westphalls' memorial at Angel Fire, readers may benefit from a brief comparison of the Vietnam Veterans Peace and Brotherhood Chapel with a more familiar structure built in response to the same conflict—namely, the National Vietnam War Veterans Memorial in Washington, DC, also known as the Wall. Almost from the moment of its inception, the latter has represented nothing less than a full-blown cultural phenomenon. Designed by the Chinese American architect Maya Lin, who was just twenty-one years old at the time, the monument has attracted more attention—and controversy—than any other war memorial in American history, including the Tomb of the Unknowns at Arlington National Cemetery and the USS *Arizona* Memorial at Pearl Harbor.[6]

And if imitation truly is the highest form of flattery, then the appeal of Lin's creation is beyond question. The number of derivative designs, each featuring a wall of some sort inscribed with names, built on university campuses and next to courthouses and city halls across America, must run in the hundreds, and even memorials to the veterans of later conflicts, such as the Iraq War, typically invoke the same basic aesthetic.

Differences between the chapel designed by Luna and the Wall could not be starker or more revealing. Although avant-garde, Lin's initially controversial design, frequently likened by its critics to an unsightly wound or gash (because of its location below ground level), was nevertheless vetted by the federal Fine Arts Commission, scrutinized by Congress, and ultimately situated on coveted ground just yards from the Lincoln Memorial. The memorial's success as one of the most cathartic and talked-about commemorative structures in the world stems in part from the fact that the American public *had* to come to terms with its cryptic black surface. The weight of official sanction (albeit sanction secured by a determined grassroots movement) demanded no less.

In contrast, the chapel at Angel Fire exemplifies historian John Bodnar's notion of "vernacular remembrance"—remembrance, in other words, that is organic, spontaneous, and created by individuals with a direct connection to a past historical event and a deep emotional stake in its representation.[7] To push the Southwestern connection a bit, one might even assert that the Angel Fire memorial, a national shrine established without the support or endorsement of the federal government and in an out-of-the-way mountain location, falls into the category of outlaw or renegade commemoration. Part of its appeal resides in the sheer audacity of its creators.

Moreover, the designs of these two memorials are literally as different as night and day. Constructed of black granite, the Wall confronts its viewer with a set of names—and little else, apart from the viewer's reflected image. (The statue of three American infantrymen located nearby was, we should recall, erected as a concession to critics and does not derive from the architect's vision.) At least explicitly, Lin's memorial neither justifies nor condemns the events that produced the 58,183 fatalities recorded in chronological order, year by year, on its surface; however, the architect's choice of color and her decision to situate the memorial so that visitors must *descend* into it do perform a rhetorical function (as opponents of the design were well aware), setting the monument apart from all others on the Mall.

The chapel at Angel Fire, on the other hand, functions as a far more ambivalent piece of visual rhetoric. A tribute to veterans *and* a hymn to peace (or, rather, to "Peace and Brotherhood"), the memorial's curved white form, so strikingly distinct from the straight lines and sharp angles that characterize so many Vietnam War memorials, expresses both grief and hope. The structure is at once ghostly *and* inspiring. The chapel's dramatic peak, which draws the eye skyward and mirrors the surrounding mountains, makes a defiant statement, symbolizing liberation from the false promises of war.

The chapel's west wall with the Moreno Valley in the background. Photograph by Robert Rook.

In contrast, the Wall is almost oppressively horizontal.[8] Its point of maximum elevation, precisely at the center, draws its meaning from statistics: the top edge of the monument rises gently to accommodate the list of fatalities from 1968, America's bloodiest year in Southeast Asia, and then descends, mirroring the onset of Vietnamization. Thus, while one memorial seems determined not to engage with the question of what the Vietnam War means, arguably as a way to avoid reopening old cultural wounds, the other plaintively insists that meaning *must* exist, that a better world is yet possible through the study and interpretation of the past.

Played out on a grand scale against the backdrop of the American Southwest, the Westphall family's effort to translate personal tragedy into enduring physical commemoration is an ageless tale of elemental emotions and impulses—none more basic, perhaps, than the desire to memorialize a lost family member. To study the Chapel at Angel Fire is to study remembrance in its rawest, most urgent form.

But like the gnarled history of the conflict in which David Westphall died, the story of the place that honors his memory is, at the same time, complicated and multilayered. Indeed, it is many things at once—a poignant family drama, a testament to the power of place, and an especially revealing case study in the malleability of collective memory over time. Each transfer of the memorial's title (from the Westphall family to the DAV, from the DAV to the David Westphall Veterans Foundation, and from the foundation to the state of New Mexico) has resulted in modifications to the site that alter its original message and, to some extent, reflect the process through which Americans have come to terms—or, if one prefers, have *avoided* coming to terms—with the Vietnam War.

Built up over time, like sedimentary rock, the layered meaning of the Angel Fire memorial begins, of course, with the opinions of its formidable chief creator. As shaped by Victor, who enjoyed the freedom to build whatever kind of monument he liked, the original, unmodified Vietnam Veterans Peace and Brotherhood Chapel was a place not of suspended argument and common ground but of iconoclastic protest and radicalism. For Victor, who saw a direct link between the wanton destruction unleashed by the United States on North and South Vietnam (and their neighboring countries) and the specter of nuclear Armageddon, healing from the cultural wounds of the Vietnam War would come only when Americans recognized the conflict as a fateful mistake, as an ominous "hinge of destiny" opening on an age of national irresponsibility and decadence.

The chapel that Victor completed in 1971 served three functions: first, to memorialize the fatalities of the Vietnam War (starting with David); second, to pay tribute to the conflict's American veterans (whom Victor perceived, with good reason, as grossly mistreated by the American public and by their government); and, third, to underscore the waste and futility of armed conflict in general, an especially urgent message during the era of mutually assured destruction via intercontinental nuclear weapons. Victor could not have felt more deeply the need to honor citizen soldiers who had unfairly borne the blame for an unpopular, morally ambiguous conflict, but he also wanted the chapel to signify something much greater than patriotic tribute. Thus, less than a year after his son's death, he wrote to North Vietnamese president Ho Chi Minh, requesting photographs of

NVA soldiers who had been killed while fighting American forces. The photographs, he explained, would go on the wall of his chapel, next to those of his son and the other marines slain near Con Thien. (Since Ho died the day before Victor penned his letter, nothing ever came of this request.) And as if this remarkable gesture were not enough to demonstrate his conciliatory attitude toward the North Vietnamese, Victor made the following remark during an interview with a *New York Times* reporter two years later: "If I found out that the person who had killed my son . . . in turn had been killed, I would put his photo in the chapel."[9] In short, Victor's conception of the Angel Fire memorial spotlighted American veterans, to be sure, but at the same time ventured into new and uncharted territory by daring to reach out to the enemy. It's hard to think of anything else quite like this in the history of American war commemoration.

In Victor's mind, at least, these aims worked together harmoniously. Nevertheless, it could be argued that from the outset his goals for the chapel were at odds with one another. Even if we set aside the tension between the national and international dimensions of his vision, a difficult question remains: How can a memorial honor those who served while simultaneously denouncing war as the ultimate evil? According to the writer Chris Hedges, public sites identified with war memory simply can't stand up to the strain of such conflicting objectives. Thus, whatever their intentions, monuments to the "fallen" (to use one of the many euphemisms that constitute the rhetoric of remembrance) invariably wind up concealing the suffering and waste produced by military violence: "War memorials and museums," Hedges writes, "are temples to the god of war. The hushed voices, the well-tended grass, the flapping of the flags allow us to ignore how and why our young died."[10]

Hedges's assessment arguably fits most American war memorials with some degree of accuracy (one thinks, in particular, of the neocelebratory National World War II Memorial), but certainly not the chapel that the Westphalls created at Angel Fire. Even today, surrounded by more familiar commemorative apparatus such as the engraved bricks and the bronze statue of the in-country soldier writing home, the chapel remains an eerie place like no other. Its unique atmosphere derives primarily from a disorienting blend of public and private space. The rather cryptic poetry from David Westphall inscribed on the entrance (in place of the sort of official rhetoric that one would expect) and the prominence of his photograph, displayed alongside twelve other fatalities, give one the uncomfortable impression of having intruded upon a family shrine. There is nothing abstract about the grief signified by the chapel; this grief comes across with such raw, intimate force that a visitor cannot help but feel, at least for a moment or two, like an interloper or a voyeur.

However, while the chapel continues—palpably, even unnervingly—to convey Victor Westphall's original antiwar message, the rest of the commemorative apparatus found at Angel Fire today promotes various, sometimes competing meanings that have been grafted onto the memorial over time. As we will see, how and why the memorial changed is an important part of its history, one that raises some big questions: What does this site in New Mexico tell us, in microcosm, about the evolution of Vietnam War memory in the United States and, just as importantly, about the ways in which twenty-first-century Americans think about conflict and peace in general? Is a true peace memorial, one free of internal contradictions and rival ideological agendas, even possible in post-9/11 America? And is the Vietnam Veterans Memorial at Angel Fire, whatever its compromises and departures from the Westphalls' original agenda, perhaps the closest thing we have to such a memorial?

For more than a decade, the Westphall family's chapel at Angel Fire stood alone, unrivaled in scale or popularity, as *the* memorial to the veterans of a war that many Americans wished to quietly forget. Then, ironically enough, another memorial to that same conflict, easily the most celebrated of all twentieth-century American war memorials, virtually obliterated public memory of this remarkable site in the Sangre de Cristos. In 2019 relatively few people beyond the Taos area realize that the Wall in Washington, DC, was (official status not withstanding) the *second* national memorial to American veterans of the Vietnam War. Propelled by grief, a desire to see American veterans appropriately honored, and rage at the stupidity of armed conflict, a New Mexico family, led by a human dynamo, got there first, albeit without governmental recognition. This book tells that family's story, which begins with the relationship between a father and son.

1

Father and Son

What was it that had seemingly put me out of step with America's current mood of indifference and was instead driving me with a passion toward an experience that would exceed what I had envisioned?
–*Jim Brown*, Impact Zone: The Battle of the DMZ in Vietnam, 1967–1968 (2004)

Then I will fly up into the clear, washed air of spring and soar over the eagle's nest and over my home under the crag.
–*Ingri d'Aulaire and Edgar Parin d'Aulaire*, Wings for Per (1944)

In November 1952, the *New Mexico Sun Trails* magazine featured on its front cover a magnificent house recently custom-built in the rugged Sandia Mountains overlooking Albuquerque. Selected as the "*Sun Trails* House of the Month," the two-story structure was like no other. Steel columns lifted the house from its "solid rock base," thereby allowing the front portion to protrude over the edge of a hillside, while its many windows, shaded by custom awnings, looked out on "a vista of mountain, mesa, and valley."[1]

No power lines ran up to the residence. Instead, butane gas, stored in a thousand-gallon tank located outside the main structure, fueled the generators that provided electricity and furnace heat for the interior, as well

The Westphall family's home as pictured in the New Mexico Sun Trails *magazine, November 1952.* New Mexico Sun Trails, November 1952.

as temperature control for an indoor swimming pool. The same system pumped water from a nearby spring. Like the building's precisely chosen elevation and well-engineered power system, its floor plan reflected great care. The most dramatic space was the living room, with its high ceiling, fireplace, and lofty front windows, which took up an entire wall and filled the room with high-desert sunlight. From a balcony that wrapped around two sides of the living room, one accessed the main floor of the home, which consisted of the study, the kitchen and baths, and the bedrooms. One of these bedrooms, designed for two sons, faced the Rio Grande Valley and sensibly featured a folding door in the middle, which, when closed, gave each boy the same amount of private space.

Although owned by a recently successful Albuquerque entrepreneur, the house had none of the ostentation or conspicuous consumption associated with the nouveau riche. Instead, clean lines and an absence of clutter defined the structure, which was notable for the practicality and common sense of its floor plan. It was the setting, more than the design (ultra-modern though it was), that turned this mountain home into a grand gesture.

Father and Son 17

The living room of the Westphalls' custom-built home; Victor Westphall on balcony.
New Mexico Sun Trails, *November 1952.*

In one of the photographs that accompany the article, the home's owner, Victor Westphall, stands at the balcony in the living room "look[ing] with pleasure" at the largest interior space.[2] He is a muscular figure—a habitual weightlifter, in fact—with sleeves rolled up over his large biceps. At a glance, one can see that the camera has not captured a man gloating over a status symbol. Instead, Victor's physical attitude is one of satisfaction over a thing done right—to his demanding specifications.

The *New Mexico Sun Trails* captured more than a remarkable building in this article. A snapshot of success, the piece celebrates the attainment of the so-called American dream amid a Southwestern landscape of seemingly limitless possibilities and resources. And Victor Westphall—a homebuilder and developer, appropriately enough, who made his fortune in the postwar New Mexico housing boom—is the article's pioneering, self-reliant Western hero, the creator of a thoroughly modern domicile set apart from the rest of suburbia, off the grid, literally anchored to the seemingly inhospitable terrain of the Sandia Mountains.

No one among the Westphalls—not Victor, nor his wife, Jeanne, nor their two sons, David and Walter—could have predicted how events in a then little-known territory of French Indochina would conspire to shatter this sunlit picture of the American dream obtained. Sixteen years after his appearance in the *Sun Trails* article, on May 22, 1968, David Westphall, one of the two boys who shared that bedroom overlooking the Rio Grande Valley, joined the more than fifty-eight thousand American soldiers killed in Vietnam, and, through his death, sent the rest of the family on a journey they could never have anticipated.

One is tempted to write that the Vietnam War shattered everything captured by the *Sun Trails* photographer in 1952. But this wouldn't be entirely accurate. For the Westphall family, the war certainly changed a great deal, and with great cruelty. Beyond the grief it inflicted, a grief that only parents who have outlived a child or siblings who have lost a brother or sister can fully understand, David's death also meant the end of Victor Westphall's successful business and, ultimately, his hard-earned fortune. The American dream, which he had gripped so securely in the years before David's demise, quickly slipped from his fingers, replaced by a nobler dream that unfortunately sometimes also smacked of destructive monomania.

However, from another perspective, the construction and maintenance of the memorial at Angel Fire, Victor's raison d'être from 1968 onward, simply represented his formidable energies and skills redirected toward a new and not altogether dissimilar object. He felt this himself and remarked on several occasions that everything in his life up to and including the loss of David prepared him for this colossal remembrance project. The once successful home builder became, if you will, a full-time architect of his son's remembrance, as well as public memory, which he approached with the same focus and flair for design so compellingly displayed in the *Sun Trails* Home of the Month.

People who met Victor Westphall while he lived at the Angel Fire memorial often came away from the encounter feeling that they had undergone a religious experience (and not simply because the memorial took the form of a chapel). Especially during his senior years, Victor displayed a rare gift for establishing rapport, and he seemed, by all accounts, to instantly—sometimes uncannily—understand virtually everyone he met. An often repeated note of awe, combined with a sense that the man's larger-than-life personality somehow eluded description, dominated the remembrances of Victor offered by veterans interviewed for this book. However, to understand the complicated young man memorialized at Angel Fire, we must first try to understand his equally complicated father, a father whose struggles and achievements become all the more impressive if we view him not as a saint but as a flawed human being with immense talents and equally immense blind spots.

The son of Vic and Sadie Westphall (a family name that went all the way back to the time of William the Conqueror), Victor Walter Westphall II was born on October 13, 1913, near the tiny town of Hebron, Wisconsin. An event from the earliest years of his life, just barely remembered, perhaps played a significant and enduring role in his character and values. When he was just two years old, his parents embarked upon a three-year adventure in the wilderness of north-central Montana, where they joined Sadie's parents and siblings on a large homestead twenty-two miles north of Great Falls, then the fastest-growing boomtown in the American West. Even though he was a toddler at the time, Victor seemed to absorb the toughness, ingenuity, and work ethic that the experience demanded of his parents, qualities that became central to his personality.

In Big Sky Country, there were blizzards to contend with—weather that could literally kill—along with rattlesnakes, coyotes, and swarms of mosquitoes that brought misery during the otherwise all-too-brief spring and summer seasons. The family lived in a tar-papered shanty with a single cookstove for heat. And the labor necessary for even basic tasks was unending. To find water—a priceless commodity for homesteaders—Vic Westphall hand-dug no fewer than five wells, one of which descended more than thirty feet (without ever yielding a single drop).[3] Picking up the family mail meant a forty-mile round trip by horseback.[4]

Then, almost as soon as it had begun, the adventure was over. Insufficient crop yields, combined with free-falling grain prices (triggered by the end of the Great War), forced the family to retreat to Great Falls. Several months later they returned to the family farm in Wisconsin, where Victor would spend the rest of his childhood and adolescence.

In the fall of 1919, Victor and his younger sister Laura entered the Monroe Public School, a one-room schoolhouse. As some of his friends later wrote, Victor's eight years of study in this modest academic environment marked the initial stage of "his formal education and a quest for knowledge that would never end."[5] From the start, this future PhD was a voracious reader and a compulsive writer.

Following a memorable family vacation in Montana in 1927, Victor became a freshman at Fort Atkinson High School, where he soon caught the attention of a teacher named Mary Spry, who recognized his potential as an educator and historian. With her encouragement, he successfully applied to Whitewater Teachers College. After completing the single year of study required at Whitewater for a rural teaching certificate, the eighteen-year-old decided to extend his education by entering Milwaukee State Teachers College and working on an undergraduate degree in art history.

Photographs of Victor in his late teens and early twenties show that he quickly developed an extraordinary physique. Though not a tall man (at just five feet six), he was nevertheless an imposing figure with massive thighs, a barrel chest, and well-defined shoulder and arm muscles. More than anything, he wished to excel at football. But when this didn't happen, because of injuries sustained during his senior year in high school and his freshman year of college, he focused on weightlifting and became a champion in the light heavyweight division.

Physical fitness remained one of Victor's manias throughout his entire life. Visitors to his office at the Angel Fire memorial noted the chin-up bar that ran between two walls. Victor used it well into his seventies. Even as an elderly man, he also jogged and bicycled—religiously, regardless of weather or trail conditions.

In 1937 the college junior fell in love with Jeanne Vivian Mary Watson, a vivacious, good-humored young woman who first met Victor while she was working behind the counter of a Milwaukee ice cream parlor. The lithe brunette and the brawny weightlifter made a striking couple, and Victor was characteristically dogged—one might say relentless—when it came to courtship. Jeanne later joked, "Victor chased me so much, I couldn't get away."[6] In some respects their relationship proved the old adage that opposites attract. Jeanne was outgoing and enjoyed a good laugh. Victor could sometimes come across as rather severe. Yet they complemented each other well, and their partnership over the next half century would triumph over every challenge but one, the most terrible challenge a couple can face.

Victor and Jeanne married on September 15, 1938. The following June, Victor completed his art history degree. To say that the newlyweds' income was meager at first would be an understatement. Jeanne continued to work in the ice cream parlor for a time, but the responsibility for covering living expenses, including the rent for their one-room apartment, fell primarily on Victor, who passed through a series of jobs conspicuously unrelated to art history. After overseeing a local playground and community center, which of course paid a pittance, he accepted a position with the Cutler-Hammer Manufacturing Company, where he assembled electrical components for US Navy submarines. From Cutler-Hammer, he quickly moved on to a modest managerial position with the Milwaukee branch of the Lien Chemical Company, a producer of cleaning products for toilets.

The Westphalls welcomed their first child, Victor David Westphall III (seven pounds, four ounces), on January 30, 1940. Unlike his father and grandfather, this particular Victor would go by his middle name and spend most of his life outside the state of Wisconsin. He would also be the first Westphall in generations to die on a continent other than North America.

During the summer of 1941 Victor seized the chance to apply at least some of his education to a full-time job. He accepted a position as program director for the YMCA office at Fort Dodge, Iowa, and moved his growing family south. There, on December 31, 1942, Jeanne gave birth to the couple's second son, Walter Douglas Westphall, who would go by

Victor in one of his strongman poses, holding David aloft. Courtesy of Walter Westphall.

Jeanne Westphall, July 1944. Courtesy of Walter Westphall.

his middle name until his early twenties and by his first afterward. This narrative uses the latter throughout.

The Westphalls remained in Iowa until the winter of 1943, when Victor entered the US Navy. At that point Jeanne and her two sons returned to Wisconsin, where, apart from a few trips to meet up with Victor at various training posts in the United States, they remained for the duration of the war. During Victor's service in the Pacific, which lasted more than nineteen months, they would receive regular letters from him—loving letters full of details about his adventures and often decorated with well-executed pencil drawings that revealed yet another of this Renaissance man's myriad talents.

Assigned to Harbor Defense, Ensign Westphall embarked for Guadalcanal early in 1944, and from there traveled to his post on Ondanga, a jungle-covered speck of land rife with malaria and other equatorial maladies near

Ensign Victor Westphall in 1943. Courtesy of Walter Westphall.

the coast of New Georgia in the Solomon Islands chain. Fortunately, enemy activity in the air and water around New Georgia was rare by then, and Victor fought off boredom and (for a time) staved off disease by ramping up his weight training and devising new physical challenges for himself. To create a suitable barbell, he welded two 50-caliber machine gun barrels together. From scrap metal he fashioned weights. But Victor's characteristically self-disciplined attention to health and fitness could keep the jungle at bay only for so long, and in the summer of 1944 he succumbed to a severe case of fungal infection.[7] Weeks of treatment followed, first in a hospital in the Munda Islands, then in Brisbane, Australia.

By October, Victor was again ready for action, and he received orders to proceed to the island of Leyte in the Philippines, where the war was still very much in progress. In fact, Leyte was such a hot spot that it took Victor weeks to reach his destination—Tacloban, the capital city of the island and home to a vital runway only recently captured from the Japanese. Few American aircraft, other than combat planes, risked going there, and Victor managed to follow his travel orders only by catching an unauthorized ride aboard a courier plane loaded with important generals and, ominously enough, blood plasma.

Expecting another assignment in Harbor Defense, Victor learned, upon arrival, that the navy now had a different role for him—that of military postmaster. (A similarly unexpected shift in command responsibilities would happen to David when he arrived in Vietnam almost a quarter century later.) Victor became good at his new job, and proud of it, but he now lived in a lethal war zone, a place far different from the sleepy (if uncomfortable) backwater of Ondanga. A sign at the entrance of the American base at Tacloban read "World's Busiest Airstrip," which, whether true or not, conveyed the magnitude of the air power quickly concentrated there—and the attractiveness of the place as a target for the enemy.[8]

Whenever possible, the now dwindling but still defiant Japanese air force pounded Tacloban, sometimes appearing to aim directly for Douglas MacArthur's headquarters, and dogfights between American fighter planes and Japanese Zeros periodically swirled overhead. On November 24, 1944, a pair of larger-scale air raids, one conducted in broad daylight and the other at night, plastered the Tacloban runway with bombs, left several aircraft ablaze, and killed eight Americans. Victor watched the daylight raid from underneath his mail truck. On another occasion, a Japanese twin-engined bomber swooped down on the airstrip carrying a "suicide demolition squad."[9] Antiaircraft fire hit the plane and sent it careening into a parked American night fighter, killing all nine of the would-be saboteurs, as well as two Americans on the ground.

Such incidents began to run together, combined with senseless accidents and snafus straight out of Joseph Heller's *Catch-22*. In an instance of so-called friendly fire, an American bomb once accidentally landed exactly where Victor usually parked his truck. Several days later, he watched as two American aircraft—one landing, the other taking off—collided on the runway. The world's busiest airport was often far too busy.

Before long the atmosphere of death and disaster at Tacloban touched Victor on a personal level. While rushing to help a group of navy men wounded by Japanese antipersonnel bombs, he saw a Filipino boy run over by an American jeep, a moment of horror that would stay with him for the rest of his life. And in January 1945 he received word that his mother, Sadie, had died of pneumonia more than week earlier. Prone to superstition, Victor often looked for patterns in random events, and in his wartime journal he speculated on a possible link between these two tragedies: "I wonder if Mother's death was somewhat predicted by the horrible death of the little Filipino boy I saw killed by a jeep."[10]

Still shaken by loss, Victor then witnessed the worst runway collision yet at Tacloban: fearful of hitting an approaching aircraft, a transport pilot aborted takeoff at the last moment and slammed the plane into several parked bombers, including two gigantic B-24s. The resulting explosions and fires killed thirty-six Americans and wounded fifty others.[11] Although the Japanese military presence in the Philippines was by now decimated— the battle of Leyte Gulf in October 1944 cost the Imperial Navy nearly thirty irreplaceable war ships and several hundred aircraft—Lieutenant Westphall's corner of the war remained a dangerous and unpredictable place.[12]

Meanwhile, back in Wisconsin, David missed his father intensely (though he formed few lasting memories of this period), and he greeted the postman each day with an anxious inquiry. Nothing made him happier than

David and his father prior to Victor's deployment in the Pacific. Courtesy of Walter Westphall.

to receive Victor's skillfully illustrated letters from the Pacific. The Westphalls' eldest son was a complex child, made even more so by his father's absence, and as he entered kindergarten he developed a lively intelligence and an outgoing nature that made him popular with other children (though he could also be perfectly content spending time alone).[13]

But there were also dark moments in David's early childhood—moments that Victor later interpreted as warning signs of the inner turmoil that would characterize so much of his son's adult life. During a visit to the Westphall home in Hebron, David repeatedly closed the door to his recently deceased grandmother's bedroom because, as he calmly explained, there were "ghosts in there." To Jeanne it sometimes seemed eerily as if the boy saw and understood things that adults could not: "He just talks and thinks above our heads."[14] David's self-consciousness over his appearance, a source of torture for him later, also separated him from other children. Indeed, although not unattractive, David never reconciled himself to his appearance. At age twenty-one he wrote of "a feeling of being lost" that enveloped him whenever he looked in a mirror, and throughout his adulthood he made wistful references to plastic surgery.[15] The shape of his nose bothered him especially and became something of a fixation.

A far more positive behavioral pattern established during David's early childhood was his overwhelming attraction to the written word. David loved books, and his mother read to him constantly. After being introduced to a collection of bible stories one morning, four-year-old David carried the book around with him "for the rest of the day and went to sleep with it under his pillow."[16] But this was nothing compared with David's attachment to his favorite book, an attachment that tells us much about the circumstances of an early childhood spent in the shadow of the Second World War, as well as the kind of man David would later become. Among the children's books Jeanne acquired during Victor's absence, one title stood out from the start—*Wings for Per* (1944), by Ingri d'Aulaire and Edgar Parin d'Aulaire. Four-year-old David could not get enough of this particular narrative, which gripped his imagination even more firmly than bible stories. As Jeanne reported in a letter to Victor, "he and the book were inseparable from the moment he got it."[17]

A husband-and-wife team, the d'Aulaires were European émigrés (from Norway and Germany, respectively) who, after settling in Connecticut,

Wings for Per. *Author's collection.*

collaborated on a series of vividly illustrated titles for young readers. In *Wings for Per*, they created a memorable war story. Set in Ingri's native Norway, the book tells the story of Per, a boy who grows up happily on a magical farm overlooking a fjord. But soon war clouds darken Per's once bucolic childhood, as unspecified invaders—obviously German—seize control of his land.

Per and several of his companions take to an eagle's nest in the high mountains, where they operate a forbidden radio. Then, warned that the enemy has learned of their activities, they secure a fishing boat and make a daring escape to Great Britain. From there, Per journeys to the United States, and then on to Canada, where he enters a training program for bomber pilots. The book ends with the young warrior's dreams of soaring above his liberated homeland: "Then I will fly up into the clear, washed air of spring and soar over the eagle's nest and over my home under the crag. Mother will stand in front of the house and clasp her hands in wonder. She will say: 'Look, Per has wings.'"[18]

In 1967, as David prepared to leave his parents' home in New Mexico for a combat assignment in Vietnam, he gave his mother instructions to donate a number of books from his childhood collection to a local library. But he could not bring himself to part with *Wings for Per*. According to Victor, his son's "last action before going to the bus" was to hand the book to Jeanne. "I can't give this book," David said. "It's worth a million other books."[19] Characteristically, Victor and Jeanne discerned the presence of the supernatural in all this. *Wings for Per* ends with the image of its hero soaring above the "eagle's nest," where Per and his friends once stashed their secret radio. The Westphalls' property at the Val Verde Ranch, where the Angel Fire memorial would later be erected, overlooked a community in the Moreno Valley named none other than Eagle Nest. For the two grieving parents, the coincidence was too great. The ending of David's favorite children's book seemed eerily to predict his death or, rather, his spirit's return to the mountainous land of his parents.

Whatever its connections to the unseen world, *Wings for Per* perhaps also predicted—or even helped to establish—the core political convictions that inspired David's decision to serve in Vietnam. As the d'Aulaires made clear in their text, the invaders who ravaged Per's homeland managed to do so because "the fathers [of Norway] were too few and not well enough armed. They had believed in freedom and justice and had not been prepared to fight."[20] In other words, beyond its broad depiction of the Second World War as a contest between good and evil, *Wings for Per* offered its young American readers a more specific message: lack of military preparedness and naiveté about the aggressive motives of other nations spelled disaster for countries such as Norway.

Not surprisingly, given their generational status as so-called baby boomers (as the sons and daughters, in other words, of veterans discharged in 1945), many Americans who volunteered to serve in Vietnam viewed the war on communism through the lens of World War II—or, rather, the collective memory of the so-called Good War, reinforced by Hollywood, that permeated American culture in the 1950s. For example, author Philip Caputo, who arrived in Da Nang with a detachment of marines a full three years before David, reported that as a young man in the early 1960s he saw potential service in Vietnam as a way of "living out a fantasy" inspired by popular culture images of the island-hopping campaign in the Pacific. Caputo imagined himself "charging up some distant beachhead, like John Wayne in *Sands of Iwo Jima*, and then coming home a suntanned warrior with medals on [his] chest."[21] Another marine, artilleryman Dan Brown, remembered "taking it for granted" that *Sands* offered a model of patriotic service for all "'red-blooded Americans.'"[22] Historian John Bodnar reports that Caputo and Brown were not alone: a number of American enlistees in the Vietnam War later identified this particular John Wayne film as an "inspiration."[23]

In David's case, seductive cinematic imagery probably mattered less than the foreign policy lessons that World War II seemed to offer. After all, he studied history formally (like his father), and, as we will see, completed a bachelor's degree in the humanities—in Spanish, Russian, and history—at the University of Montana shortly before entering officer training. David even managed—posthumously—to place an article on Southwestern American history in a scholarly journal. Although this young historian may or may not have thought back to his favorite childhood book when forming his foundational political opinions, his conservative assessment of the situation in Vietnam reflected convictions not unlike those expressed by the d'Aulaires in 1944. For David, as for many Cold War volunteers, stopping the spread of aggressors bent on world domination (communists, in this case) depended on the recognition that, as stated in *Wings for Per,* "right does not stand without might."[24]

Once confronted directly with the confidence-draining ambiguities of the war in Southeast Asia, David's hawkish worldview, arguably formed at a young age and against the backdrop of World War II, suffered more than a few blows. Whether it would have collapsed altogether, had he survived his service in the field, is, of course, a question that cannot be answered.

In February 1945 Victor received transfer orders and said goodbye to the American base at Tacloban. Over the next several months, he established mail centers in Samoa, Mindanao, and Balikpapan, a port city (left in ruins by the Japanese) on the east coast of Borneo. The latter was to be a temporary assignment, but a snafu somewhere in headquarters kept Victor in Balikpapan, with comparatively little to do, for the remainder of the war.

But Victor had hardly seen the last of death and tragedy, and an experience on the eve of VJ Day left him with some of his bitterest memories of the war. With time on his hands, he became acquainted with a native doctor who supervised a civilian hospital "in a former Dutch Army barracks."[25] Victor never forgot his tour of this overcrowded facility, which held more than a thousand patients, most of them suffering from maladies, including vitamin deficiency, that could easily have been treated in peacetime. Among the people laid out on the concrete floor—for there were simply not enough beds—he saw "emaciated living skeletons," as well as islanders with gruesome wounds caused by military ordnance, human collateral damage left behind by the military contest between the Allies and Imperial Japan.[26] Shocked by this final spectacle of misery, Victor hardly knew how to feel when news of the Japanese surrender reached Balikpapan.

But his reunion with Jeanne and the boys several months later was a joyous event. Victor arrived home in time for the family to enjoy Christmas together and to celebrate the birthdays of David (now five) and Walter (three). Although he had not served in a combat role, the discharged lieutenant knew that this happy reunion might never have happened. He had seen too many disasters at Tacloban—and too much suffering, especially at Balikpapan—not to know that he was lucky.

Next to David's death, probably nothing affected Victor Westphall more than his service in the Second World War, and so it is worth pausing for a moment to consider the role that wartime experience may have played in his later philosophy of "peace and brotherhood." In many respects, the Second World War was a grand adventure for Victor, who had, after all, never set foot outside the United States before. Although it required a painful separation from his family and exposed him to considerable death and destruction (punctuated by boredom), his experience in the Pacific was, on one level, extraordinarily fulfilling—a chance for this son of homesteaders to demonstrate, more fully than he had ever had the opportunity to do back in Wisconsin or Iowa, his unique combination of talents.

But Victor also noted—and was haunted by—the waste and barbarity of armed conflict, and his radicalization, for want of a better term, following David's death in 1968 represented not a departure from his core values but an intensification of long-held beliefs. Indeed, Victor's moral qualms about war surfaced even before his service in the Pacific. Walter Westphall believes that his father quickly left the Cutler-Hammer Manufacturing Company in Milwaukee at least in part because "he did not like the idea of working for a company that built electrical components for military submarines."[27]

During his time in the Pacific, Victor felt all the emotions that one might expect, including satisfaction over the destruction of enemy ships and planes. For example, while stationed at Tacloban, he once received permission to "relay intelligence information freely" regarding the American invasion of the nearby island of Ormoc.[28] Thus, when a Japanese convoy tried to reinforce the island and was cut to pieces (with the loss of all fourteen vessels), he called out each and every victory to his comrades "minute by minute," displaying all the enthusiasm and excitement of a sports announcer.[29]

But more typically the conflict inspired somber reflection, and never more so than at its conclusion, when Victor witnessed something extraordinary that later became central to his thinking about peace and war. In 1981, he described the scene this way:

> This whole matter of friends and enemies is . . . an ephemeral thing. Given the complexities of international relations as they are practiced by the human race, today's enemies may become tomorrow's friends.
>
> This point was graphically illustrated to me immediately following cessation of hostilities in World War II. I was in Balikpapan, Borneo, at the time. The hatred of Australian soldiers for the Japanese was proverbial there, yet that same afternoon I saw Australian soldiers and Japanese prisoners of war bouncing along in an American Jeep laughing and joking as though they had been friends for years.[30]

According to Walter Westphall, this visionary moment stayed with his father, helping to fuel his "true and strong feelings about war" from 1945 to 1968.[31] However, two factors caused those feelings to recede temporarily into the background of Victor's life: first, like many discharged servicemen, this father of two put family, self-improvement through education, and the establishment of a successful business ahead of everything else. And, second, his "faith that [our] government would resort to war only when the need was great and the cause was just" helped rein in these reflections on the tragedy of armed conflict.[32]

In February 1946, the sudden discovery of tuberculosis lesions in Jeanne's lungs prompted the Westphall family's fateful decision to relocate, per doctor's orders, to a "high, dry climate." Albuquerque offered that climate, along with an opportunity for Victor to pursue a master's degree in history at the University of New Mexico. And so, after purchasing a camper trailer, the family embarked upon the epic 1,500-mile trip, repairing no fewer than eleven blown-out tires along the way.

At the end of the ten-day journey, they found themselves in a strange land as different from southern Wisconsin as any part of the United States could possibly be. New Mexico in the postwar era was a place of disorienting contrasts, of antiquity and desolate beauty juxtaposed with modernity and accelerated development. Six years before the Westphalls' arrival, Albuquerque was already the largest city in the state, but its population stood at less than thirty-five thousand. By 1950 the postwar boom in housing construction (to which Victor would energetically contribute) had lifted

Victor and his two sons in front of the family trailer. Courtesy of Walter Westphall.

the number of inhabitants to nearly one hundred thousand. And by 1960 the population topped two hundred thousand.[33] Over this twenty-year period, the total value of residential building permits rose from $2.35 million to $43.4 million, and the physical space occupied by the city grew from eleven square miles to sixty-one.[34] David and Walter would grow up in an environment where everything seemed new.

Or, rather, almost everything. Amid the runaway development and the population influx stood a city older than most places in America. Albuquerque could trace its official founding to 1706, long before New Mexico ceased to be part of Mexico proper (actually, long before there was even a Mexico), and Native American communities called the location home centuries before that. Moreover, despite the homogenizing influence of suburbanization, the city remained what it had always been—a cultural crossroads where Mexican, Native American, and Anglo cultures intersected and enriched one another (albeit not without tensions).

Changes came quickly for the Westphalls. As David would remark in 1967, within just a few years of their move to Albuquerque, the family "went from what today we would call poverty to wealth."[35] Accustomed to a meager lifestyle, they lived at first in their trailer on a patch of land acquired inexpensively near the university. Jeanne worked for a time outside the home, before focusing all of her attention on the two growing boys, while Victor collected a modest stipend as a graduate teaching assistant. Combined with his veteran's benefits, this support from the university brought his income to just $200 per month. But such austerity soon ended. When not studying for classes or teaching, Victor honed what would become impressive skills as a builder and, ultimately, as a developer, turning the plot of land where the family parked their trailer into a marketable property. First he constructed a garage from scratch, then the house to go with it. Westphall let the property go at a profit, purchased another lot, and built a larger home upon it, which he also eventually sold. This became a pattern. By now it was clear that Victor not only had the talents of an intellectual steeped in the humanities and of a carpenter; he was also a highly effective businessman.

In 1947 he received his master's degree and took a position teaching history at Albuquerque High School. But the position was short-lived. Victor had decided to go on for an interdisciplinary PhD in "American civilization," and he could see that the building trade would offer a far more lucrative platform for graduate study—and far greater security for his family—than teaching. By 1949 he had acquired enough capital to partner with Clyde Davis, a painting contractor, and the two went on to ride the housing boom for all it was worth, constructing more than two thousand tract houses in the Albuquerque area. The resulting wealth enabled the Westphalls to move into the custom-built home—known as the Juan Tabo house (because of its proximity to a picnic area that bore that name)—featured in the November 1952 issue of the *New Mexico Sun Trails* magazine.

David quickly made friends with other boys in Albuquerque, and one of them, Fidel L. Baca, later shared his memories of their Tom Sawyerish escapades together in a letter to Victor. He recalled that by the sixth grade he and David were the "fastest kings of biking" in their neighborhood, and they rode their ten-speeds everywhere—even up to the base of the Sandia Mountains, where they once killed a rattlesnake.[36]

Then, without warning, Fidel lost his friend. The Westphalls suddenly vacated their residence at the corner of Morningside and Claremont and not long afterward moved into their new home in the mountains. Fidel

The Westphall family in 1949. Courtesy of Walter Westphall.

remembered that from his own home he could see the Juan Tabo house in the far distance and would "frequently wonder what Dave was doing that day."[37] Obviously, the distance that now separated them was both physical and social.

The plot of land that Victor purchased for his new home was an astonishing eighty acres, which meant that there were no close neighbors, and for David and Walter those acres—essentially the side of a rock-strewn high desert mountain—offered adventure galore. The boys enjoyed climbing on the countless boulders and often caught glimpses of bighorn sheep, deer, bobcats, coyotes, roadrunners, and—unnervingly—rattlesnakes. At 6,950 feet, the house was still below the zone at which the reptiles thinned out. The Westphalls kept horses, which the two brothers often rode bareback, as well as two dogs—Josefa and Tucum—who accompanied the boys on their various expeditions into the higher elevations.

Walter recalls that one of these expeditions was nearly one too many. When David was perhaps sixteen, he led Walter on a circular hike to the summit of the Sandia Crest, the highest point in the mountains (at 10,700 feet). The boys calculated the total distance at about twenty miles and figured they could cover it in two days. So, with packs and sleeping bags, and Josefa and Tucum for company, they set out—only to discover that the terrain was much more rugged than they had anticipated. By the time the hikers stopped for the night their canteens were completely empty, and Walter, a self-described "worrier," began to fear for their safety.[38] David, he recalls, "didn't show any great concern about our predicament." The next day, dehydrated and utterly exhausted, they pressed on to the summit, still without any water in sight. Then, on the descending portion of their route, they finally found a spring. It was not a moment too soon—as anyone who has felt the desiccating New Mexico sun will appreciate.

The Juan Tabo location also provided the boys with their own running track of sorts. Not far from their house stood an abandoned building reportedly once used by the Civilian Conservation Corps. The road circling the structure was flat, unlike all the others in the area, and so the two brothers often ran sprints there, launching themselves from homemade starter blocks.

A natural-born coach, Victor kept time with a stopwatch, logged the results of each trial, and often joined in the races. (Walter recalls that his father ran sprints "until he was at least 50 years old."[39]) Needless to say, athletics and fitness played a central role in the boys' lives, as Victor pushed them to emulate his personal model of physical self-improvement. With such a father, neither son questioned whether he would excel at sports, especially track and football. It would have been unthinkable to do otherwise. And so, perhaps not surprisingly (given Victor's mania in that regard), it was athletics that soon brought David great unhappiness.

David's introduction to organized athletics during junior high school went well enough and demonstrated his tremendous natural talent and potential. Between seasons of flag football, he won a weightlifting competition at the local YMCA, beating out many adults. And he was fast. For example, at age fourteen, he ran 100 yards in just 10.8 seconds. A year later, his 50-yard dash clocked in at 5.7 seconds.[40] In the ninth grade, he transitioned to tackle football and quickly racked up an impressive record. Victor's account of these early gridiron achievements in *David's Story* is so meticulously detailed that it bears quotation. The following passage suggests both the loving father's pride in his son and, more disturbingly, a level of parental scrutiny and expectation that could hardly have been entirely healthy:

> David's statistics in several categories of the games played [while he was in the ninth grade] tell how completely he dominated the play of his team. He gained 429 yards in 49 carries from scrimmage (8.75 yards average), completed 6 of 17 passes for 175 yards, caught 3 of 5 passes for 86 yards, intercepted 2 passes for 73 yards, returned 1 punt for 15 yards, as well as 2 kick-offs for 48 yards. In the 76 times he handled the ball, he gained 836 yards for 10.9 yards per effort. This was 30 percent better than the second best in this category on the team.[41]

In fairness, Victor served for a time as an assistant to his son's junior high football coach (this detail in itself is revealing), and so he may well have kept track of such statistics for all the players on the team. Nevertheless, his unwavering conviction that David's abilities far surpassed those of his teammates, while probably warranted in some respects, soon caused serious problems.

David's first football season at Highland High School in Albuquerque was a disaster for reasons that had nothing to do with his father. A pulled hamstring kept him from participating in a single game. By his junior year, David had fully recovered (Victor personally oversaw his physical reconditioning), but his delight in rejoining the team soon ended when the head coach, Hugh Hackett, made him a tackle—a position ill suited to David's speed and build. Victor was furious, and from this point on little that Hackett did met with his approval. Worse, he openly shared this attitude with his son, who as a result sometimes acted insubordinately toward his coach. A vicious cycle formed.

David, number 35, playing for Highland High School. Courtesy of Walter Westphall.

Such a knowledgeable and self-confident man—and a formidable sports statistician to boot—would likely have been a difficult parent to please under any circumstances. Under *these* circumstances, Victor revealed an enormous blind spot in his personality, as he himself later recognized. Continually second-guessing the coach and engaging in paranoid speculation about David's lack of opportunity on the playing field turned what should have been an enjoyable athletic experience into agony for father and son alike.

Fortunately, when David subsequently joined the track team, which was also coached by Hackett, things went surprisingly well. David's reputation as one of the most talented up-and-coming runners in Albuquerque preceded him, and the coach welcomed him enthusiastically. David went on to triumph in nearly every race he ran, and together with his father, who promised to stay out of the way this time, he looked forward to a fresh start where football was concerned.

But it was not to be. Just a few games into the season, Victor detected the usual onslaught of injustices and humiliations directed at his son. However, the culprit this time around was not Coach Hackett but a "clique of players who influenced the selections of plays."[42] By this point, David had had enough, and following a family meeting, during which Victor and Jeanne pledged their support, he decided to transfer to Oklahoma Military Academy (what is today Rogers State University). He selected this institution, in part, because of an emerging ambition (nurtured by Victor) to attend West Point.

During his single season at OMA, David played the best football of his life and achieved the star-player status that had eluded him at Highland High. However, when he sat down to take West Point's formidable entrance examinations, he enjoyed less success. Highly verbal and enamored of history, languages, literature, and music, David's was a mind clearly geared to the humanities, and in the end, despite special tutoring by OMA faculty, he could not achieve the necessary scores in the math and science exam sections. It was a bitter disappointment.

Then, while still basking in belated football glory and still smarting from his performance on the entrance exams, David did something remarkable—something that was perhaps, in retrospect, a mistake, but nevertheless an admirable expression of his character. Near the end of David's year at OMA, Hackett left Highland High School to become the head track coach at the University of New Mexico. Despite their previously strained relationship, David wrote to congratulate him, and in response Hackett encouraged the high school senior to come to UNM and join the track team. Although he could easily have found a spot on any one of a number of college teams, David accepted. It was an extraordinary gesture, made for reasons that are not entirely clear. Perhaps David did not like feeling that he had run away from a difficult situation. Or perhaps the bond between athlete and coach had been stronger than Victor, in the midst of his dissatisfaction and anger, had fully realized.

Whatever the case, David enjoyed considerable athletic success throughout his first few months at UNM. During a series of intersquad track meets, he won every race, and his promising performance on the freshman football team earned him a slot for the coming year. By the spring semester of 1959, he faced another major decision; namely, "whether to continue uninterrupted with track or participate in spring football practice."[43] David chose the latter, thereby signaling, once again, his commitment to a sport that had thus far brought him, on balance, far more misery than joy. Nothing at the moment suggested that old problems would reemerge, but Victor felt so much anxiety on his son's behalf that he hired a private investigator to look into the "earlier intrigue" at Highland High.[44] The detective's report revealed what the father had alleged all along: a "cabal" of jealous teammates had undermined David while the coaching staff, led by Hackett, did nothing to rectify the situation.[45]

Although Victor must have felt vindicated by the results, this private inquiry (focused on the nefarious inner workings of a high school sports team) was perhaps not the best way to give David a fresh start with football, and what happened next smacks of self-fulfilling prophecy. To Victor's horror, David's handling of the football became an issue during his sophomore year, and UNM head coach Marv Levy soon came to occupy the same hated position, in the father's eyes, previously inhabited by Hackett.

In the end, David's football career came down to a single game—UNM versus Colorado State. Warned repeatedly by his coaches not to fumble, David did just that—and on a crucial play. Then, while there was still a slim chance of recovering the ball, he "froze into uncertainty."[46] No one on the coaching staff spoke to him afterward.

To David, it seemed as though his entire life had gone to pieces, and so in the summer of 1959, eager to leave Albuquerque and its now painful associations, he impulsively enlisted in the Marines. He would go on to spend two stints in the Corps, with an interval of three years between them, and they would be nothing alike. Even more than rank (David would first serve as an enlisted man, then as a junior officer), the war in Vietnam would make all the difference.

Looking back on his fatherly behavior from the vantage point of the early 1980s, Victor realized that "his enthusiasm for excellence for his sons may have actually done [David] a disservice."[47] It was a painful conclusion to draw, but probably not inaccurate. Indeed, one has to wonder whether the various shortcomings that David's coaches detected in his performance resulted, at least partly, from his father's unrelenting scrutiny and impossible expectations. Did that disastrous fumble occur because of his coaching at school *and* at home, because Victor demanded perfection and, statistics-covered notepad in hand, studied his every move? Might David have done better and been happier without all the extra training and microanalysis offered by his father?

Either way, Victor saw a change in David as the once happy-go-lucky companion of childhood friends like Fidel Baca became more and more yoked to athletics. Or, rather, the father detected this change years later as he reviewed David's life. In *David's Story*, he wrote that photographs taken of his son in elementary school and junior high school capture a boy who is "smiling, trusting, and outgoing." But as David "progressed through high school . . . his photos often showed him somber with a tinge of wariness."[48] Given the curious way in which Victor narrates this passage, one wonders whether he necessarily observed this progression at the time. Did David take pains to hide this "wariness" and depression from his father? And how much did Victor, so focused on helping his son to achieve "excellence," allow himself to see?

However, while Victor's actions as a parent probably didn't help matters, the chief cause of David's growing unhappiness perhaps resided elsewhere: he had a broader range of interests and a more serious attitude toward learning than most of his classmates and fellow athletes. As Victor later remarked, "David was different than his peers. He wrote poetry, played musical instruments, [and] enjoyed classical music."[49] In other words, David—like his home-building, weightlifting, history-studying father—combined the physical and the intellectual in ways that must have seemed disorienting to other teenagers.

As David entered his twenties, this sense of apartness remained with him. Evidence of this exists in a particularly revealing sample of personal writing. In July 1964, following David's first period of service in the Marine Corps, he applied to the teacher education program at the University of Montana (UM). He had already tried, for two semesters, to make progress on a UM forestry degree, but the required science and math courses proved, as usual, excruciatingly difficult for him. Wisely, David turned to the humanities, always his strongest area. History, he indicated on the teacher education application, would be his major teaching field, Spanish his minor. (Ultimately, he would reverse these and add Russian as an additional subfield.) Along with a questionnaire, the application called for two pieces of prose—a "planning paper," intended to address aptitude for teaching, and an "autobiography." David submitted well-written essays in response, and they provide a remarkable window into his personality.

From the planning paper, we learn that he viewed life from the standpoint of what he called a "cynical idealist." He had seen plenty of the "hypocritical and bad in people" but continued "to believe that man is inherently good and not evil." David's disciplined childhood, and resulting impatience with slackness in others, came across when he described his greatest potential handicap as a teacher—"a quickness to condemn seemingly rude, unruly youths as ill-bred punks." But, characteristically, he expressed confidence that he could see past his strict upbringing and any resulting impatience by "keeping in mind the social backgrounds of [his] students."[50]

David's sense that his avid interest in books and history put him out of step with many other young men his age appears in the autobiography. Consider, for example, his humorous account of reading habits among the marines with whom he served during his first period of enlistment, a passage that also reflects his broad (for the time) racial outlook:

> One day in the barracks I was reading *Arrowsmith* and wanted to discuss it with someone. On that entire floor if the majority thought Sinclair Lewis was anyone, they thought he was a barber over in the PX. The only people in that platoon with whom I could talk about the book or its author were two Negroes. This example is typical. On a per capita basis not only were Negro Marines better informed than were whites about jazz and sports, but also about politics, geography, world happenings, and literature. Whites *might* have held an edge in a discussion of automobile engines. (Both races claimed to know all there was to know about women.)[51]

No less impressive than the content of this passage—and the force of personality behind it—is the style. David's prose in these typo-free essays *flows* in a manner that suggests careful planning, multiple drafts (in the pre-word-processing era, no less), and a writerly sensitivity to the nuances of language that may even have exceeded his well-published father's.

And so, from this pair of fifty-year-old artifacts (combined with Victor's biography and Walter's recollections), a picture of a complex and interesting young man emerges. Like most people, when you look at them closely enough, David Westphall was full of contradictions. He could be self-assured and free of worry, a calming presence around others and a natural leader. And he could be neurotic, filled with self-doubt, revolted by his image in a mirror, obsessed with the shape of his nose. Periods of black depression stalked him. Statistics leave little question that he was a born athlete of truly exceptional talent. And yet, if we are to believe his coaches, he could sometimes also be physically clumsy and preoccupied. Accustomed to a life of structure and self-discipline, he could come across as arrogant; at the same time, however, he was, for a man of his generation, remarkably free of racial or ethnic prejudice. He held a conservative, hawkish worldview, while delighting in all things related to the humanities, more typically the refuge of young liberals.

In the final analysis, David's father, whom he loved and who most certainly loved him, helped end his athletic career through well-intentioned but disastrous meddling. David must have known this and felt conflicted as a result, torn between his eagerness to please Victor and his frustration with the unanticipated personal weaknesses that football revealed in his suddenly fallible parent. Despite occasional fights, however, there is no record of deep bitterness between the two of them. After all, like many eldest sons, David was that apple that doesn't fall far from the proverbial tree. By his early twenties he had become a Renaissance man like his father, and the two men could scarcely have had more in common.

But dissatisfaction and restlessness gnawed at David, the result most directly perhaps of the football debacle, but also indicative of a deeper (if vague) concern that his life was not turning out as it should. *Something*, he increasingly felt, was wrong with him. For now, however, he sought to adjust his external circumstances. And so, after abandoning football and abruptly leaving the University of New Mexico, David turned to the structure and security of two time-tested institutions—the US Marine Corps and marriage. Unfortunately, neither would provide a solution to his growing unhappiness.

In April of 1960, just a few months after joining the Corps, twenty-year-old David announced his engagement to nineteen-year-old Mary Lynne Willmarth, a former classmate from Highland High School who had also gone on to the University of New Mexico. To Victor and Jeanne, this engagement must have seemed impulsive and more than a little unwise, even though David and Lynne saw each other regularly during their freshman year together at UNM. After all, David was a lowly enlisted man now, and hardly in the best position economically to support a wife.

Signs of trouble developed early on. Just a few weeks after their engagement, for example, David announced to his father that he planned to write to Lynne about her one and only blemish: she was "too chubby." He would ask her to "reduce," so that her figure would correspond with her attractive face.[52] Whether Victor tried to wave his son away from this particular matrimonial no-fly zone or whether his enthusiasm for physical fitness blinded him to the likely consequences is unknown. What we do know is that David subsequently broached the topic with Lynne, with results that may easily be imagined. Then, strangely, David's concern over Lynne's appearance became somehow entangled with his own insecurities. The old fixation with his nose reemerged. If Lynne were to trim down, he would surely lose her. He was ugly and unworthy. This "mental turmoil" also led David to question whether the two should marry at all.[53]

Whatever was going on inside David went well beyond the cold feet that young men customarily feel on the eve of matrimony, and so in February 1961 the couple broke off their engagement. But a month later, when David returned to Albuquerque from Hawaii, where he was now stationed, they reconciled and set a new date for the wedding—March 11.

On the evening prior to the ceremony, David suffered what can only be described as a nervous breakdown. According to Victor, the groom-to-be spent most of the night in a state so wretched and "incoherent" that his father felt compelled to remove all possible "tools of self-destruction from his presence."[54] Walter was also on hand, and his brother's frighteningly erratic behavior that night stood out vividly in his memory more than fifty years later: "I made what feeble effort I could to comfort him, but it was one of those absolutely terrifying experiences of a lifetime. I remember sobbing and praying to God that he would remove this pain from David and give it to me."[55] The ceremony the next day went smoothly enough—a wonder given the groom's state of mind.

Nothing made David fundamentally ill suited for marriage. He had a robust interest in women, excellent interpersonal skills, and, in his parents, a model of a harmonious union. More than anything, incompatibility seemed at the root of the crisis he now faced with Lynne. In several letters written prior to the wedding, David confessed to his father that he thought it best if he and Lynne parted before making a serious mistake by marrying. But he feared hurting her, and his sense of obligation overpowered the desire for escape.

Despite such an inauspicious start, the young couple enjoyed a brief honeymoon in California, where they visited the mission at San Juan Capistrano and spent a day at Disneyland, fitting in as much travel and enjoyment as they could before David's leave ended. Throughout their holiday, David held himself together—thanks, in part, to "some pills his mother had given him."[56] Four months later, Lynne joined her husband in Oahu, their car and household belongings in tow, and displayed great skill and persistence when securing an affordable apartment. Indeed, she proved an accomplished housewife and made David's modest income go further than anyone thought possible. By the time the couple's first wedding anniversary arrived they had settled into a comfortable routine, and their relationship seemed (at least on the surface) free from turmoil.

Then everything turned sour. David received an unwelcome transfer to Camp Pendleton in Southern California, and a heartbroken Lynne had to make do with a cramped apartment far inferior to their home in Hawaii. The Westphalls' second wedding anniversary came and went, and, sadly, Lynne spent it alone in their hated residence. David was deployed at the time on a field exercise at 29 Palms, a desolate training base in the desert east of Los Angeles. A freakish snowstorm added to the discomfort he experienced from the nonstop wind and blowing sand.

But the couple had a fresh new start to look forward to: David's four-year period of enlistment was now nearing its end, and, determined to follow through with his promise to complete his degree (which his veteran's benefits would, of course, cover), he began to consider various universities. In the end, he selected the University of Montana in Missoula, where he planned to major in forestry.

After David's discharge in September 1963, the couple resettled in Missoula, barely arriving in time for David to begin his work on his baccalaureate degree. By all accounts, his professors encountered in this serious, relentlessly curious, and already well-read former marine the kind of student who makes a teaching career in academia, despite its low pay

David studying in his house in Missoula. Courtesy of Walter Westphall.

and attendant humiliations, ultimately such a joy. David met regularly with faculty members during their office hours, sometimes challenged the content of their lectures, and when faced with liberal dogma in the classroom staunchly and eloquently defended his conservative views. After concluding that he was not as "outdoorsy" as he thought, or as capable of forging his way through math and science courses as he had hoped, he switched his major from forestry to teacher education and focused on Spanish, history, and Russian, subjects with which he could not have been more fascinated or more attuned.[57] Educationally, at least, he had found his place.

And then, just as David began to hit his stride as a student, his marriage to Lynne, long imperiled, went to pieces, triggering one of the worst crises of his life—worse, perhaps in some respects, than anything he would later face in Vietnam. Victor later recalled that the first signs of trouble appeared in a letter from his son dated May 20, 1965. David confided that he and his wife were living in a "state of armed truce" and that he planned to spend the summer back in Albuquerque while Lynne, now an art major, completed some courses in Missoula.[58]

It wasn't long before the truce ended. Lynne filed for divorce on June 20, by which time all of David's obsessions and insecurities, especially regarding his appearance, had come crashing down on him. In a letter to his parents sent a couple weeks before the formal divorce announcement, he confessed that he had spent two days "quaking and sobbing" and that he felt a "persistent urge to kill himself."[59] With this news in hand, Victor and Jeanne wasted no time. They immediately drove to Missoula, picked up their son, and returned to Albuquerque, where David began a series of sessions with psychoanalyst Dr. Henry W. Blake.

Walter speculates that the divorce, which Lynne handled with relative equanimity, had multiple causes, possibly including David's intense focus on his education, his emerging desire to reenter the Marines (now that the Corps was fully engaged in Southeast Asia), his mental illness, for which Lynne had unsuccessfully urged him to seek treatment, and Lynne's understandable resentment over David's request that she lose weight. But the couple may also have simply "drifted apart."[60] David did not report—either to his brother or anyone else—any major fights, just a growing coolness, masked by "elaborate courtesy."[61] Nevertheless, it is clear from the letter that so alarmed his parents that the end of the marriage awoke all the old demons.

In Dr. Blake David found an able and sympathetic therapist, and he later described his period of treatment as "a very interesting and worthwhile experience."[62] Throughout the summer of 1965, which he spent largely in a state of contented inactivity, his spirits improved, and when he returned to Missoula in September he entered what was perhaps the happiest phase of his adult life, the closest he ever came to an idyll. That fall and spring, he earned A's in all of his classes, and in the summer of 1966, he apparently fell in love, perhaps for the first time in his life. To improve his Spanish, David attended a language institute in Saltillo, Mexico, and there he met a young schoolteacher, Irene de la Rosa Fuentes. The two dated very briefly, but they corresponded throughout the fall—both writing in Spanish, of which David had quickly acquired an exceptional command—and while their relationship remains mysterious in many respects, Irene's surviving missives, later translated into English, can only be described as love letters.[63]

Remarkably, while everything in David Westphall's life seemed at last to be falling into place, including love, he was quietly preparing to go to war. At some point during the 1965–1966 academic year, well before meeting Irene, he had made up his mind to reenter the Marine Corps and to seek a commission as an officer (the latter required that he first complete his undergraduate degree at the University of Montana). We know this in part because of a surviving letter from his psychiatrist dated May 19, 1966. David must have applied to the Officer Candidate School (OCS) by this point because Dr. Blake was asked by the Marine Corps to confirm his patient's soundness of mind. In his note to the medical department representative at Fort Douglas, which was carbon-copied to David, the therapist offered the following appraisal:

> The above mentioned individual was seen in therapy by me from June 16, 1965 to July 23, 1965 for a total of ten hours for the purpose of aiding him in working through a mild situational depression. It is my opinion that he showed evidence of good maturity in working through his problem and should be less subject to this type of reaction under stress in the future than the average young person of his age.[64]

Assured of David's mental health, the Corps accepted his application for officer training, and on November 1, while wrapping up his final semester at UM, David received orders to report to the Marine Corps base at Quantico, Virginia, on January 23, 1967.[65] There he would complete the OCS, followed by rigorous instruction in the Corps' legendary Basic School, which trained newly commissioned officers how to lead men in the field.

Why did he reenlist? One explanation comes directly from David, and we even have it in his own words. As part of his application to the Basic School, he provided an autobiography not unlike the personal narrative he submitted to the teacher education program at UM. In this case, his primary purpose was to explain why he wanted a command position, and his candor when describing his earlier experiences as an enlisted man probably came as a surprise to the officers who reviewed his application. He even confessed that he had been disappointed in the Corps. However, this attitude had lifted when he received the opportunity to lead: "I continued to be disillusioned with my career in the Marine Corps until I made corporal and became a squad leader with the Fourth Marines in Hawaii. One of the reasons I'm here today is that the interest and challenge of working with even as small a group as a squad were so great that I want to try it with larger units."[66] No one who knew David well would have found this passage surprising. Fidel Baca had noticed David's innate leadership ability when they played together as children. So had Walter. And, despite the vicissitudes of his ultimately disastrous athletic career, David's charisma and ability to inspire often came across on the football field.

As we will see more fully in the next chapter, additional factors, unrelated to David's first four years in the Corps, arguably played a role in his reenlistment as well; these included his hawkish views on foreign policy, his general faith in American virtue, and his patriotic conception of war experience (formed during the Second World War and colored by Victor's bittersweet adventure in the Pacific). But David's prior service, which gave him the taste for leadership that he described in his autobiography, probably also inspired a strong sense of obligation, perhaps even feelings of guilt. After all, when he received his discharge in 1963, there were no marines in Vietnam. Now, three years later, many of the men with whom he had served in Hawaii and California were deployed, and the conflict in which they found themselves bore little resemblance to the "splendid little war" that Caputo, one of the first marines to land in Vietnam, had expected to find in 1965.[67] By 1966 marines were dying every day in Southeast Asia—none faster than junior field officers—and there was no immediate end in sight.

David completed his bachelor's degree in December 1966 and soon after headed south to visit Irene, stopping to see his parents along the way. By this point Victor and Jeanne no longer lived in Albuquerque. Victor's business ambitions had shifted to the Moreno Valley, an up-and-coming resort area in the Sangre de Cristo Mountains and overlooked by Wheeler Peak, the highest point in New Mexico. The homebuilder had sunk much of his fortune into a massive tract of land, located on the west side of the valley, which he planned to develop into a subdivision named after the Val Verde Ranch, the property's original title.

The site was nothing less than stunning. From the forested west end of the property, nestled at the base of the mountains, jutted a barren, windswept prominence, which offered dramatic views of the nearby ski community of Angel Fire and Eagle Nest Lake. David greeted his parents in their new house, which came with the property, and—chilling thought—the young man walked for the first time on the ground where his future memorial would stand. Then he was off to Mexico, where he spent several precious days with Irene and their mutual friends in Saltillo. It was the last time he would see her.

David reported to Quantico, as ordered, on January 23, and if he had any doubts about his decision to rejoin the Marine Corps, they certainly didn't surface during his training. He was, by all accounts, exceptional officer material. In March 1967 he completed the OCS—he was thus Second Lieutenant Westphall now—and received orders to proceed to the Basic School, where would undergo immersive instruction in, among other things, amphibious operations, field engineering, first aid, infantry weapons, map and aerial photo reading, marksmanship, and current Marine Corps operations—twenty-two subject areas in all, each critical to the performance of a marine officer in the field.[68] David mastered them all. When graduation arrived in August, he stood twenty-sixth in his class of 516.[69] By this time, of course, his upcoming departure for Southeast Asia was official: after twenty days of leave, he was to report to Camp Pendleton in California for two weeks of reconnaissance replacement training, then proceed to Camp Butler, where he would receive his assignment to FMFPac WestPac Ground Forces (MCC 159).[70] Or, in English: the war in Vietnam.

Walter drove to Quantico from Indiana University in Bloomington, where he was completing a college program for enlisted air force men, and attended the Basic School graduation ceremony. He found his brother "proud and happy" and did not detect any "sense of foreboding." David displayed the same cool nerves that had impressed Walter years earlier during their nearly disastrous hike to Sandia Crest. At no point did he talk "about the dangers of Vietnam or about the chances that he would survive."[71] Moreover, the freshly minted second lieutenant had made new friends, including his roommate Kim, a South Korean national sent by his government to train with the US Marine Corps. (The United States, it is often forgotten, did not act unilaterally in Vietnam; thousands of South Koreans and Australians served there as well.)

After the ceremony the two brothers decided to drive, in separate vehicles, to the Val Verde Ranch at Angel Fire, where David had decided to spend his leave. The nearly two-thousand-mile journey turned into a mild adventure. In Ohio they became separated, but somehow managed to find each other. "Hooking back up was not easy in the days before cell phones," recalls Walter. And at a restaurant off the Kansas turnpike, David's brother made an innocent comment that nevertheless haunts him to this day. When David became irate over a "messed-up" food order, Walter quipped, "I can't believe you exist."[72] It was nothing more than a friendly joke, but when Walter later reviewed the list of remarks he wished he had never made, he regretted this one most of all.

David might have done many things during the twenty days that separated him from his imminent journey into war, and why he didn't visit Irene in Mexico during this period is something of a mystery. Perhaps their romance had cooled by this point. We simply don't know. Or perhaps he felt, instinctively, that instead of another exciting trip south of the border, he needed an interval of calm in order to collect himself for what was to come.

After just a few days at Angel Fire, Walter had to leave—his new term was beginning at Indiana University—and so he said goodbye to his brother in the driveway of their parents' house: "I told David to keep his head up while he was keeping it down, shook hands and left. I don't recall that he said anything; likely he just nodded an acknowledgment." [73]

As his own departure drew closer, David spent more and more time in the high mountains. To test his skills as a field marine, he hiked, off trail, on a direct line from the Val Verde Ranch to a "point midway up the formidable southeast flank of Wheeler Peak."[74] Amazingly, he made the round trip in a single day. For his next adventure he set his sights on the mountain's summit (more than thirteen thousand feet in elevation), and Victor decided to join him. It was a memorable outing for so many reasons, but it did not begin auspiciously. The two decided to travel by jeep to a trailhead at the base of the peak, and on the way their vehicle became stuck in a marsh. Hours passed before they could they free it, and so they spent the night camped out in sleeping bags that they had brought along for just such an emergency.

The next day they reached the trailhead and climbed the steep switchbacks that led higher and higher through the timber pines and then up into the barren, boulder-strewn zone above the tree line, where patches of months-old snow still lingered. Near the summit, father and son gazed down upon a sight considered sacred by the nearby Taos Pueblo and withheld to all but the intrepid few who ventured this high into the alpine wilderness—the azure water of the Blue Lake, a mirror of the sky ringed by dense pines and set against the Blood of Christ Mountains like a gem.

2

A Casualty of Vietnam

It had been eerie, frightening, invigorating, chaotic, and surreal.
Welcome to combat.
It was not like in the movies.
–Jack McLean, Loon: A Marine Story (2009)

That was the third lieutenant we lost. Talk about officers and luck . . . I don't think they had too much.
–Lance Corporal Tom Ryan, No Shining Armor: The Marines at War in Vietnam, an Oral History, by Otto J. Lehrack (1992)

As historian Ron Milam has written, whatever else it may or may not have been, Vietnam was "not a gentleman's war."[1] There was nothing gentlemanly about the Vietnamese climate, which David would experience in the open, for days on end, at the height of the annual monsoon season and during periods of heat so intense that in some cases it quite literally cooked the brains of young Americans and killed them. And there was certainly nothing gentlemanly about the enemy, who had deftly mastered the art of asymmetrical warfare against a global superpower. The two things—the only things—that American soldiers could expect from their adversaries were intelligence and absolute ruthlessness.

The specific military circumstances that David came to know along the ironically titled Demilitarized Zone (DMZ), a "thirty-five-mile-long buffer" that separated North and South Vietnam, were much like those throughout the conflict, but with some important differences.[2] Unlike many US Army units to the south, whose principal enemy, at least prior to the Tet Offensive, was the Viet Cong, the Marines consistently faced well-trained units of regular soldiers from the North Vietnamese Army (NVA), who operated from bases located north of the DMZ. Thus, heavy artillery and rockets, both unwieldy for guerrilla fighters, often figured significantly in North Vietnamese operations in the area. Some of the heaviest barrages of the war (those fired by the NVA, that is) occurred in the Marines' sector—as seen, most vividly, in the four-month-long artillery siege of Khe Sanh that started in January 1968 and the six-week-long bombardment of Con Thien the previous fall.

However, proximity to the border also brought a modicum of relief from one of the conflict's worst scourges. Enemy land mines and booby traps, though still a menace, were, at least by this point in the war, less common along the DMZ than they were in the south. Why? Because such weapons would have posed a danger to NVA forces that needed to maneuver, sometimes en masse, over the same ground as the Americans. And, finally, encounters with the rural Vietnamese population, often tense and sometimes conducive to brutality (to say nothing of atrocity) born of frustration and fear, occurred less frequently in this northernmost of sectors. By the time David arrived in the fall of 1967, the Marines, together with South Vietnamese soldiers, had rounded up most of the area's civilians and deposited them in the American bases at Dong Ha and Cam Lo, which functioned essentially as "refugee camps"; cleared of its indigenous inhabitants, the area along the DMZ became a free-fire zone, where marines on the ground—and American jets and helicopters in the air—had license to shoot at anything that moved.[3]

On a map, if not in reality, the state of affairs on the DMZ resembled the more conventional warfare for which Vietnam War-era American commanders, schooled in World War II tactics, longed. Here the situation appeared more coherent than the ever-shifting patchwork of friend and foe that confronted troops in the southern Corps zones. After all, the

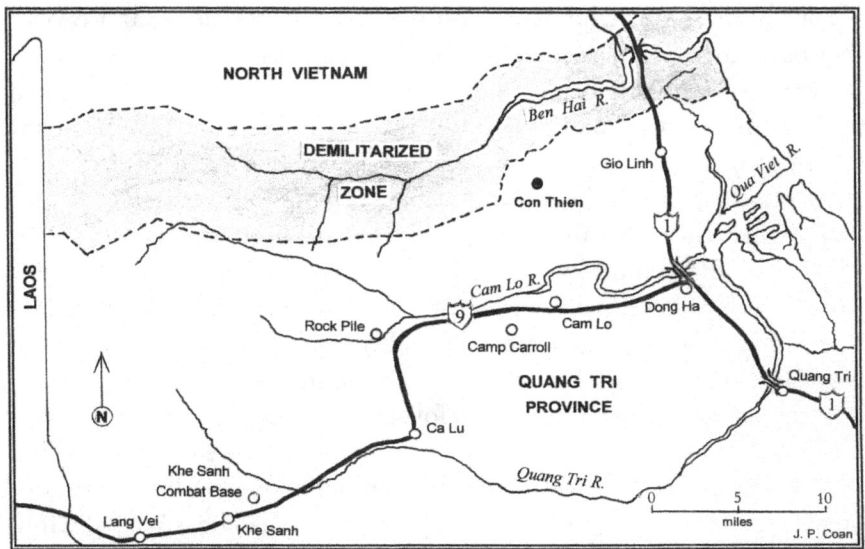

Map of northern Quang Tri Province showing Marine strongpoints along the DMZ. Map by James P. Coan. Courtesy of the University of Alabama Press.

DMZ itself seemed to make things simple. The NVA held one side, the Marines the other—at least in theory.

To keep the enemy from moving easily into South Vietnam, the Corps relied on a first line of defense comprising fortified strongpoints, some closer to the DMZ than others. If one were to fly over these bases from the west, traveling from the mountainous border with Laos to the South China Sea, the first to come into view would be the legendary outpost at Khe Sanh, then the Rockpile (aptly named for the granite mountain summit used by the Marines for long-distance observation), and then, in the eastern half of this defense system, the sandbagged hamlets of Con Thien (the "Hill of Angels") and, next to the coast, Gio Linh. To the rear of these strongholds, serving as a logistical lifeline, ran Highway 9, the main east-west road, which connected near the coast with Highway 1, the primary north-south artery. Farther south, an additional set of bases—Ca Lu, Camp Carroll, Cam Lo, and Dong Ha—provided support for those closest to the enemy.

Four of these strongholds, two on the first line of defense and two farther back, formed the corners of what came to be known as Leatherneck Square. Every marine could find it on a map: you just drew a line connecting (in clockwise motion) Con Thien with Gio Linh, Dong Ha, and Cam Lo. Inside the square was some of the most dangerous country in Vietnam, country that David would come to know all too well.

And then there was the so-called McNamara Line (also known as the "Trace"), a fifteen-mile-long clearing established just south of the DMZ along its eastern half, right in front of Con Thien and Gio Linh. Over Marine objections, the Department of Defense, via General William Westmoreland, mandated the creation of this fixed line of defense in 1967. The idea was to have a zone, denuded of foliage, through which the NVA could not possibly advance without being detected and mowed down, and like most ideas in Vietnam that originated from on high, it wasn't a very good one. As historian Otto J. Lehrack remarks, "From the Great Wall of China to the Maginot Line, the history of warfare is replete with examples of the successful circumvention of barriers."[4]

Not surprisingly, the ever-capable NVA proved masters of such circumvention, as every marine assigned to Leatherneck Square realized within two seconds of arrival. For example, Lieutenant Jim Brown, an artillery observer attached to the 2nd Battalion, 4th Marines, spent forty-five days in 1968 helping to defend a vital bridge on a road that led into Con Thien from the south. Brown and his comrades endured daily mortar barrages and rocket fire, all of it delivered by NVA troops who operated miles below the supposedly impregnable McNamara Line. David would have a similar experience at C-2, a camp just five miles or so south of Con Thien. As Brown recalls, marines regarded the Trace as a "farce . . . because the NVA were everywhere to begin with."[5] Ironically, David's death would occur not only near the Hill of Angels but also in the vicinity of this patently porous line of defense, a symbol, if ever there was one, of foolhardy tactics imposed from above. Or, if one prefers, a symbol of the entire mismanaged American war effort.

No place in the vicinity of the DMZ could be considered safe. While the NVA sieges of Khe Sanh and Con Thien were especially terrifying, subjecting the inhabitants of these strategic bases to long intervals of shelling and helplessness (and raising the specter, via television, of an American version of Dien Bien Phu), there were still plenty of ways for marines to get killed or wounded in less famous locales.[6] Search-and-destroy missions conducted beyond the relative safety of strongholds often proved costly (David would, in fact, die on just such a mission), as did the establishment of smaller, more vulnerable outposts, such as the one occupied by Brown south of Con Thien.[7] Such operations produced terrible losses. Indeed, Brown recalled hearing at "some [stateside] briefing . . . that Marines spending a full tour on the DMZ during the peak of the war had a 50 percent chance of becoming a casualty."[8]

David knew this risk. Of that there is no question. As fellow marine Jack McLean later explained, any member of the Corps inducted in 1967 knew exactly where he was going and the lethal conditions he would find there. The news from Vietnam—"escalating troop deployments and skyrocketing casualties"—left little doubt.[9]

Second Lieutenant Victor David Westphall III arrived in Da Nang—via Okinawa—on Halloween, 1967. By his side was his new friend Captain Rocky Wirsching, an Annapolis graduate one year David's junior. Rocky had hoped to become a Marine Corps pilot, but when he failed the final vision test just a few weeks before receiving his wings, the Corps gave him two options: he could stay on in aviation as a commissioned crew member only, which meant that he would occupy the back seat (rather than the front) of an F-4 Phantom, or serve in the infantry. Rocky chose the latter. Like David, he was not inclined to shy away from difficulty, and one can easily imagine the kind of rapport that developed between this well-educated, strong-willed professional soldier and the bright, incessantly curious New Mexican.

The two men had met during the intensive reconnaissance training, specifically focused on "supporting arms," which David received at Camp Pendleton just prior to his deployment. Thus, both marines fully expected that their duties in Vietnam would involve stealthy insertions into enemy territory, as well as forward observation—that is, visually locating the enemy, recording his coordinates as carefully as possible, and then calling in artillery fire or air strikes.

However, David's first surprise in Vietnam—the first of many—came when he and Rocky checked in with the major responsible for distributing field assignments. Just the day before, NVA troops had ambushed Bravo Company of the 1st Battalion, 4th Marine Regiment (henceforth referred to, per Marine usage, as B/1/4), and killed or wounded a number of Americans, including the company commander. So, instead of an assignment to a recon battalion, as planned, Rocky was put in charge of Bravo Company. For a moment it seemed the two friends would be parted. The badly shot-up unit required a number of replacement officers, but the major's orders mentioned a captain only. However, Rocky was insistent—he needed a platoon commander he already knew and trusted—and in the end the major relented. For the rest of his time in Vietnam, David served at the head of a platoon in B/1/4, a job far tougher, in many respects, than the one he had envisioned for himself in reconnaissance. He was now responsible for the lives and welfare of more than forty men.

The next day, the two officers reached Bravo Company at Camp Evans, a Marine base located near the coast (south of the DMZ sector where David would later see so much action), about twenty-five kilometers from the city of Hue. The unit was a mess. Fourteen marines had died during the ambush; many more were wounded—including every noncommissioned officer (NCO), the radioman, the corpsman, and all the officers but one. (David knew two of the wounded second lieutenants from their time together at the Basic School.) And, understandably enough, morale among those marines who had avoided getting hit couldn't have been worse.

What these survivors thought of David and Rocky, greenhorn replacements who had never heard a shot fired in anger and who had been in Vietnam less than forty-eight hours, isn't difficult to surmise. But both men would soon have a chance to prove themselves, and for David his new assignment to B/1/4 was—through a remarkable coincidence—a kind of homecoming. Though the personnel were now different, he had once served in this very same unit as an enlisted man.

David received the command of the 1st Platoon, which fortunately contained an exceptionally able NCO, Sergeant Tom McKinney, who helped the new second lieutenant learn the ropes, and by November 16 he had survived his first search-and-destroy mission. It was, he reported in a letter to his parents, "a real bitch."[10] Accompanied by "some engineers, . . . interpreters, snipers, and a scout dog team," Bravo Company had gone looking for the enemy—or, short of that, enemy provisions (namely, stashes of rice)—along a river that ran through some mountains southwest of Hue.[11] David's platoon had the dubious privilege of traveling in rubber boats and protecting a team of scuba divers as they searched the river bottom for hidden supplies. The expedition also gave him his first taste of what travel by foot in the Vietnamese cordillera would be like. At one point, in order to provide better cover for the divers, 1st Platoon tried to scale a "slippery" mountainside covered with "vines with thorns like barbed wire."[12] The marines gave it up. The jungle had beaten them back.

After three days in the mountains, Bravo Company returned, via helicopter, to Camp Evans. Then, less than twenty-four hours later, the unit was airlifted into the nearby Kobi Tan Tan Valley for another search-and-destroy mission, and it was here that David came upon the enemy for the first time. In a way, that initial encounter captured the entire war in microcosm. As the men crossed a rice paddy, a sniper opened fire on them. To his parents, David described the soon-to-be-familiar sound of the AK-47 as a kind of "*chug-chug-chug.*"[13] While the marines hit the deck, the rookie second lieutenant kept his head. He directed his 60mm mortar team to lob white phosphorous at what he thought was the sniper's position, and then he ordered the forward observer to call in an artillery barrage.

Whether the resulting avalanche of explosives, which did end the sniping, killed the enemy soldier isn't clear. In his letter, David made no mention of a corpse—a perhaps telling omission given the focus on body count as a measure of military success. But this detail simply adds to the incident's accuracy as a miniature version of the entire conflict. Surprise and stealth versus overwhelming firepower, with an unclear outcome: the essence of the American war in Vietnam.

Over the next four days, Bravo Company enjoyed other brief flirtations with the phantomlike NVA. At one point a marine spotted a group of enemy soldiers through his infrared nightscope, but did not receive permission to fire upon them—much to David's disappointment. Soon, however, the marines could barely focus on their human adversary. With the "monsoon now [beginning] in earnest," the physical environment of Vietnam—the real enemy—enveloped them in misery. Always the writer, David described his rapidly deteriorating physical condition during this ordeal with characteristic vividness and attention to rhetorical effect, sparing his parents nothing:

After a couple more days we were all feeling really miserable. My feet were beginning to bleed from being constantly wet, my hands were a mass of red welts from thorn cuts, my face was all swollen from mosquitoes, I had a rash on my legs where leeches had bitten me, my flak jacket was biting into my shoulders, pulled down even tighter by a pack which included extra machine gun ammo and mortar rounds, I was trembling with cold, and I had diarrhea. For an instant, I thought I'd throw down all my gear, slump into the water of the rice paddy, and sob.[14]

David fully expected that he would have to march all the way back to Camp Evans in this wretched condition, but the torrential rains that helped created such hardship also brought unexpected relief: as the marines wrapped up their mission and started the long trudge home, they soon realized that the streams separating them from Camp Evans, mere trickles before the deluge, had become impassible. Thus, after some bickering over the radio between Rocky and battalion headquarters (which apparently couldn't understand B/1/4's predicament), they were airlifted back to their base. David had survived his first real encounter with war. But it was just the beginning.

In his next letter to his parents, dated November 26, David described still more outdoor hardship and additional ambushes by a largely unseen enemy, standard fare (as he was coming to realize) for American infantrymen in Vietnam. After a brief recovery at Camp Carroll, B/1/4 moved to the nearby combat base of Phu Bai, and from there proceeded—once again aboard helicopters—into the mountains to the west. Among other things, the mission gave David his first introduction to the American media presence in Vietnam, and he was amused when—in a scene that might have come straight from *Apocalypse Now*—three NBC photographers jumped onto the landing zone ahead of the marines and "snapp[ed] flicks of us as we ran by."[15] Fortunately, there were no enemy troops present; otherwise, David quipped, "the joke would have been complete." To reach their first objective, the men hacked their way through the jungle with machetes, and when night fell the only way they could get any sleep was by tying themselves to tree trunks. Without this precaution, they would roll right down the rain-drenched mountainside.

The next day, Delta Company walked into an ambush that left six marines wounded, and the day after that it was Bravo's turn. The VC or NVA (no one seemed to know which) caught B/1/4 stretched out along a mountain trail and opened fire at the back of the column, exactly where David's platoon was located. For the novice second lieutenant the incident represented, as he explained to Victor and Jeanne, an important rite of passage: "I had one man wounded and one man killed. It was the first time I'd ever watched anyone I knew die. I guess I conducted myself as an officer is expected to because after that when I came around the men, especially veterans, stiffened a little bit straighter and said 'sir' with a little more deference."[16] In this instance, David's ordinarily crystal-clear prose arguably hid more than it revealed, perhaps because he was quickly learning that some details were best withheld from his anxious parents. There is something more than a little jarring about the way his letter leaps from the deeply personal declaration "It was the first time I'd ever watched anyone I knew die" to the far more distanced and official language that follows ("conducted myself as an officer is expected to").

In a longer letter to Walter, which he composed on the very same day, David was much more candid about the obviously traumatic nature of the episode. He reported that once the firing stopped, the man who had been wounded "came back by me with a look of unbelief on his face. I turned to my radio man and snatched the handset from him. He was round eyed and pale as a sheet." One suspects that the second lieutenant, still a relatively new arrival in the field, probably looked much the same. As for the dead man, an African American marine named Willie Broadnax, David described how "everyone in the company must have taken a turn carrying [the corpse] before we got out of the mountains. Down in the rice paddies we floated him on an air mattress."[17] Marines never leave their dead behind.

From the mountains, Bravo Company pushed on to a makeshift camp, halfway between Da Nang and Phu Bai, where the marines had orders to protect some sailors in a naval construction battalion (also known as "CBs" or "Seabees") who were building a bridge on Highway 1—exactly the sort of target coveted by the VC and the NVA. By the time David and his companions arrived, they could barely stand. "We were," David told his parents, "a sorry lot—drenched, blistered, sore, hungry, and without good water. The CBs took pity on us. They fed us hot chow and used their back hoe to help us scoop out 'hooches' (shelters) in the hillsides to finally get out of the rain."[18] Here the young man in whose memory the Angel Fire memorial would later stand made a commemorative gesture of his own: since the camp had no name, David dubbed it Camp Broadnax, and the men put up a sign.

Despite the ever-present discomfort presented by the monsoon, David's confidence as a platoon commander continued to grow. The unflappable, devil-may-care side of his personality, which Walter admired in his brother, now seemed ascendant.[19] Soon a battery of 105mm guns parked near the camp, and the jittery artillery commander "begged Captain Wirsching for a professional infantryman to set up defenses." Even more than the bridge, American artillery pieces presented a tempting target for the enemy—especially this far out in the bush. The VC, David reported, "receive special rewards if they can destroy a 105 with a satchel charge."[20]

Rocky had sent most of Bravo Company on a search-and-destroy mission in the surrounding hills, but fortunately 1st Platoon was still in the camp. David enthusiastically accepted the challenge of defending a half-mile perimeter with a patently inadequate number of men—basically his platoon, the artillerymen, and a handful of noncombat personnel (supply troops and so forth) against whatever force the enemy decided to send his way. Everyone remaining in the camp felt vulnerable, but by the time David had worked out all of the positions and fields of fire, he "almost hoped the VC would come up."[21]

While meeting and taking pride in his professional responsibilities, David was also quickly learning (in the fashion of all foot soldiers in all wars) to seize and to savor what small pleasures came his way. One never knew what tomorrow would bring. So, after sorting out the defense of the 105mm guns, he took advantage of a rare break in the weather to join a group of marines bathing and washing their clothes at the bridge. It was glorious. "That river," David told his parents, "must be a sewer for half of Vietnam and what's more it was filled with barbed wire and dud grenades, but for an hour while we washed and swam it was our paradise."[22] To top things off, the Seabees cooked up a ham Thanksgiving dinner that evening, which they shared with the ravenous marines.

Then, at a little past 3:30 a.m. that night, David Westphall's adventure in Vietnam took a terrifying turn. He woke in the early hours of the morning in order to inspect the defensive perimeter he had established the day before. He found his own men alert and on the ball, their eyes trained on the razor-wire-covered no-man's-land in front of them. Likewise the artillerymen. But some of the soldiers from the rear were sound asleep. David kicked them awake, lined them up, and bawled them out. Obviously enjoying himself, the furious second lieutenant didn't mince words: "I swore to them and myself that if they weren't still standing there when I came back at daybreak, I'd have them shot."[23]

David moved on in the pitch blackness to check on some more foxholes, and as he groped his way from one position to another, he suddenly felt a sensation unlike anything he had experienced up to this point in his young life. He had been hit—but not by a VC saboteur or even by an enemy booby trap. A pit viper had planted its fangs in his left index finger.

David thought quickly. It would help the doctors in Da Nang, where he was now surely heading, if he caught the snake. That way they could prepare the proper antivenom. But he could no longer see or hear any trace of the creature in the inky predawn. He'd have to take his chances without knowing the species. He found a corpsman, who applied a tourniquet, and for a moment the two men considered the pros and cons of the "cut and suck" treatment (slicing an X over each fang incision with a scalpel or razor blade and then drawing out as much of the venom as possible with a plastic suction cup). The procedure sometimes helped, but just as often led to "complications."[24] They decided against it. The air force forward observer attached to the camp immediately called in a medevac flight from Phu Bai, but the heavy rain delayed the helicopter's arrival for three hours.

By the time the chopper finally landed at Camp Broadnax, David's hand had swollen to the size of a "boxing glove," and his arm "was like a sausage up to the elbow."[25] His stomach had emptied. Up came the Thanksgiving dinner, followed by thin streams of bile. And he was delirious. Once hospitalized at the Naval Support Activity Hospital in Da Nang, he received, as he recounted to his brother, "20 some shots of anti-venom" before the swelling finally began to subside.[26]

In his next letter to his parents, dated December 4, 1967, David revealed that he was still in the hospital with at least three more days to go before he could rejoin his unit. Apparently he had suffered one of the most serious snakebites the doctors had seen, with greater than usual damage.

Even a week after the incident, the venom continued its toxic work. David reported that he still felt "quite a bit of soreness." Moreover, the fingers of his left hand remained "immobilized," and he had "lost ten pounds."[27] And no one could say for certain which variety of reptile was the culprit.

But much as it may have seemed to David (at the peak of this ordeal) that he was on the verge of joining the namesake for Camp Broadnax, his life had probably never been in danger. A report on internal medicine in Vietnam, released by the US Army Medical Department in 1982, revealed that "only one snakebite death . . . occurred" among American forces during the entire conflict.[28] The vast majority of bites—including, most likely, David's—came from the white-lipped bamboo viper, a reptile whose green coloring made it unnervingly invisible in the foliage and whose venom produced serious sickness. For understandable reasons, this creature soon assumed mythic proportions among American foot soldiers, giving rise to imaginary cousins like "the cigarette snake" (meaning that the recipient of the snake's venom would live just long enough for one cigarette) or the "two steps snake" (that is, two steps and then you were dead).[29] In reality, however, surprisingly few reptiles in Southeast Asia—cobras, mainly—were as dangerous as the Western diamondback rattlesnakes that David had frequently encountered back at home in the Sandia Mountains of New Mexico.

David rejoined Bravo Company on December 8, 1967, and the next day the unit made the fateful move north to what David called the "famous DMZ."[30] Ironically, David undertook the journey without his friend and commanding officer Rocky Wirsching, the person who had brought him to B/1/4. In fact, the two men never met again. During David's hospitalization, Rocky had heroically pulled two machine guns from a downed chopper while under fire, reopening an old knee injury in the process. As a result, he would fight the rest of his war from behind a desk in Saigon. His replacement, Captain Robert E. Harris, never produced the same warmth of feeling in David, but Harris was unquestionably courageous and, like the second lieutenant from New Mexico, he had risen through the ranks, serving initially as an enlisted man. He could identify with the soldiers he commanded.

David pressed on in the field, and the fall-off of detail in his subsequent letters to his parents and brother perhaps reflects his growing adjustment to a dangerous but also monotonous routine. Before taking up defensive positions at C-2, a sandbagged strongpoint just five miles or so south of Con Thien, Bravo Company embarked upon yet another field operation, but this time David scarcely bothered to describe his experiences to his parents or brother. Instead, he summarized, somewhat numbly remarking to Jeanne and Victor in a letter dated December 28 that over the past forty days they "had just enough killed and maimed to keep [them] alert."[31]

Bravo Company settled in at C-2, and for some weeks David had relatively little to report—an irony given the headline-generating excitement experienced by American troops elsewhere during this phase of the war. In one of her letters to her son, Jeanne had apparently predicted that a major North Vietnamese offensive would hit at the end of the monsoon. On February 3, 1968, David wrote to tell her that she had, of course, been right. The famous Tet Offensive had exploded in late January, and ever since David and his comrades had been "at it tooth and nail," filling sandbags and reinforcing bunkers in preparation for an NVA assault in their area.[32] But he had no direct contact with the enemy to report—just shelling from NVA artillery, which managed to inflict some "bad wounds," but no deaths, among the men stationed at C-2.[33]

Two weeks later, this period of relative calm ended, and David participated in his biggest firefight yet. As he subsequently explained to his parents, the 2nd Platoon of Bravo Company received orders on February 16 to locate and protect a downed helicopter, which had spun to earth while trying to extract a recon patrol, just a few miles from C-2. When the platoon reached the crash site, NVA troops who had taken shelter inside the chopper opened fire, killing several Americans and wounding several more. The marines pulled back and soon found themselves surrounded. They fought all night, struggling to defend a perimeter so terrifyingly constricted that called-in artillery or air strikes were out of the question. The NVA were (almost literally) right on top of them.

The next morning, the rest of Bravo Company, including David's platoon, set out to rescue the besieged marines. Everyone wanted to reach the crash site as quickly as possible, but as David explained, a march straight from point A to point B invited an enemy ambush. So, when David and his men reached a position about a half mile from the surrounded platoon, they "circled around," hacking their way through "a jungle of thorn bushes."[34] David admitted that he became so impatient that he seized a machete himself and tore up his hands on the thorns. Once the marines passed through this natural fortification, they "deployed along a tree line," pointed every M-16 rifle and M-60 machine gun at their disposal toward the sound of the enemy AK-47s, and opened fire. The resulting hail of bullets apparently killed a number of the NVA, who offered only "sporadic fire" from that point on.[35] Confident that they need no longer fear an ambush, David and his men proceeded to link up with the trapped marines, who had barely held on.

The ground where the 2nd Platoon made its stand was a hellish sight—bullet-riddled bodies, discarded weapons, blood-soaked field dressings, all the detritus of battle. And the survivors were mostly in a state of shock. David encountered a wounded marine who stared at him vacantly for a moment before recognizing him and asking for water. The second lieutenant shared his canteen. Then the commander of the encircled platoon came up and seized David by the hand.[36] When the chopper arrived to remove the wounded—always the tensest moment—Bravo Company opened fire in every direction, but the NVA, true to form, had already disappeared back into the countryside.

Remarkably, David's platoon made it through this particular mission without any casualties, and the next few weeks passed without anything quite so dramatic—just more patrolling, which failed to result in any significant contact with the enemy, and occasional NVA artillery and rocket fire directed at C-2. It was nearby Con Thien, David often remarked, that typically took the real beating.

The relative lack of NVA activity in David's immediate vicinity gave him at least a little time, amid his daily duties, to reflect and to write. And so, ever the student of history, he offered his personal assessment of Marine strategy along the DMZ in a letter to Jeanne and Victor dated February 28, 1968. The United States, he maintained, had learned nothing from the French:

> McNamara's "strip" [the McNamara Line] up here is ridiculous. We're tied to a number of bases, exactly like the French were, with no one,

not even one company in this whole division, as nearly as I can tell, left for a blocking force. As soon as the sun goes down as many gooks as take a notion can walk in between the bases anywhere they want to. Two things are supposed to bring the whole project to fruition: 1. Sophisticated surveillance devices will be installed in depth. 2. the ARVNs will be taking over the bases, freeing U.S. forces for maneuvers. From here it's most obvious that neither of these two things . . . will for months, if not years—years—take place. So . . . we're no smarter than the French.[37]

David's analysis couldn't have been more prescient, and criticisms of the US military's high command abound in his letters.[38]

Like his father, David could be eloquently outspoken and unsparing in his judgments when confronted with what he deemed incompetence or laziness. He did not, as they say, suffer fools gladly. From his letter of November 26, 1967: "Maybe there is something to the popular caricature of the 'the military mind' that I've always resented so. I hope I can avoid the pattern."[39] From December 28, 1967: "Under other circumstances I'd call most of our field grade officers incompetent oafs; under the present ones they're stinking bastards."[40] February 20, 1968: "Not even our bn. [battalion] commander, who is objectively a filthy bastard and a senseless swine, can upset me."[41] February 22, 1968: "Three quarters of my NCOs need a boot up the tail three quarters of the time and most of the officers deserve the same."[42] March 28, 1968: "Today I'm being royally chewed out by the co. CO [Company Commander] and XO [Executive Officer] because my platoon is all fouled up right now. Things will get straightened out, but in the meantime my inclination is to tell those two to go to hell."[43]

However, David's commitment to the war effort never wavered (even as his criticisms of American strategy and tactics became more frequent), and the following summation of his situation, offered in a letter to Walter dated January 18, 1968, appears in several variations throughout his correspondence from Vietnam: "This business is frustrating as hell, and I can see why most can't stomach a career in the military. But despite damnable frustrations, they're outweighed by the satisfactions and fascinating aspects."[44] The word that leaps from this passage (the quintessentially Westphallian word, if you will) is *fascinating*, hardly the adjective that most soldiers would select. Once again, we see the curiosity and intellect that set David apart—whether on the high school running track and football field, in the college classroom, or amid the northernmost front lines of the war in Southeast Asia. And we see how similar his mind was to his father's. "Fascinating" is exactly the way that Victor Westphall would have described World War II in the Pacific, a frequently repugnant display of brutality and suffering that he nevertheless found consistently engrossing and intellectually stimulating.

On March 9, Bravo Company moved even closer to the DMZ and occupied the outpost known as Yankee Station, just a quarter mile or so southeast of Con Thien. Enemy activity in the area remained light, and David grew increasingly restless. Eager for a chance to see the war from a different perspective, he applied—no doubt much to the horror of his parents and brother—for an aerial observer position, which meant flying over hostile territory in a slow-moving Piper Cub–type aircraft and reporting the coordinates of any NVA troops he spotted. To Walter, he explained the perks of this particular job, which included more contact with the enemy (he saw this as a good thing) and a pay increase of "$110–$160" per month.[45] Hazard pay, apparently. But of course David didn't mention that.

Ultimately, the aerial observer post went to someone else, which meant that David would see his war through to the end, which was now fast approaching, as the leader of 1st Platoon. Though disappointing, his continuance in this modest role did not reflect a lack of ability. Quite the contrary. The two fitness reports submitted by his battalion commander, Lieutenant Colonel E. A. Deptula, offered glowing (if somewhat generic) praise. The first report, dated December 31, 1967, describes David as a "spirited, aggressive, mature officer who produces excellent results."[46] The second, dated April 25, 1968, characterizes him as "level headed, thorough in his duties, and determined to excel."[47] Both reports conclude with the observation that David had what it took to become "an outstanding Marine officer."

An even more important signal of David's value to his superiors reached him on April 13, when his promotion paperwork finally came through. From this point on, he was First Lieutenant Westphall. Ironically, as he explained to his parents in a letter dated April 22, 1968 (exactly one month before his death), the celebration that customarily came with such welcome news inadvertently put him in the path of an NVA artillery projectile. David's account of the incident reveals his robust sense of humor; he was not always the somewhat stern officer we see elsewhere in his correspondence:

> The other day I went up on the hill i.e. from Yankee Station to Con Thien to deliver to the battalion commander the beer and cigars that are traditional after a promotion (being lucky enough to have wrangled some from the rear for this purpose). Strolling along with my sandbag of goodies over my shoulder and my helmet cocked to listen for the freight-train rush of incoming from the North that's exactly what I heard. I dropped my bag, sprinted for the nearest trench, and dived. For the third time since I've been in Nam a round landed right where I'd been standing. When I got out of the trench I went to look for the precious beer. One can was PIA (punctured in action), one can was DIA (dented in action), the other 15 were MIA (missing in action). Everyone thought it was a fine joke. My spirits remain high.[48]

On a more serious note, David revealed in the same letter that he had signed up for a six-month extension of his tour of duty in Vietnam. Perhaps to make his parents feel better about this decision, he carefully underscored the perks that came with his longer enlistment; these included a thirty-day paid leave in Spain (travel costs included), scheduled for September 1968, in addition to his regular thirty-day furlough, and the R&R that he was still owed. He seemed eager to present additional time in harm's way as a good deal.

Obviously, however, the chance to travel—and to practice his Spanish—at government expense hardly represented the main reason why he chose to remain at war. Why, then, did he make this commitment? For one thing, as the son of a World War II veteran, David may have felt that honor demanded service "for the duration." After all, Victor didn't get to enjoy the option of heading home after thirteen months (the Marine Corps, always eager to prove its toughness, added one month to the twelve required by the army, navy, and air force for a full tour of duty in Vietnam), and so why should he? In addition, as we have already seen, David felt that the "satisfactions" of his position in Vietnam outweighed the "frustrations."[49]

Among the former, he would likely have included the respect that he received from his subordinates. At several points in his letters, David underscored his delight in learning that the men of 1st Platoon felt safe with him in the field and comfortable with his strict-but-fair style of leadership. As Terry Middleton, a soldier in David's unit, later wrote to Victor, "Your son was always on us. Maybe that's why we made it home."[50] Had David lived, he would, in all likelihood, have eventually left the platoon. But perhaps he now felt that confidence in his leadership was something that he could count on wherever he landed. Clearly, that confidence meant a great deal to him.

And, finally, we can speculate that this often-tortured young man discovered in the intensity of war experience at least some temporary relief from the inner demons of depression and insecurity that had tormented him since childhood. Whether the extension of that experience into 1969 might have ultimately worsened his psychological condition is yet another question we cannot answer. Or perhaps we can: among the marines who later wrote major book-length accounts of their field service in Vietnam, none escaped at least some degree of PTSD. Had he come home, David would not have been the same man, most likely in ways both positive and negative.

For Bravo Company in April 1968, the war remained a sluggish affair, a seemingly unending cycle of anxiety followed by anticlimax and then more anxiety. It was easy, under such circumstances, to become bored, but everyone knew that boredom led to complacency, which led to death. As David was learning, the toughest moments in war don't necessarily come in the thick of the fighting. Throughout the first three weeks of the month, Con Thien continued to take the brunt of enemy artillery fire, which landed sporadically, and at nearby Yankee Station, David and his men continued to prepare for the worst, constantly building up their defenses along the perimeter in case of a ground attack.

On May 9—now just thirteen days from his death—David wrote with some details about a recent action that underscored the very real threat to Marine bases along the DMZ (despite the deceptive atmosphere of stalemate and lethargy), as well as the competence and resolve of the Americans stationed there. In response to a question from Jeanne about news reports of fighting near Con Thien, he described what had happened there just a short time ago. Though his own platoon was kept at Yankee Station, part of Bravo Company participated in the firefight; thus, David was in a good position to learn what had transpired. Essentially, just outside Con Thien, the marines ran into a large enemy force, which was apparently massing to overrun the Hill of Angels (just as NVA troops had done a year earlier).

This time the Americans cut them to pieces. David reported 72 enemy dead "at a cost of 9 Marines." Moreover, the battle reached its climax with "a tank-infantry charge so stirring that the next day six clerks and motor transport people, who normally have nothing but jibes for 'the grunts,' volunteered to go on patrol with my platoon."[51] Even now, in the third year of the United States' large-scale troop commitment in Vietnam, the year that would prove deadliest for Americans, and as resistance to the war skyrocketed at home, tearing the nation apart, there could still be moments that seemed to come from a John Wayne movie.

In all, David wrote thirty letters to family members while in Vietnam—twenty-two to his parents and eight to his brother. All show the Westphall flair for composition. Those written to Walter often cover the same material as those addressed to Jeanne and Victor, but they typically run longer and perhaps offer a somewhat more candid record of David's experiences and attitudes. Understandably, there were things he couldn't bring himself to tell his parents, and Walter, he knew, would be discreet. For the historian seeking to reconstruct the experiences of marines along the DMZ in 1967 and 1968, this body of correspondence represents a veritable treasure trove. But David himself comes most to life in the details, in the little things that have nothing to do with his accounts of ambushes, defense preparations, or tallies of enemy dead.

For example, he frequently asked—sometimes pleaded—for his parents to send him things. Sometimes the items are minor creature comforts, but just as frequently they were pieces of equipment that the resource-starved Marine Corps could not issue or did not think to issue. In his letter dated November 16, 1967, David requests:

a good whistle, w/chain, preferably not shiny, another pair of leather gloves, preferably black, just a dab of red cellophane [for use as a night filter on a penlight, perhaps?], vitamin C, notebook paper as per the enclosed sample, a giant size, fineline, black papermate pen refill, mustache wax (very important!), a small calendar, contac[t] paper, which is clear adhesive sheets—rolls, rather—of thin plastic indispensable for protecting maps. Most important and with the highest priority: 3 or 4 boxes of Bit-O-Honey candy bars, & if possible some raisins, some almonds, & if possible some beef or deer jerky or the like.[52]

By December 28 most of the requested items had arrived, but some appear to have been stolen. Could Jeanne and Walter send the following? "Another '68 calendar, + more socks, also the same size notebook paper you sent, green dye, candles, automatic grease pencils, 4 or 5 prs. of size 11 innersoles (emerging priority, separate packages/pr might ensure quicker delivery, as well as might absence of any special arrangements other than regular air mail) and batteries both penlight and regular size."[53] He explained that the mustache wax he requested earlier was a joke.

In his letter from February 3, 1968, David hates to "be always importuning," but he is in desperate need of, among other things, "hankies" and "Hoppy's #9 gun cleaning solvent," as well as "45 cal. bore cleaning patches, Q tips, pipe cleaners," some "kool aid or Tang," and "more Bit-O-Honeys." In the same letter, he asks his parents to check on his subscription to *Playboy* magazine and to send along "a bottle of Kahlua and some glasses (or a bottle of brandy)."[54] Having now acquired a taste for liquor, he would, along with his fellow officers, receive a number of libation-bearing care packages over the next few weeks, until divisional headquarters put a stop to the practice.

Perhaps the most ironic item that David requested from his parents is a poster-size map of Vietnam from *National Geographic*. Military maps, he explained, gave absolutely no sense of his location in relation to the country as a whole.[55] When the map finally arrived, David couldn't wait to pin it to the wall of his dugout. His place in Vietnam now made a little more sense—at least geographically.

Walter also sent him large boxes of provisions and received a grateful response. "Opening your packages," David wrote, "was more fun than

Christmas time. I unpacked goody after goody to the oohs and ahs of an astounded audience."[56] To his brother, David wrote passionately about books. He urged Walter to read *The True Believer*, by the then popular American philosopher Eric Hoffer, and well as its sequel, *The Ordeal of Change*. Later he reported that he was reading Pascal's *Pensées* ("it's fascinating and very thought-provoking") and looking forward to perusing *Mein Kampf*.[57] And in his final letter to his brother, he recommends Ayn Rand's *Atlas Shrugged* and *Capitalism: The Unknown Ideal*.[58] Hardly light reading.

Matters of personal finance also find their way into his letters, often as a source of worry. Since he had yet to go on R&R, David had no place to spend his monthly salary, and so he sent most of his money home. He repeatedly asked his parents to confirm that they had received the checks. Transactions with the local Vietnamese, he explained, were conducted on a barter basis. He traded extra cans of C rations—when not in the field, the Americans had plenty—for souvenirs and local goods, including a "bush hat" and "some bread," and wished that he had studied Vietnamese.[59] The haggling would have been much easier that way.

Since there was no point in making monthly payments on an automobile sitting back home in a garage, he decided to sell his Datsun—the car he drove during that epic trip with Walter from Quantico to Angel Fire—and was satisfied with the price that his parents managed to sell it for. And like all Americans, he dreaded filing his taxes. As the April 15 deadline approached, he wrote to Jeanne and Victor that "the stresses and strains over here don't bother me much, but things like my W-2 form do, so I'm sending you mine."[60]

Reminders of his father's war experience in the Pacific surface from time to time. Sometimes eerily. In his very first letter from Vietnam, David explains to his parents that he may be sending "for a lot of gear"—this partially explains the lengthy wish lists that came later—because "one of my sea bags may have been lost on the truck coming north from Phu Bai. This truck hit a Vietnamese bus in Hue, and I think a little boy was killed."[61] One can't help but think of that terrible moment—one of the lowest points in *his* war—when Victor, utterly horrified, saw a Filipino child run over by a jeep.

Another reminder of civilian suffering crops up in David's reports during his hospitalization following his snakebite. In the ward next to his was "a Vietnamese girl (yes, a female in the ward with all these men) who has malnutrition along with other complications. The wretches have put a sign on her bed saying 'Twiggy' [a notoriously thin British fashion model of the period]. But she's beautiful."[62] David never saw anything like the hellishly overcrowded civilian hospital on Borneo toured by Victor, but here, as elsewhere, he began to understand what war must mean for the people caught in the middle. The term *gook* he usually reserved for the NVA and VC, and—racial offensiveness notwithstanding—employed with a mixture of fear and grudging respect.

Like his father, the son also experienced the anything-but-friendly phenomenon of "friendly fire." At C-2 he became especially close to a fellow New Mexican in his platoon, a Corporal Jacobs from Taos (just a forty-minute drive from Angel Fire), and they talked longingly of Wheeler Peak and Taos Mountain. Jacobs shared some photos from home, which showed the magical landscape of the Sangre de Cristos. But then came "a beautiful snafu."[63] An American artillery round fired from Dong Ha fell short and exploded, and one of the red-hot metal shards struck Jacobs in the knee. The wound didn't seem serious, and David hoped his comrade could avoid being evacuated (perhaps Corporal Jacobs hoped for the opposite). But it turned out that there are "too many moving parts in a knee to accommodate a piece of shrapnel," and so this "Taoseño" dropped out of the second lieutenant's life.[64] In Vietnam, as with any war, human error and defective equipment sometimes proved just as dangerous as the enemy.

Meanwhile, life at Angel Fire went on, and though thousands of miles away, David remained connected to his parents' interests and routine. He showed little sign of the estrangement from family—from home—that some frontline soldiers experienced. Perhaps that would have come later. Throughout his letters he inquires after friends, relatives, the family dogs, and a stray cat his mother has adopted. He asks for updates on the Val Verde Ranch development project, which Victor was now thinking of selling off.

David's letters to his brother reveal a close bond. He frequently congratulates Walter on his academic successes—the latter was just a semester away from completing his bachelor's degree at the University of Indiana (prior to entering officer training in the air force)—and advises his sibling on affairs of the heart. When Walter announced possible wedding plans,

David didn't hold back: "Marriage? No, no! You're your own best judge of this, but beware, beware! In any case there are thousands and thousands of women, plus 'world enough, and time.'"⁶⁵ (And, as it turned out, Walter would not marry in this instance; he would wait until much later in life and then do so quite felicitously.)

On the subject of his own love life David remained silent. His letters from Vietnam contain no mention of Irene or of any other girlfriend. Perhaps he felt that in his case too there would be, per Andrew Marvell's "To His Coy Mistress," "world enough, and time" for love and marriage. He was, after all, just twenty-eight years old. But "Time's wingèd chariot"—to quote from the same poem—was approaching faster than he knew. His advice against matrimony appears in his very last letter to Walter. It is dated May 15, 1968, just seven days from the ambush that would end his life.

For Bravo Company at Yankee Station, the month of May opened with more of the same—occasional shelling and infrequent, inconclusive encounters with the NVA. Overhead, however, the war took on a different character. The molasses-like pace of peace talks in Paris, characterized by delays and disingenuousness on both sides, resulted in a temporary halt to American bombing of North Vietnam. As a result, the marines noticed increased air activity in their area. David speculated that American pilots probably flew "the same number of sorties as previously," only now they concentrated their efforts along the DMZ.⁶⁶

With the six-month anniversary of his arrival in Vietnam just passed, Lieutenant Westphall's prospects appeared to be looking up. He was back on good terms with his superiors (after restoring his platoon to tip-top shape), and he could—per the Marine Corps policy of rotating field officers once their tour reached the half-year mark—expect a transfer soon. He anticipated that by May 25 he would become the new XO for Bravo, with the real possibility of a company command a month or so after that. He also held out hope that he would eventually find a place in a reconnaissance unit, thereby fulfilling an ambition that he had nursed from the start of his tour.

On May 12 he wrote the last letter his parents would ever receive from him. He addressed it to Jeanne in recognition of Mother's Day. Even the

The last-known photograph of David Westphall. Taken May 1968, at Yankee Station. Courtesy of Walter Westphall.

Marine Corps, he explained, was sentimental when it came to this holiday, and he apologized for being unable to include an appropriate gift: "We had a chance, last pay day, to fill out forms for sending flowers by mail, but I missed the opportunity because I was taking the pay roster back to Dong Ha."[67]

Then, in a passage of scene painting unlike anything else in his wartime letters, David describes a moment of sudden, aching beauty. For a brief interval at least, Vietnam became something very different from the sinister landscape of concealed threat that he scrutinized with a soldier's eyes:

> You're probably having pleasant weather there now. It rained here today which cooled things off some, although the temperature still got up to a muggy 95 [degrees] with the hot months still to come. After a rain here the air seems to be more clear and you get a good view of all the mountain ranges to the west of us, and from the observation post on the "the hill" you can see the ocean to the east. There was a

really beautiful gold, pink, and light blue sunset over the mountains in Laos this evening.⁶⁸

David went on to apologize for not writing more frequently, and he quoted a passage from a recent letter from Kim, the South Korean soldier with whom he had become friends at Quantico. Kim teased him about being promoted too quickly. Soon, he joked, his American comrade would reach an exalted rank even higher than his own.

Near the bottom of the letter, David offers "greetings and good wishes" to his father. Then he refocuses on Jeanne and quietly closes with, "Mom, I hope you had a good day today. Take care. Love, David." Someone—Victor, presumably—later made a notation at the top of the first page, indicating when the letter was received. It arrived at the Westphall household on May 21, 1968, the day before the ambush and one of the last good days Jeanne would ever know.

The disaster that befell Bravo Company on May 22 came with terrible suddenness, and involved more enemy firepower—more chaos and violence—than anything 1st Platoon had experienced over the preceding six and a half months. As a result, those marines who were lucky enough to survive later remembered the incident in different, sometimes conflicting ways. What follows sticks to the broadest possible outline of what happened; as Walter Westphall has discovered in his decades-long effort to reconstruct the battle as precisely as possible, many of the details have already been lost to time or will remain forever speculative.

To understand the story of Bravo Company on this fateful day, we must first turn to another Marine unit. Before sunrise that morning, a neighboring outfit, India Company of 3/3, filed out of A-3, a firebase five miles or so to the east of Con Thien, and embarked on a search-and-destroy mission. The marines headed southwest toward a spot in Leatherneck Square exactly on the line between their "Tactical Area of Responsibility" (TAOR) and that of David and his companions at the Hill of Angels and Yankee Station. Border areas like this, where one unit's TAOR ended and another unit's began, invited enemy infiltration, and India Company planned to set up several ambush sites at this potentially vulnerable location.

But before they could do so they collided with an unknown number of NVA heading toward the DMZ. The company CO, Captain Matthew G. McTiernan, called in a helicopter gunship, and the enemy force—outgunned for the moment and caught without any fixed defenses—withdrew westward in the direction of a hamlet named Phu Oc.[69]

As news of these developments—half-understood though they were—worked their way up the chain of command, a delicious prospect began to form: with the NVA unit's approximate location known—it *had* to be somewhere between Phu Oc and the McNamara Line now—there was a chance to trap it and annihilate it. All the trap would need would be for a group of marines to swing below the Trace, thereby blocking the NVAs' movement north and hopefully pushing them back toward McTiernan's men. As it turned out, that group would be Bravo Company.

By midafternoon David and his fellow officers had received their orders. Led by Captain Harris, who was just days away from the end of his tour, the men of Bravo Company climbed on top of eight tanks and held on for dear life as the armored vehicles barreled eastward along the south edge of the Trace. At a point about two miles east of Con Thien, the infantrymen jumped off and lined up alongside Route 561, a "tree shaded, narrow dirt road" that led straight south into Phu Oc.[70] At 4:10 p.m., they set out cross-country, moving east parallel to the Trace and toward—they hoped—an enemy unit that would be on the move, desperate to reach the DMZ and home, and thus vulnerable to an unexpected American ground attack. The tanks remained on the Trace, ready to destroy anything that emerged from the south side of the McNamara Line between Con Thien and Route 561. To all appearances, the NVA were trapped and within minutes of being massacred.

David's thoughts during all this may easily be imagined. He had missed out on the big fight three weeks earlier, when Marine tanks working in concert with infantry had killed more than seventy NVA soldiers. Now he was in the thick of an operation that promised comparable glory. As a chess aficionado, he perhaps thought of the situation in terms of that cerebral game. As the Marine forces, like so many rooks or bishops, closed in and cut off escape routes, the NVA unit, like a cornered king, was quickly running out of squares on which to land. And David would be right there for the inevitable checkmate.

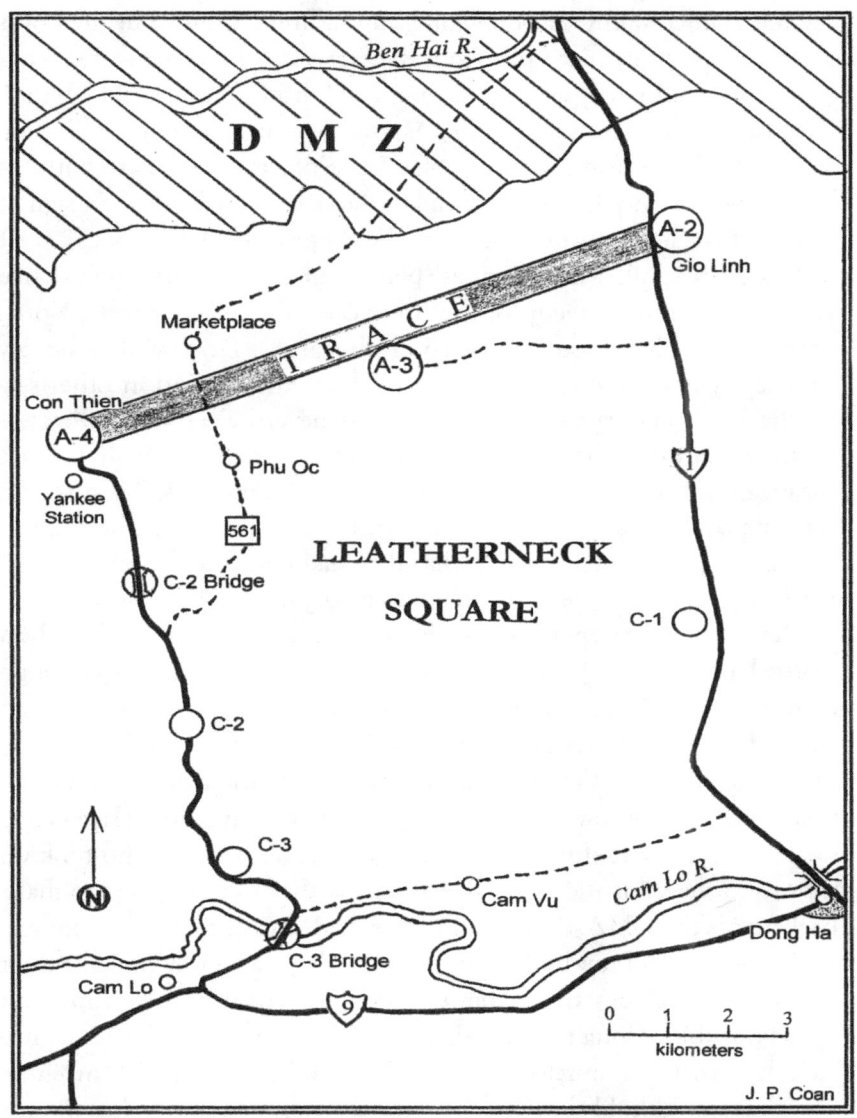

Map of Leatherneck Square. Note the position of A3, Phu Oc, and the Trace. Map by James P. Coan. Courtesy of the University of Alabama Press.

He felt fear, certainly. Anyone going into a firefight did. But there was also that perverse joy that came from the certainty of contact—actual contact!—with an ordinarily wraith-like enemy. Philip Caputo would later admit to this strange emotion.[71] Other Marine veterans remembered feeling it as well. And on the afternoon of May 22, 1968, as he advanced with his men and peered into the foliage ahead of them, waiting for the first sign of an enemy that he *knew* would be there, David probably felt it too.

Two factors spoiled the marines' plans and turned what looked like certain victory into a tragedy for the Americans (the tragedy for the North Vietnamese involved would come soon thereafter). First, while a far cry from the impenetrable jungle that David had encountered in other sectors, the landscape east of Con Thien was nevertheless an intelligence nightmare featuring "waist-high Kunie grass interspersed with patches of heavy brush and hedgerows that divided the countryside."[72] In such a place, one couldn't see beyond a small area or be sure of anything. Thus, the marines guessed at this point that they had cornered a sizable enemy force, but just how sizable no one could say for certain. The best estimate, after the fact, put the enemy's strength at roughly a battalion—a battalion of battle-hardened troops in the NVA 320th Division, more than enough men to hit back hard, as David's unit would discover.[73]

Second, after their encounter with I/3/3, the NVA withdrew to the area northeast of Phu Oc for a reason unknown to the marines: a hidden bunker complex, set low to the ground and so expertly camouflaged as to appear invisible, waited to shelter them. The NVA soldiers who took up positions in these fortifications perhaps knew they weren't going to make it back across the DMZ—the attention they had already attracted from marines in the area did not bode well—but now they had a way to make their sacrifice count for something: they would take as many of the enemy with them as possible. Along the top edge of each bunker ran narrow slits into which they stuck the muzzles of their AK-47s and drum-fed RPD machine guns. They would hold their fire until the marines were just a dozen yards or so away.[74]

At about 5:20 p.m., Bravo Company came in range, and the foliage on a rise in front of the Americans exploded with small-arms fire. At the moment of contact, 2nd Platoon, under Lieutenant Joe Johnston (the experienced, highly competent officer who had led his men through that all-night siege near the downed chopper three months earlier), was closest to the enemy, with the 1st and 3rd Platoons perhaps a hundred meters or so behind on the right. The volume of NVA fire, stunningly unexpected, almost immediately pinned down Johnston and his men, and bullets raked the other two platoons as well. Right away, marines started getting hit. An enemy grenade landed near Lieutenant Johnston and exploded, blowing fragments into his face. And Captain Harris went down with multiple fatal wounds. His radio operator joined him in death perhaps an hour later.[75]

Bravo had achieved contact with the NVA, all right, and now the company was fighting for its life. The protection of darkness couldn't come too soon. When dusk finally arrived, 2nd Platoon was still pinned down and continuing to take casualties. The other two platoons did what they could, squeezing off rounds that traveled over the backs of their trapped comrades, and then received orders to pull back. Lieutenant Johnston's men eventually made it out of the inferno by crawling away from the bunker complex on their bellies.[76]

By 7:30 p.m. the fight was over, at least where Bravo Company was concerned, and those marines who could still function moved to a nearby clearing, where they formed a defensive perimeter around the several dozen wounded—many barely clinging to life—and waited for the medevac helicopter. David Bilbrey, the chopper pilot who swung in to pick up the worst cases, later wrote to Victor Westphall that "the extent and the type of wounds on display" was overwhelming. He had already logged two thousand hours of combat flying and had two Hueys shot down while he was at the controls. But the gory spectacle that greeted him on the evening of May 22 took the horror of it all to a new level.[77]

At this point, Bravo Company's exhausted, nerve-strung survivors also tried to sort out who had made it and who had not, and David's name wound up on the list of the missing. No one found this information encouraging. It simply meant that his body was too close to the NVA bunkers to be recovered just yet.[78] Why David reached such a forward position—recall that at the moment of the ambush 1st Platoon was perhaps a hundred meters behind Lieutenant Johnston's outfit—remains something of a mystery. All we know, based on the testimony of several eyewitnesses, is that at some point early in the ambush David left his platoon under the command of Sergeant Roger Boyd and followed by his faithful radioman, Lance Corporal Charles Kirkland, raced toward Captain Harris's position, which was right behind 2nd Platoon. Harris may have summoned David by radio. Or perhaps the first lieutenant saw his CO go down and instinctively moved forward, wanting to help. In any event, David and his comrade apparently reached Harris's position, or at least got close, before a burst from an NVA machine gun or assault rifle killed them both.[79]

As combat veterans know, the phrase "died instantly" often signifies the opposite—a gruesome, lingering demise too terrible for disclosure to family members. But in David's case the phrase probably fit. Multiple rounds hit him at once and likely ended his life within seconds, if not "instantly." The official cause-of-death paperwork filed on May 24, following a standard examination of the body, indicated "W/M [wounds massive] penetrating back and upper and lower extremities." As for Lance Corporal Kirkland, he expired from a "gunshot to the head."[80] Both bodies presumably remained where they fell until May 23, when circumstances finally allowed the recovery of marines killed the day before.

Less than twenty-four hours earlier, tanks had hauled David and his companions—high-spirited warriors who smelled blood—to their dropoff point on the Trace. Now those same vehicles carried the dead.[81] Men whose vacant stares still registered the overwhelming shock and intensity of the previous day's combat lifted rag-doll bodies with familiar faces— Captain Harris, Lieutenant Westphall, Lance Corporal Kirkland, and eight others—onto the M-48s, which then returned to Con Thien with their grisly cargo. In all, the 1st Battalion, 4th Marines lost seventeen men as a result of the fighting on May 22—fifteen killed in action and two additional solders (including Sergeant Boyd) who subsequently died of wounds. Thirteen of these marines served in Bravo Company.[82]

But what of the NVA troops who had inflicted so much damage? By the time David's comrades recovered his body, almost every single North Vietnamese soldier who had fought Bravo Company the day before was dead, including, presumably, the man who pulled the trigger on the weapon that ended Lieutenant Westphall's life. They had never had a chance. At 8:00 a.m. on May 23, Alpha Company of 1/4 located the NVA at a tree line roughly 1,500 meters northeast of the ambush site, right next to the McNamara Line.[83] American artillery and air strikes pulverized the position. Then groups of frantic enemy troops made a break for the Trace—six hundred yards of cleared, murderously open ground—where they became proverbial sitting ducks for the marines' tanks, which were waiting with antipersonnel canister or beehive rounds (ghastly bundles of steel darts, or flechettes). As the beehive rounds hit the NVA, helicopter gunships and Phantom jets simultaneously rained destruction from above.

It was a slaughter. Afterward, the marines estimated that of the 150 enemy soldiers who tried to cross the Trace, fewer than a handful made it.[84] Just a few hours earlier, in a skillful maneuver, these same NVA troops had caught Bravo Company off guard. Now an entire battalion of the North Vietnamese 320th Division had basically been wiped off the face of the earth. In Vietnam, the fortunes of war could change with terrifying swiftness.

One state over from New Mexico, in the mining town of Morenci, Arizona, those same fortunes brought a terrible concentration of loss. In 1966, nine young men from this rugged, working-class community—five Anglos, three Mexican Americans, and one Navajo—joined the Marine Corps. By Christmas 1969 six were dead, most of them killed the year before, the deadliest period of America's war in Vietnam. And for the three who came home, grief, survivor guilt, and PTSD would take a terrible toll.

These nine Arizona boys—for that's what they were, really, all but one still in their teens—enlisted for a variety of reasons, none of which had much to do with the geopolitical complexities of conflict in Southeast Asia. Some viewed military service as an essential component of manhood and wanted to emulate fathers and uncles who had fought in World War II or Korea. Others saw opposition to atheistic communism as a mandate of their Catholic faith. Two of the enlistees were Mormon and perhaps sought, in historian Kyle Longley's words, "to fit into mainstream American society and overcome suspicions of their secretive practices, as well as their legacy of polygamy."[85] Hollywood probably played a role as well. A Morenci Vietnam veteran tellingly described the nine enlistees as "gung ho John Wayne boys."[86]

Representing a racial and ethnic cross-section of the American Southwest, the Morenci Nine, as the group came to be known, inevitably grew into a symbol of working-class patriotism and heroic sacrifice or (depending on one's point of view) exploitation and waste on the part of politicians married to a delusional foreign policy. So much death and suffering inflicted on one community, in the service of such a controversial war effort, cried out for interpretation, for a processing through collective memory. "Even today," Longley writes, "the Morenci Nine are a prominent part of the historical consciousness of the Southwest."[87]

And so, from 1969 onward, the town of Morenci—a name synonymous with nine Marine Corps enlistees and their tragic fates—became one of two prominent sites of Vietnam War memory in the region. The other was a windswept hill overlooking the Moreno Valley in the Sangre de Cristo Mountains of northern New Mexico, where a shattered family would struggle—against every imaginable obstacle and at dreadful personal cost—to preserve the memory of another lost marine and to connect that memory to the needs of an entire nation.

3

Terrible News in a Beautiful Place

> As the government-issue car wound its way through the community, people prayed that it would keep moving.
> –Kyle Longley, The Morenci Marines: A Tale of Small Town America and the Vietnam War (2013)

In Arizona, the gut-wrenching task of contacting the families of marines killed in Vietnam fell to a Phoenix-based captain in the Marine Corps reserve. It was a duty perhaps worse than anything faced overseas. The most terrifying NVA rocket attack or massed infantry assault would have been preferable.

As Kyle Longley recounts, the process, repeated again and again, began with a phone call to the officer in Phoenix from the Marine Casualty Section at Quantico. The voice on the line would offer "details on either the death or the wounding of an Arizona Marine," as well as an address for the soldier's family.[1] The captain would carefully take notes before hanging up, knowing full well that the family he was about to visit would—after their initial shock—want every scrap of information, no matter how seemingly insignificant. If his destination was unfamiliar, he consulted a road map. Then he set off on a drive that could take five minutes or five hours, depending. Regardless, it could hardly have been a comfortable journey for many reasons. For one thing, the officer's appearance needed to be immaculate, without a single crease or sweat stain on his distinctively tight-fitting, dark blue dress uniform—a difficult thing to achieve in the Arizona heat. He also needed to be mindful of his black shoes, buffed to a high sheen, and his dress cap, whose black leather visor would likewise be expected to gleam in the desert sun.

In the case of a killed-in-action (KIA), the captain would, upon arrival in the soldier's community, seek out a local minister or priest to accompany him to his destination, a household that would be changed forever even before he could speak—changed by the sudden apparition of his deathly dress uniform or a quick glimpse of the government license plates on his car. By 1968 the families of combat marines knew how to read these signs.

We can assume that the process was similar, if not identical, in the neighboring state of New Mexico. But on the afternoon of May 27, 1968, two Marine Corps captains, not one, made their way from Santa Fe to the home of Victor and Jeanne Westphall at the Val Verde Ranch in Angel Fire. The homebuilder and his wife were still relative newcomers to the north-central region of the state, and they did not attend regular services at any of the local churches. Perhaps this explains the presence of the second captain. In any event, as the officers' car entered the Moreno Valley, and the Westphalls' hilltop property swung into view, with Wheeler Peak and its phalanx of surrounding mountains towering in the background, the two men must have been struck by the splendor of the scene. They could scarcely have brought their awful news to a more stunning locale.

In recent letters to David, Victor had indicated that he might sell off the Val Verde Ranch and launch a different project. But while he pondered his options, the development work proceeded as planned, much of it undertaken singlehandedly by Victor. On this particular day, he was busy digging a trench for a water line that would irrigate the subdivision's golf course. Thus, the two marines found the muscular fifty-four-year-old operating a backhoe, which he had parked at the "bottom of a steep slope."[2]

From his perch in the cabin atop the machine, Victor had a "clear view" of the main road that led into his property, but he was so focused on the operation of the mechanical shovel that he didn't notice the officers' car until its occupants were already walking toward him.[3] He shut off the motor on the backhoe and, with what he later described as "numbing apprehension," waited to hear what they had to say.[4]

The two messengers knew from experience that delaying the announcement only made the situation more difficult. If the blow must come, better to deliver it at once.

"Are you Doctor Westphall?" asked one of the officers.

"Yes."

"Your son has been killed."[5]

Victor sat in silence for several moments, and his weightlifter's body suddenly seemed frail, as if all the youth he had preserved through his daily exercise regimen had evaporated. The officers twice offered to help him climb down from the cab. He refused and awkwardly descended on his own. As he stood facing the two marines, a faint hope surfaced in the father's mind. Perhaps they had confused his son with someone else. Perhaps there was still a way out. He asked if the soldier in question was named David, which was actually his oldest son's middle name. One of the officers answered by speaking David's real first name, as given on his birth certificate. Victor submitted to the inescapable reality. The two emissaries had come to right place, to the parents of Victor David Westphall III.

One of those parents did not yet know the news, and Victor immediately took it upon himself to inform his wife. He rode with the officers to his house, which was a half mile away, and then went inside alone. The announcement left Jeanne "stunned nearly to insensibility," but she quickly pulled herself together, knowing that Walter, who worshipped his older brother, would need every ounce of strength she could muster.[6] Victor phoned his surviving son right away.

Like David the year before, Walter was in the midst of his last round of final examinations, eagerly wrapping up his undergraduate degree before entering officer training (though in the air force, not the Marine Corps). Thus, the news of his brother's death landed like a bomb in the midst of what would otherwise have been a happy and exciting period of transition. And for Victor, nothing on this terrible day stood out more in retrospect than Walter's horrified reaction over the phone, which "lacerated" his father's "soul to the well-spring of [his] being."[7] Knowing that Walter would be alone with his grief during his plane ride home from Indiana made the situation even worse.

After offering what consolation they could, the two Marine captains quietly departed. Other visitors quickly took their place. While Victor manned the telephone, spreading the word among relatives and friends in Albuquerque and Wisconsin, a stream of considerate neighbors from Angel Fire and Eagle Nest—friends that the recently resettled Westphalls didn't know they had—stopped by to offer their condolences, a welcome distraction for Jeanne.

And then, finally, with the departure of the last well-wisher, the utterly worn-out parents were left alone, face to face with an incomprehensible disaster—and the most painful of mysteries. For on top of everything else, it didn't take long for the fog of war to settle around David's death. The two officers who delivered the news on May 27 indicated that David had died during a rocket attack. But the official telegram, which arrived the next day, attributed his demise to a single "gunshot wound."[8] More confusion followed. A letter from the new commander of David's company, dated May 31, absurdly maintained that Lieutenant Westphall had expired due to wounds in his arms and legs. This preposterous claim sent Walter, who had now arrived at his parents' side, into an understandable rage. However well intentioned, the Marine Corps seemed determined to insult the Westphalls' intelligence. After all, Victor had seen the carnage of war firsthand in the Pacific and harbored no illusions about the gruesome nature of death in combat. All the family wanted was the truth.

David's body arrived in Albuquerque on June 6, four days before the funeral, which his parents had decided to hold in the city. And, sadly, the return of his remains, the best evidence of what had happened to him, only deepened the mystery. In horror, Victor and Jeanne discovered that their son's casket was sealed, a measure that hardly corresponded with the information they had received so far.

For Victor, this latest development supported his growing conviction, based on a series of dreams, that David had died from a head wound. And it would not be the last time that he employed dream interpretation to understand David's death or the direction his commemoration should take. Indeed, as we will see more fully in a moment, both parents were about to descend into a terrible, grief-driven struggle to hold on to reality, a battle that would be especially hard on Jeanne. In Victor's case, the loss of David, a tragedy that he saw coming only in retrospect, amplified his long-standing habit of forcing often tenuous patterns onto events. And as he read more and more meaning into his dreams (while also discovering signs and portents in the waking world), his "behavioral patterns" increasingly seemed, to use his own words, "tinged with madness."[9] As for Jeanne, a vague certainty that mysterious evil forces had singled out David for destruction—or were closing in on his family—soon evolved into a deep dread of certain individuals and certain places, including, ultimately, the site of her son's memorial.

Grief, as we know, is a complicated emotion—or, rather, a set of often incongruous emotions that change and move in and out over time—and it would push all three surviving members of the Westphall family toward an extraordinary expression of remembrance, operative on a national level, as well as deep empathy with others left scarred by the war in Vietnam. But it also carried a destructive side.

At times during the days immediately following the announcement of David's death the waking nightmare became too much for the Westphall family. When Jeanne first approached her son's flag-draped coffin at the funeral home in Albuquerque, she collapsed onto her knees and asked—in what Victor described as a "wrenching, dry-eyed tone"—"What have I done to deserve this?"[10] Bearing smelling salts, the funeral director helped her to her feet. Victor maintained a numb composure—there was, after all, so much to take care of—until the day of the funeral, when, observing the tears streaming down Walter's face, he too was overcome. "I broke down completely," he later recalled.[11]

Conducted by Chaplain William J. Cooper, the service in Albuquerque was made all the more poignant—and all the more agonizing—by the inclusion of a passage from one of David's college papers, which had, of course, earned an A from a dazzled professor. Titled "The Prophets and Their Times," the paper drew a characteristically well-articulated contrast between the civilization of the ancient Greeks and that of the Hebrew prophets, and it featured—in the portion read by the chaplain—a line that would later appear prominently on the Vietnam Veterans Peace and Brotherhood Chapel: "If we are to stand on our feet in the presence of God, what, then, is one man that he should debase the dignity of another?"[12] This question stuck with Victor. For what was war, he concluded, but the ultimate debasement of other human beings and the ultimate form of arrogance in the face of God? A political hawk and a proud combat marine, David might not have agreed, but his language nevertheless pointed the

The National Veterans Cemetery in Santa Fe. David's grave is in the foreground on the right. Photograph by Richard Dickerson.

way to what would become some of Victor's most deeply held convictions about peace and war.

To the large crowd of mourners that day, which included dozens of David's high school and college friends, this demonstration of David's formidable writing ability served as both a moving tribute and a bitter reminder of what the world had lost. A half century later, looking back on his brother's life and what might have been, Walter doubted whether David would have stayed in the Marine Corps beyond his second tour in Vietnam: "It is more likely that he would have become a teacher and a writer. . . . Had he lived, I think he would have written significant books about history, including the Vietnam War."[13] All of the writings by David Westphall cited in this book—his papers for college classes, personal statements, letters, and an impressive article in the *New Mexico Historical Review*—support that conclusion by evidencing an exceptional facility with language, as well as a love of history and the arts, that could hardly have remained in the background of his life indefinitely.

After the funeral, the mourners formed a procession of vehicles and slowly drove the sixty-mile stretch of I-25 that connects Albuquerque to Sante Fe, where the Westphalls had elected to have David buried at the

National Veterans Cemetery, a swath of peaceful green northwest of the historic downtown square. Surrounded by men and women who served in conflicts ranging from World War I to the Iraq War, Lieutenant Westphall remains there today—in section U, grave number 520—beneath a white headstone inscribed with lines as terse as rifle volleys:

VICTOR
DAVID
WESTPHALL III
NEW MEXICO
1ST LIEUTENANT
US MARINE CORPS
VIETNAM
JANUARY 30 1940
MAY 22 1968
PH [Purple Heart][14]

Visitors to the memorial at Angel Fire are often surprised to learn that while Victor and Jeanne are both buried next to the chapel, David is not. There is a simple explanation: at the time of David's interment in Santa Fe, the Westphalls had not yet decided to erect a large-scale, physical memorial to their son, or to tie his memory to larger cultural concerns. They were, in fact, seriously pondering other, more conventional forms of remembrance, including a university scholarship (perhaps tied to one of the humanities fields that David so loved) endowed in their son's name. Given Victor and David's shared love of academics, as well as the family's ample (at that point) finances, this option made a great deal of sense—so much so that to friends and family members it probably seemed like a foregone conclusion.

Then, on June 12, just two days after the funeral, Jeanne presented a new idea to her husband and her surviving son, one that would change all three of their lives profoundly, perhaps no less profoundly than the loss they had just suffered: What if they built a chapel in David's memory atop the dramatic prominence—overlooking the valley—that formed the eastern side of the Val Verde property?

On the surface, the notion seemed to come out of nowhere. After all, the Westphalls were not exceptionally devout. Walter recalls that during the early years in Albuquerque the family actively participated in the First Congregational Church on Lomas Boulevard. The two sons attended Sunday school, and Victor, ever ready to take on another construction project, "even helped build an addition to the church."[15] But the Westphalls' church attendance fell off once they relocated to the Juan Tabo house and ultimately ceased altogether. Earlier in Victor's life, a mystic streak had surfaced in his personality. When first married, he was active in the Order of the Magi, a supposedly ancient brotherhood possessing arcane spiritual knowledge. However, this interest faded as his business career and scholarly writings came to consume more and more of his time and attention. (His attraction to mysticism will reemerge, with greater intensity, later in this narrative.) As for Jeanne, who was born a Catholic, she showed little interest in organized religion, outside of her brief membership in the Congregational church, and preferred to identify herself, broadly, as a Christian. Likewise indifferent to dogma, David listed his faith on Marine Corps paperwork as Unitarian.[16] Walter has remained, for some decades, an agnostic.

In short, as a family, the Westphalls hardly manifested the kind of conventional religious fervor that one would expect of individuals associated with one of the most dramatically designed church buildings in North America. But in other ways, remembering David through the establishment of a place of worship made perfect sense. Victor's study of art history had, after all, immersed him in Christian painting and architecture, and the idea of *building* something in response to David's death must have struck a deep chord within him. Over time, it would also become clear that the chapel offered the grieving father something that an endowed scholarship would not have—a place where he could teach (or, if one prefers, preach) the lessons he had drawn from tragedy. Though sidetracked from a career in education thanks to his business success, Victor remained an educator at heart, as the thousands of Vietnam veterans soon to come his way would discover.

More than anything, however, it was Jeanne's belief in a spiritual connection between David and the Val Verde Ranch that inspired the memorial. Ten months earlier, as he walked toward the bus that would take him on the first leg of his journey to Southeast Asia, David had placed his copy of *Wings for Per*, his favorite childhood book, in his mother's hands. It was the one title he could not bring himself to give away. As she pondered the best way to memorialize her son, Jeanne's thoughts returned to the closing sentences of the d'Aulaires' narrative: "Then I will fly up into the clear, washed air of spring and soar over the eagle's nest and over my house under the crag. Mother will stand in front of the house and clasp her hands in wonder. She will say: 'Look, Per has wings.'"[17]

Weird parallels seemed to abound between this passage and the locale to which Victor and Jeanne had recently moved. Gazing north from the Westphalls' hilltop property, Jeanne could see a body of water known as Eagle Nest Lake and, beyond that, the village of Eagle Nest. Other specifics matched up as well. The Val Verde Ranch stood beneath the nearby "crag" of Wheeler Peak, to which Victor and David had hiked on that memorable final outing. And, of course, there was no shortage of actual eagles wheeling and hovering over the Westphalls' mountain home. Surely, Jeanne concluded, something mysterious was at work in all this, a conclusion quickly shared by her husband and surviving son. Destiny, Walter would later call it.[18]

As the notion of constructing the chapel quickly took hold—just four months would pass between Jeanne's first mention of the memorial and the ground breaking—its commemorative agenda also came into focus. The building would serve as more than a memorial to a single individual. It would honor David, certainly, but also recognize all who had served and died in the Vietnam War (presumably at this point thought of exclusively as American fatalities) and express the hope for universal peace. Walter recalls that this three-pronged mission came together with astonishing swiftness, perhaps on the very day when Jeanne first expressed her idea. The building's title, which reflected its multiple functions and multiple levels of meaning, was agreed upon from the very start. The Westphalls would call their memorial the Vietnam Veterans Peace and Brotherhood Chapel.

And although a handful of other Vietnam War memorials appeared first, there would be nothing else quite like this grand conception—nothing with the same unsettling blend of personal and public memory or quite the same expression of respect toward the fallen combined with longing for an end to war. Arguably nothing with the same power and complexity—except, perhaps, Maya Lin's design for the Wall in Washington, DC, which deploys a very different kind of visual rhetoric. With its strata of messages, the chapel would stand alone on the American commemorative landscape and thus become a focal point for controversies and conflicts that Victor, Jeanne, and Walter could not, at this point, even begin to imagine. But first it had to be designed and built. And the ordeal of its construction—two and a half years of setbacks, disappointment, and financial freefall—would push the family to the breaking point.

Through a mutual associate, one Tony Perry, Victor contacted Santa Fe–based architect Ted Luna, an up-and-coming artist with a flair for the dramatic, and invited him to design the chapel. On July 2, the architect signed a contract with the Westphalls. Victor's vision of the project took the form of a broad directive. He asked Luna to see "that the structure should be such that no person entering it could leave with quite the same attitude toward peace and war."[19] Beyond that, the only specifics he requested were the inclusion of an eternal flame (a nod, perhaps, to John F. Kennedy's famous tomb at Arlington National Cemetery) and the mounting of two inscriptions drawn from David's writings.

The first of these came from a poem titled "The Ultimate Curse," a meditation, at least as Victor interpreted it, on the kinds of societal failings that lead to war:

> Greed plowed cities desolate
> Lust ran snorting thru the streets
> Pride reared up to desecrate
> Shrines, and there were no retreats.
> So man learned to shed the tears
> With which he measures out his years.

The second appeared in that extraordinary student essay, showcased at David's funeral, titled "The Prophets and Their Times." It included the statement about human dignity that Victor found so memorable:

> At the sight of the heavenly
> throne Ezekiel fell on his
> face, but the voice of God
> commanded, "son of man, stand

upon your feet and I will speak with you." If we are to stand on our feet in the presence of God, what, then, is one man that he should debase the dignity of another?[20]

Less than a week later, Luna visited the Westphalls at Val Verde and unveiled his plans. What Victor and Jeanne saw stunned them. The architect's blueprints presented a soaring structure with three curved walls, two of which swept upward to form "twin pinnacles" fifty feet off the ground—the lofty front end of the chapel, that is, which overlooks the valley.[21] The third wall, arranged on the one-room floor plan like the base of a triangle, formed the rear of the building. In the narrow gap where the first two walls nearly met—the top, if you will, of the triangle—a slender window, the only source of natural light (apart from two glass doors), ran vertically from the floor to a point twenty-eight feet in the air. Seen from the side, the design looked something like a miniature glacial peak: "The roof line follow[ed] the downward curve of the two main walls to normal room height at their juncture with the third wall."[22]

Featuring a "relatively petite interior compared to the truly massive exterior," it was a simple but spectacular conception—and exactly what Victor had hoped for.[23] He was, in fact, in awe of the architect's uncompromising design, which would surely result in "one of the most beautiful buildings in the world."[24] Several weeks later, Luna presented the Westphalls with a scale model of the chapel, which also met with their approval.

While representing a complete departure from *traditional* approaches to church design, the architect's vision expressed a modernist idiom that was not entirely unfamiliar to residents of the American Southwest or the Rocky Mountain region. Indeed, the Vietnam Veterans Peace and Brotherhood Chapel shares some affinities with two midcentury ecclesiastical structures, both regional icons—namely, the Chapel of the Holy Cross outside Sedona, Arizona, and the famous Cadet Chapel at the United States Air Force Academy (USAFA) in Colorado Springs. Dedicated in 1957 by the Catholic church, the former sits atop a massive red rock formation two hundred feet above the Sedona Valley, its glass front divided into four panels by a ninety-foot-tall crucifix that juts out of the space between two stone monoliths. Seen from the sides or rear, the structure looks boxlike, its severe vertical and horizontal lines relieved only by a tilted roof, which, like the shark-toothed front end of the Westphalls' chapel, rises to form the semblance of a church spire. But when viewed from the valley below, the building takes on a far more inspiring aspect. From this vantage, the Chapel of the Holy Cross seems at once an apparition (a "dreamy vision" impossibly situated in the high desert landscape) *and* a natural extension of its red rock foundation.[25] It's a human structure that gives the eerie appearance of not having been made by humans at all, as if fashioned out of the landscape directly by nature or by God—a description that parallels comments made by many visitors to the memorial at Angel Fire.

Conceived by the architect Walter Netsch and completed in 1962 (following a prolonged controversy over its radical design), the Cadet Chapel at the USAFA likewise achieves an otherworldly effect while also connecting with its natural setting. The building's pyramidal form evokes Pikes Peak and other nearby mountains, part of the Colorado Rockies Front Range, that form a backdrop for the academy on its western side. But there's also a science fiction feel to the structure, which looks a bit like seventeen futuristic aircraft—or spacecraft—stacked side-by-side, each resting with its nose pointed straight into the air. Constructed of steel, polished aluminum, and glass—materials redolent of space-age flight—the Cadet Chapel fits the modernist aesthetic of the USAFA as a whole, which, as art historian Robert Allen Nauman has observed, stands apart from the other, older service academies (all located in the east) through its visual linkage to technology and futurity, as well as "ideas of individualism [and] exploration" associated with the "Western frontier."[26] Like the Chapel at Angel Fire, Netsch's brainchild is both strange—weird, even—*and* oddly harmonious with its physical and mythic space.

Once viewed alongside these earlier church buildings, the blueprints for the Vietnam Veterans Peace and Brotherhood Chapel seem less iconoclastic. Still, to some jaundiced twenty-first-century eyes, Luna's design—with its startling curvature, teepee-like spire, and overall eccentricity—may come across as dated hippie architecture, subversively aimed, through its defiance of structural norms, at the establishment. However, the architect, for his part, did not attribute to the chapel a counterculture message of any kind. Far from it. The "Architects Statement [sic]" that accompanied the blueprints opens with the following, somewhat ungrammatical declaration: "Dedicated in conception to the memorial and tribute to all young men that have given their lives so that others may live as personified by David Westphall."[27] Luna went on to identify the chapel as "a timeless statement"—of what, he did not indicate—"void of all traditional connotations of materials and their use . . . simplicity without sterility."[28] Nowhere does his brief statement mention protest or the American war in Vietnam.

It seems likely that the Westphalls' thoughts at this point likewise had little, if anything, to do specifically with American policy in Southeast Asia. As we have seen, Victor's experiences in the Pacific left him with a deeply conflicted attitude toward armed conflict, torn between pride and patriotism, on the one hand, and a haunting sense of tragedy and waste, on the other. He had long brooded over the contradictory realities of war, but he was hardly a pacifist. Thus, his charge to the architect—to design a structure that would leave no visitor's attitude toward war unchanged—may have carried, at least on one level, a somewhat more conventional, even patriotic meaning than one might assume given the grieving father's later, more radical pronouncements. Indeed, there is no evidence to suggest that Victor saw any contradiction between the memorial's honoring of Americans who had fought and died and its message of peace. And this applies to Luna as well, as indicated by his anything-but-radical Architect's Statement, with its conventionally patriotic reference to "young men who have given their lives so that others may live."

Moreover, Walter's decision to move forward with his own deployment in Vietnam, despite a provision that allowed exemptions for siblings of servicemen killed in action, also suggests that the family's investment in traditional notions of military honor and patriotic service survived the initial shock of David's death. Both men, father and surviving son, would later speak out against the Vietnam War with great eloquence and anger, but that moment had not yet arrived.

On August 31, 1968, Luna submitted a cost estimate for the chapel, which he had worked out with Sante Fe-based contractor Georg Vedeler. Except for the architect's 7.5 percent fee, the quote was reasonably complete, and it set the price of the finished building at $43,345.[29] The actual cost came out considerably lower. According to Walter, the final price tag for the chapel—not including ongoing maintenance, external features such as landscaping or parking, or repairs—was $32,699, a not-astronomical figure that equals the buying power of $237,399 today.[30] The amount of construction labor that Victor and Walter took on themselves largely explains the difference.

Characteristically, the former homebuilder joined in the work to ensure that it was done correctly. And in this regard, given his personality, he could hardly have helped himself—much, as we will see, to Vedeler's chagrin. But physical labor also offered Victor a therapeutic application for his formidable energy, as well as a desirable distraction. Savings had little to do with it at this point. The Westphalls had the money for this unusual venture—the settlement from David's life insurance policy added an extra $30,000 to their resources—and they could take comfort in the potential earnings represented by the Val Verde property, into which Victor had sunk most of the modest fortune that he had made in Albuquerque. At the time, it probably all seemed manageable. In reality, however, the family was stepping into a financial abyss, as they would soon discover.

Things began to move quickly. Just two days after receiving Luna's cost estimate, the Westphalls entered a formal agreement with Vedeler, who, in the manner of all contractors before or since, offered an overly optimistic schedule for the project's completion: just forty-five days.[31] Twenty-four hours later, the family established a nonprofit corporation (known today as the David Westphall Veterans Foundation) as the sole owner of the Vietnam Veterans Peace and Brotherhood Chapel. The articles of incorporation opened with the following vision statement: "Article 1. Purpose and Function. The fundamental purpose and function of the corporation shall be to erect and maintain a memorial Chapel to VICTOR DAVID WESTPHALL, III and to others who have served and fallen in the Vietnam War to the end that peace and brotherhood will eventually be attained for all mankind."[32] Despite the legalese, the final fourteen words of this statement could not have been more audacious—or, depending on one's point of view, fanciful. Either way, they expressed an aspiration that would be integral to the chapel, along with its mission of personal and patriotic remembrance, throughout the next decade.

On September 9 Vedeler and his crew measured and staked out the location of the exterior walls, and the excavation of the site, performed by Victor atop his backhoe, began the next day, a fateful moment that marked a point of no return for David's surviving family members. From this day forward, the Westphalls' brash decision to turn their private tragedy into a public statement, via an avant-garde, fifty-foot-tall structure that no one visiting the Moreno Valley could miss, would become the central, looming fact of their day-to-day lives, a source of pride (even, on occasion, joy) but also tremendous hardship and disappointment.

Just as the climate of Southeast Asia had been an implacable foe during David's deployment in Vietnam, weather conditions in the Sangre de Cristos would prove a perpetual enemy of his commemoration. One of the highest-altitude church buildings in North America, the chapel stands at 8,500 feet, and is thus subject to all the unpredictable extremes associated with an alpine setting.[33] In the winter, temperatures sometimes dip to forty-five degrees below zero. Howling down the Moreno Valley with near-hurricane force, blizzards periodically produce whiteouts and leave several feet of snow at a time. And even in the summer, flurries or ice storms can hit without warning, sometimes as late as August, along with near-daily rain showers (at least during years that do not see drought conditions, a growing problem throughout the Rocky Mountains region presumably linked to climate change). Temperatures during the warmest months sometimes fluctuate by thirty degrees or more over the course of a single day, and nights are frigid year-round. The fauna associated with this high-mountain locale also present unique challenges. According to Walter, "elk herds occasionally travel over the memorial grounds," sometimes damaging obstacles inadvertently placed by humans in their path, and "black bears are [sometimes] a nuisance."[34]

As the rugged denizens of Eagle Nest and Angel Fire can attest, living in an area of such ferocious weather and abundant, sometimes even menacing, wildlife requires a level of fortitude that not all Americans possess—or would necessarily care to possess. Even in the second decade of the twenty-first century, when the mountains of northern New Mexico are far less remote than they were in the 1960s and somewhat tamer, the region is not for everyone. Of course, Victor, the son of homesteaders, matched this sometimes inhospitable environment perfectly. However, even he underestimated the difficulties involved in erecting a structure of such epic dimensions atop a prominence completely unshielded from mountain winds and subject to such intense winter conditions. And in retrospect, breaking ground in September, as opposed to waiting until the spring, was perhaps not the best idea. As befitted the bleak tragedy that had descended upon the Westphalls, the cold and snow came on fast in 1968.

Completion of the basic structure, confidently scheduled for a month and half, took nearly a year. As noted, poor weather was to blame, but so were the unique challenges posed by Luna's audacious design, with its curved ceiling and walls (Vedeler, it is safe to say, had never constructed anything even remotely like it before), and the sundry screw-ups and oversights that attend any substantial building project. Of course, Victor found the latter intolerable, and consistent with his strong-willed, high-achieving personality he soon came to regard Vedeler and his crew in much the same light as he had earlier viewed David's football coaches.

Later, after the job was finally completed and his anger cooled, Victor would reach out to Vedeler and thank him warmly for his work and for his "dedication to the ideals expressed in the beauty of the structure and the worthiness of the cause for which it stands."[35] But in the fall of 1968 that moment was still far in the future. Throughout the dark months that followed the ground breaking, Victor wrote repeatedly to Luna with complaints about the contractor, whom he had hired based entirely on the architect's recommendation. (Vedeler was not, apparently, among the large circle of New Mexico builders that Victor had come to know through his business in Albuquerque.) On November 10, Victor described the project, now more than two weeks past its projected completion, as a "two months fiasco in which not even the walls were completed."[36]

Ten days later, a plumbing issue drove him to explode. Apparently, he had insisted, when helping with the excavation, that deep trenches would be required for the water lines. Vedeler had brushed the advice aside. Now, sure enough, the plumbers indicated that they would need to set their pipes at least four feet in the ground (to avoid freezing), a task complicated by the partially completed walls, which would make it difficult, if not impossible, to use a backhoe. But it was the contractor's reaction to the situation that Victor found most infuriating: Vedeler seemed "incredulous that [the earlier conversation] had ever taken place."[37] "The whole sorry performance . . . has left its mark on me," lamented Victor, but in a strained effort to be fair, he remarked that he had "almost come to the conclusion that, in their way, the crew that was here this summer meant well."[38] Almost.

Despite his disappointment with the work so far, Victor extended Vedeler's contract into 1969 (he had little choice), and according to Walter the two men agreed upon terms for two additional tasks beyond the completion of the basic structure or shell: installation of "roof framing members" and construction of the "plywood deck."[39] For a contractor, time truly is money, and so Vedeler, who had already hemorrhaged a vast number of hours beyond his original calculations, must have looked forward to the advent of spring and better conditions with an eagerness equal to Victor's.

But then disaster struck. In early January, pummeled by winter weather, the half-completed structure began to give way. Victor wrote to Luna with the grim details: "The west wall of the Chapel is . . . deteriorating. Some of the blocks are completely out and the wall has leaned to the extent that the top of the window opening to the south is nearly closed. We fear that the wall may completely collapse with consequent damage to the east wall."[40] On January 19, a howling windstorm produced the damage that Victor feared.[41] More than four months in, his chapel was not just unfinished, it was literally being blown off its hilltop perch.

Vedeler's feelings about this new setback, and the additional time it would require for his salaried crew, can easily be imagined. But he honored his contract and, as weather allowed, patiently oversaw the rebuilding of the collapsed wall. In his conciliatory letter penned after the structure's completion, Victor thanked the contractor for his steadfastness in the face of this particular reversal: "I admire," he wrote, "your unflinching attitude in approaching that most disagreeable task."[42] A forceful personality, the Albuquerque businessman/historian/bodybuilder could be an irritable taskmaster and in some contexts a know-it-all who (like most of us) was not above an occasional "I told you so." However, Victor's correspondence from this period also reflects moments of hard-won self-awareness and generosity, as well as an unwavering commitment to Luna's architectural vision—not once did he consider aborting the project or downsizing the finished product—that becomes all the more remarkable when one considers what else was going on at the time.

Nearly fifty years later, as he looked back on his mother's reaction to losing a son in war, Walter had this to say: "No one escapes unscathed . . . no matter how strong you are or how you react."[43] Before David's death, when not doting on her sons, Jeanne Westphall had served as the clerical, administrative backbone of the family's home-development business. A kind woman with an outgoing and cheerful disposition, she was also hard-working and fearless. One day at the Juan Tabo house, a large snake managed to get inside and latch its fangs onto a dead rodent caught in a mousetrap. It wasn't a rattler, but the situation was alarming just the same. Walter saw the reptile first and froze. Jeanne calmly "scooted it out with a broom."[44]

She had also kept her cool and responded swiftly during a terrible incident that occurred at the house on Morningside while Walter was still a small child. A toddler from a neighboring family, perhaps two years old, somehow wandered into the Westphalls' back yard and fell into their swimming pool, where he drowned. Walter found the little boy floating facedown and alerted his mother, who after phoning the emergency personnel did everything she could to resuscitate the child. The neighbors apparently sued the Westphalls afterward, but had no case.[45]

In the winters, Jeanne loved to ski in the Sandia mountains, and she led a generally contented life in Albuquerque, which grew large enough, during the two decades or so in which the Westphalls lived there, to offer most of the urban amenities she had enjoyed in Milwaukee. Walter speculates that she was perhaps none too keen to make the move to the Moreno Valley, which meant a new start, a new existence in comparative isolation. But, as usual, she went along with her headstrong husband's plans. It was usually pointless to resist them.

On May 22, 1968, Jeanne became a casualty of the Vietnam War—no less than the physically maimed or psychologically tormented veterans who returned from that conflict only to be greeted, in all too many instances, with awkward silence and governmental neglect. She was simply the kind of war casualty that one seldom hears about, even today. A recounting of her story takes us out of the chronology observed by the rest of this chapter, but it is important to consider that story here. If anything, Jeanne was

Jeanne Westphall with David, circa mid-1940s. Courtesy of Walter Westphall.

twice wounded—first by the war, and then by the very memorial that she had proposed and perhaps came to regret. Vietnam took her oldest son. It could be argued that the chapel, a gesture of parental love that ironically drove the two parents apart, claimed her husband.

Throughout the summer and fall of 1968, Victor kept himself going, at times just barely, by fixating on the memorial project and by taking comfort, as we will see shortly, in dreams that he interpreted as communications from David. Jeanne could do neither, and she sank into a terrible state of depression and paranoia, gripped by fears that malevolent forces were stalking her family and had killed her son, or had taken him prisoner and were hiding him somewhere.[46] Like most delusions, the suspicion that David wasn't really dead made its own kind of logical sense. After all, the family had never actually seen his body. And who could trust any information that came out of Vietnam? Early one morning in July, she experienced a terrifying episode. Victor woke to hear his wife "frantically scurrying about the house pulling all the electrical plugs from their sockets." "When I questioned her," he later wrote, "she frenziedly broke from my grasp to continue her search for more plugs, explaining hysterically that the house was about to blow up. . . . Her fear appeared to be genuine and frightening."[47]

In the days immediately following the shattering news of David's death, Jeanne had found comfort in the beauty of the Moreno Valley and the magical correspondences that appeared to exist between her new home and the mountainous Norwegian setting of David's favorite book. But soon, sadly and ironically, she began to find life at the Val Verde Ranch unendurable. Evil now seemed to surround the family's lonely property, and unpleasant local characters—one in particular—took on a sinister aspect.

Before David's death, while the development scheme was still under way, a self-proclaimed representative of the "old Catholic church," one Padre Martin, had approached the Westphalls with a request to build a religious sanctuary on the very spot where the chapel would later stand.[48] Victor was amenable but insisted upon specific terms and conditions. When the negotiations began to bog down, Martin tried to convince Jeanne, who must have struck him as impressionable, that he possessed certain "powers."[49] Shortly thereafter, the supposed padre was exposed as a charlatan and sent packing. Walter recalls his father angrily taking a sledgehammer to the wooden cross that marked the location of Martin's proposed sanctuary.[50]

But in the wake of David's death, Jeanne's wounded consciousness perceived the bogus priest not as a con artist but as a vengeful, supernatural figure wielding black magic. She even wondered if Martin had somehow managed to slip a bomb into one of the care packages that she had sent to David in Vietnam.[51] If so, then could she be responsible for his death?

Terror-stricken, Jeanne could no longer stay at Val Verde, and so began a torturous series of relocations—all, as Victor would later write, "while the problems of . . . constructing the Chapel were unimaginably numerous and vexing."[52] First, Victor took his wife to Albuquerque, where she stayed for a time with her sister. Then, in the summer of 1969, the couple moved to a mobile home in Springer, New Mexico (a winding sixty-five-mile drive from Angel Fire), where they lived until March 1970, when Jeanne decided, in the midst of another panic attack, that they were still too close to the Moreno Valley. Victor hauled the mobile home to Albuquerque and tried for two months in 1971 to oversee the chapel construction from that remove.

But the distance from Angel Fire, where he felt constantly needed, was just too great. Following the dedication of the still unfinished structure on the third anniversary of David's death, he convinced Jeanne to return to Springer, where she would remain for nearly the rest of her life, a lonely figure whose existence had been turned upside down first by war and then by commemoration. Throughout the 1970s Victor would visit twice a week or so, making various improvements to the mobile home for his wife's comfort, including some room expansions and a two-car garage.[53] But his heart was clearly at the chapel, which demanded, at least from Victor's perspective, his near-daily presence.

Its hold on him became absolute. During the early years of construction, he would stay over at the site, sleeping in a camper shell parked on the windswept prominence. Later, he built a tiny cabin—he was, in a sense, homesteading yet again—located downhill, southwest of the chapel.[54] To anyone who had known Victor during the Westphalls' peak of affluence and family happiness in the Juan Tabo house, that symbol of the American dream attained, the homebuilder's new life and domicile, along with his growing distance from Jeanne, would have seemed incomprehensible.

Victor outside his cabin near the chapel, circa early 1970s. Courtesy of Walter Westphall.

The contrast was just too surreal. Only individuals similarly bereaved would have understood.

In 1986, nearly two decades of corrosive grief, combined with Victor's fixation on the memorial, finally drove the couple into more or less separate existences. As part of the terms for the memorial's takeover by the Disabled American Veterans that year, Victor demanded an apartment for himself, which was built at the rear of the visitors center. Here he stayed until his death in 2003. He would still see Jeanne from time to time, and in 2002 she even returned to the Val Verde property (or what was left of it) and lived near the chapel in a house constructed for her by Victor.[55] The two remained amiable, and there would be no divorce. But the marriage, battered by heartbreak and obsession, was no longer the intimate union it had once been.

Walter recalls his mother's long years in Springer as a time of bleak monotony and, in comparison with her former existence in Albuquerque, isolation. She did become good friends with a number of couples her own age, and each week she received a visit from the local Jehovah's Witnesses. Sometimes she went out to dinner, a special treat to which she always looked forward. But mostly she spent her days alone, watching television—she was a great fan of *Jeopardy!*—or reading. From her porch, she fed an ever-growing colony of neighborhood cats. Just to get out of the house, Jeanne would sometimes pull her car out of the garage "and drive through Springer and take the loop onto the Interstate and back."[56]

Later in life, Walter's family brought her much of the happiness that she had otherwise been denied. In the presence of her grandchildren, Kimberly and David, her spirits and mental health rebounded. Her old vivacity returned. Kimberly remembers her as a person who despite heartache "embraced happy moments and joy."[57] Indeed, to her granddaughter, she was essentially "a happy woman."[58] The two would sit side by side in the living room of Jeanne's mobile home, and Kimberly would listen to the story of how her grandmother had met her future husband at the ice cream parlor in Milwaukee. Years later, Kimberly recalled the story vividly: "Victor came in and chatted her up. Eventually they went out on a date. She was very clear to tell me that there was no funny business going on. I remember her shaking her little finger as she told me this."[59]

During the last year of her life, eighty-nine-year-old Jeanne moved to Wichita in order to be close to Walter and his family. Despite her failing health, it was perhaps the happiest time she had known since David's death. And now that her granddaughter could visit weekly, her relationship with Kimberly only grew stronger. While Jeanne reminisced, the two would root through boxes of jewelry and family papers. And all the while, Kimberly stored up memories for the future: "I would take mental snapshots and think 'I don't want to lose her.'"[60]

In August 1969, a year and three months after the two Marine Corps captains had delivered their shattering news to the Westphall family, Vedeler's crew finally completed the chapel's cinderblock shell, probably the strangest-looking building they would ever construct. Even in its rough form, the gigantic, avant-garde structure dramatically altered the skyline west of Angel Fire and could be seen for miles in multiple directions, making it the talk—not always favorable talk—of the Moreno Valley. The only question now was whether the Westphalls would be able to support themselves after the chapel was finished.

By this point, Victor fully grasped the project's potentially disastrous impact on his finances. In fact, he had worried about money throughout the previous year. Back in December, he wrote to Luna that "our financial situation here is critical in the extreme."[61] And in the same letter, he bemoaned the false impression his family gave of being "loaded."[62]

The problem was that while Victor and Jeanne had enough in their savings to cover the chapel's construction—and even, thanks to David's life insurance payment, some of the additional expenses that would come later—their income had basically disappeared. Achieving a return on the Val Verde land investment would have required fully developing the "golf course and homesites," a task for which Victor now had neither the funds nor the time.[63] Thus, in May, the Westphalls had made the difficult decision to sell the Val Verde Ranch, into which they had poured most of their assets, to a Texas-based development corporation. All of the property had to go, except for five acres set aside for the chapel.[64] One month later, the two parties closed on the deal, which provided Victor and Jeanne with a significant cash buffer just in case the long-term costs associated with the memorial grew higher than expected (which, of course, they did). But while the money was welcome, the sale marked the end of Victor's construction business, and it placed a cap on their resources. The latter caused Victor to wonder constantly whether he and Jeanne would be able to spend their "declining years with a modicum of comfort and dignity."[65] Would their memorial enterprise leave them with anything? And now, with the first phase of construction complete, Victor could see a new tidal wave of expenses rushing toward him.

The situation was overwhelming. The chapel still needed window- and doorframes, a layer of roofing material, stucco finishing within and without, flooring, a furnace, interior and exterior lighting, a sound system, apparatus for the eternal flame, a sign near the highway at the base of the hill, and a host of smaller items that even Victor, an experienced builder, could barely keep track of. And beyond everything else, the matter of upkeep loomed. The winter climate in the Sangre de Cristos had already demonstrated what it could do to an exposed building at 8,500 feet. How would the Westphalls deal with the inevitable wear and tear that mountain conditions would inflict in the future? Like all who build memorials, they wanted theirs to be permanent. This required funding for ongoing maintenance. Where would it come from?

Initially, Victor may have believed—with his somewhat customary naiveté—that his chapel would immediately be perceived as an absolute public good. Philanthropic organizations or even government offices would rush to support it, thereby allowing him to continue with his home-development business and to hold on to at least some vestiges of the private life he had enjoyed before David's death. Luna shared this conviction. But as it turned out, no one—or at least no one with deep pockets—would help the Westphalls with their half-finished project.

One of the more grimly amusing examples of Victor's miscalculations in this regard occurred during the summer of 1969 when he hosted the meeting of a "local ministerial group" at his home on the Val Verde Ranch.[66] Viewing the gathering as a fundraising opportunity, he took up a collection, which yielded (as he lamented to Luna afterward) about the same amount as the humanities-scale cash award received for David's article in the *New Mexico Historical Review*.[67] Though Victor didn't say so, one suspects that his guests were actually there to see if the presumably wealthy developer could help *them* with their various projects. A similar thing happened, earlier that year, when the New Mexico Council of Churches took an interest in the chapel. As he explained to Luna, Victor leaped at this apparent opportunity for financial backing (one of many such chimeras) but quickly learned that the organization had its own agenda, which he refused to dignify with a description. "I may," he simply admitted, "have overlooked the possibility that the New Mexico Council of Churches wanted a foothold in the Moreno Valley for their purposes, not mine."[68]

At the same time, Victor received a crash course in the Sisyphean nature of grant writing. Throughout the winter of 1968–1969, he submitted proposals to every foundation he could think of. None were accepted. Or, as Walter would later put it, rather acidly: "Not one of the great and magnanimous institutions applied to considered the Chapel worthy of its support."[69] To be sure, the whole scheme would have sounded outlandish to anyone who didn't know Victor or the kind of man he was. One perhaps needed to meet this human dynamo face to face to fully appreciate his energy or the depth of his resolve. But Victor was also a trained academic and a published author. He knew how to write a compelling grant application.

The problem, one suspects, had nothing to do with Victor's powers of persuasion (or the worthiness of the chapel) and everything to do with the American war in Vietnam, now in its post-Tet Offensive stage and the center of a cultural storm into which few foundations would willingly have ventured. Although the memorial's message of patriotic tribute *and* peace accommodated both the political right and the left, the site would be a lightning rod for controversy just the same, as the evaluators of Victor's doomed grant proposals no doubt realized. A public memorial, by definition, invites acrimonious debate since there is rarely total agreement over the meaning of the events selected for commemoration or even the form that commemoration should take. Here, then, was a memorial to America's fallen in a war that was *still under way*, with no clear outcome in sight. In retrospect, one could easily have predicted the negative responses that Victor received from those "great and magnanimous institutions."

Disenchanted with fundraising, Victor submitted to the inevitable: it would take almost everything the Westphalls had to make the memorial an enduring reality, along with contributions here and there from parties as yet unknown. As for the long-term impact on his personal financial situation, along with Jeanne's, it would be what it would be. As he later explained in *David's Story*, faith in the project began to matter more than having a precise plan for the future: "Gradually, . . . I learned that if I simply went to the Chapel and worked with my own hands—and didn't expect too much too soon—the funding would come right there. I didn't have to go out and beat the bushes for it, but I absolutely did have to have faith."[70]

He drew this faith from a series of visions involving David, and regardless of whether one interprets these "revealments" (as Victor called them) as messages from the beyond or expressions of the subconscious, there's no question about the comfort they offered the grieving father. The earliest occurred on the morning after David's funeral, when Victor saw a family friend standing on the freshly constructed golf course at the Val Verde Ranch. Suddenly, in a burst of "blinding light," the man's features became those of David. Then, as quickly as it had come, the vision passed.[71] But the brief experience was so intense that in bed that night Victor could see this split-second image of David "engraved on the lids of my closed eyes."[72]

The visions also took the form of dreams, initially cryptic scenarios that later made sense to Victor as a form of guidance from his oldest son. He experienced several of these seeming visitations between 1968 and 1975 and always around 5:45 a.m., which he estimated was close to the exact time of David's death on the other side of the world.

However, the most cathartic "revealment" came on March 13, 1969, a day of particular anguish for Victor, and it was neither a dream nor a vision exactly. It's hard to say exactly what it was. Still frightened and filled with second thoughts about the memorial, Jeanne was staying at her sister's in Albuquerque on that date. Victor was at the Val Verde Ranch alone and, as he subsequently explained in a letter to Luna, "snowed in." "My only communication with the outside," he wrote, "was skiing to the mailbox, and I had worn skin from four places on my feet in this endeavor."[73] Nothing was going right. Work on the chapel had once again ground to a halt. And Victor still had no idea how he would handle the project's mounting expenses without leaving his wife and himself penniless in their old age. As he looked through some of David's possessions, which the Marine Corps had sent home from Vietnam, his pain and frustration became overwhelming, and he began to weep. He wept for four hours.

What happened next may well have been nothing more than a minor freak of electricity, but for Victor it represented a moment of extraordinary significance: "As dusk approached, I arose wearily and turned on a nearby three-stage light. I knew that the center stage of this light had been burned out for months, and I had to turn past this burned out portion to reach the brighter light. This time that center stage came on! Right then I knew that nothing could stop the Chapel effort."[74]

At that precise moment, Victor also came up with a new idea for the memorial. Not surprisingly, given his penchant for superstition, the number thirteen had long held special importance for him. He was, after all, born on October 13, and the number "repeatedly marked significant events in [his] life," including this latest encounter with the uncanny, which occurred on March 13.[75] In a proverbial flash, Victor saw that the memorial must display thirteen photographs of thirteen different Americans killed in the Vietnam War. He would rotate the images—state by state, month by month—so that as many fatalities as possible could receive recognition. Only David's photograph would remain a constant fixture.

114   Chapter 3

The photograph of David displayed in the chapel. This was David's portrait upon completion of basic training as an enlisted man. His parents had the lieutenant's bars, ribbons (including the ribbon for the Vietnam Service Medal), and Expert Rifleman Badge painted onto the original image. Courtesy of Walter Westphall.

Over the coming years, this concept would undergo minor revisions. For example, in its original incarnation, Victor envisioned the photographs arranged in a crucifix-shaped "montage," a notion later abandoned.[76] And, for a time in the late 1970s and early 1980s, the number of images on display swelled to 135. For the most part, however, the photo display remained true to Victor's sudden moment of inspiration, and like everything else associated with the memorial it soon turned into a Herculean effort, as the Westphalls received and processed images from hundreds of families. Today housed in the memorial's visitors center, this still updated collection of images (currently around 2,200 total) is one of the very few of its kind.[77]

But there is still one more detail—no doubt just a coincidence, but eerie just the same—to note about this remarkable moment when Victor hit rock bottom and (from his perspective, at least) received a message of encouragement from his lost son: although he had no way of knowing it, the total number of fatalities suffered by David's Bravo Company during the ambush of May 22, 1968, was none other than thirteen.[78]

As Victor later recalled in *David's Story*, his youngest son "was like a rock in his support of the Chapel enterprise."[79] However, Walter's intensive air force training—he had decided to become a pilot—and subsequent service in the Vietnam War would limit his direct involvement in the building's construction. After graduating (just a few days after David's death) from the Airman Education and Commissioning Program at Indiana University, where he also obtained a bachelor's degree in business and accounting, Walter entered the Officer Training School at Lackland Air Force Base and from there moved directly to pilot training at Craig.[80] His air force career looked promising in every way.

But Walter increasingly felt he was in a "difficult position."[81] And for a very good reason. He wanted to serve and to fly; however, he could not put his parents though another tragedy. It was unthinkable. As so, as his service in Vietnam loomed (in what type of aircraft or combat capacity he did not yet know), he requested and was granted a "humanitarian deferment from service in a hostile fire zone," a provision created by the War Department for servicemen in exactly this sort of situation.[82]

As it turned out, however, by the time Walter received the deferment, he no longer saw the need, and so he waived it. The air force had selected the young New Mexican to fly KC-135 Stratotankers, massive air-to-air refueling aircraft that sometimes operated within enemy air space but without much threat from the North Vietnamese. Accidents could—and did—happen aboard these flying reservoirs of jet fuel, especially during takeoff and landing. Air force statistics report that twenty-five KC-135 crewmembers serving in Southeast Asia died in crashes.[83] But Walter believed that as a pilot he could minimize this risk. After graduating from pilot training in

Walter Westphall during pilot training at Craig Air Force Base, May 1969. Courtesy of Walter Westphall.

October 1968, he served aboard KC-135s that operated out of Fairchild Air Force Base in Washington. Then came two ninety-day tours of duty in Southeast Asia, where Walter would help refuel the B-52s that executed Richard Nixon's bombing campaigns against North Vietnam—and neighboring countries. The experience left him deeply disenchanted and ended his air force career. Or as he later put it: "My attitude toward the military and political leaders during the Vietnam War made it impossible for me to stay."[84]

Prior to his first overseas deployment, Walter spent his leaves in New Mexico working side by side with his father. In the summer of 1969, the two men installed the chapel flooring for a fraction of what a contractor would have charged. And through his service abroad, Walter was sometimes able to shave off other costs in unexpected ways. For example, while stationed in Okinawa, he purchased a "tremendously good" sound system for the memorial at a discount—"a TEAC tape deck, a McIntosh amplifier, and four columnar speaker units," all high-end.[85] As we will see later, the memorial would, at least through the 1970s and early 1980s, have an important aural dimension, a commemorative soundscape to match its stunning visual rhetoric of remembrance.

Help began to come from other quarters as well. Shortly after Vedeler and his crew left the scene, Victor discovered a local builder, Louis Ortiz, whose impressive knowledge of "roofing and plans" inspired the veteran home developer to hire him.[86] By October 1969 Ortiz had successfully weatherproofed the top of the chapel—just in time for the usual extreme winter conditions, which pushed the rest of the construction, much of it singlehandedly completed by Victor, into the summer of 1970, when the furnace was finally installed and the frames put in place for the window and doors. Plastic sheets now covered the openings, which was better than nothing.[87]

That same year, the chapel received its first significant media attention. A retired journalist in Taos, H. W. Potter, saw the obvious human interest potential in the Westphalls' beleaguered effort to complete their memorial, and he sympathetically described the project in a nationally syndicated news article published on March 30. As Walter later wrote, thanks to this unprecedented publicity, "interest in the Chapel increased markedly."[88] Victor now confronted two happy developments that he had nearly despaired of ever seeing—visitors (not friends or acquaintances, but complete strangers drawn to the chapel, sometimes from hundreds of miles away), and contributions to help with expenses. The former, a trickle at first, consisted mostly of Vietnam veterans and their families. They came to thank the Westphalls for what they were doing. And for other reasons. There was something powerful about this lonely spot in the Sangre de Cristos—soothing for some, violently cathartic for others—and the grief-battered father, still muscular but aging now, who greeted them with friendliness and understanding born of tragedy. As for the latter, it wasn't much, but it seemed to offer assurance that Victor's faith had not been misplaced.

From the beginning, the Westphalls had intended to dedicate their memorial on the anniversary of David's death. But by May 22, 1970, the chapel still was not ready. Among other essentials, it still needed doors, glass for its twenty-eight-foot-tall window, lighting fixtures, and mountings for the thirteen photographs, as well as the two inscriptions selected from David's writings.[89] The ceremony had to be delayed until the next year—and even by that point, as it turned out, the structure couldn't exactly be described as finished. But it was close enough, and with the public dedication in 1971, the story of the Vietnam Veterans Peace and Brotherhood Chapel would enter a new phase, one defined by the politics and divisions spawned by the most controversial war in American history.

4

Peace and Brotherhood

> Thank you for teaching me how to cry: I thought
> I had forgotten how.
> —*Gloria Emerson, in* David's Story: A Casualty of
> Vietnam, *by Victor Westphall (1981)*

By 1971, a year of extraordinary turbulence on virtually every front of American life, a madman led the United States' war effort in Southeast Asia. Or at least that's what President Richard Milhous Nixon, elected in 1968 on the promise that he would pull the United States out of the war, wanted the North Vietnamese to believe. During secret negotiations with the North, which went just as poorly as the official Paris peace talks, National Security Advisor Henry Kissinger threatened that Nixon was capable of anything. If Hanoi did not withdraw all troops from south of the DMZ, accept South Vietnam as a legitimate long-term state, and immediately return American POWs, the president, who was out of control, might escalate the conflict even further. Perhaps even use nuclear weapons. He was a madman with a hair-trigger.

This bizarre negotiating ploy, which made little impression on the intractable North Vietnamese, reflected Nixon's desperation as he navigated a precarious political situation of his own making. As sociologist Jerry Lembcke explains, "Nixon had won election as a peace candidate, but he was also committed to not being the first American president to lose a war. It was a contradictory agenda."[1] A *wildly* contradictory agenda, one might add, driven by a blend of wishful thinking and cynical political calculation. Recognizing widespread disenchantment with the war, the president steadily reduced the number of American troops in Vietnam and shifted the burden of military responsibility to the South Vietnamese, a policy known as Vietnamization.[2] By the start of 1971, 334,600 Americans were deployed in Southeast Asia, a considerable decrease from the peak in 1968 of more than 500,000.[3] And orders called for a further reduction of 100,000 troops before the end of the year.[4]

But Nixon assured his fervently anticommunist base that "peace with honor" would still come through victory, whether that victory was achieved by American ground troops or not. And to that end, he ramped up the bombing campaign against North Vietnam and (secretly) its neighbors, Cambodia and Laos. During a fourteen-month period in 1969 and 1970, American B-52s dropped "110,000 tons of bombs" on Cambodia.[5] (Total tonnage for 1965–1973 comes to 2.7 million tons, more explosives than were used by the Allies during the entirety of World War II.[6]) Laos suffered under a comparable rain of destruction, its historic Plain of Jars essentially carpet-bombed out of existence by the end of 1969.[7]

Controversial ground operations inside these two ostensibly neutral countries followed, starting with an invasion of Cambodia in 1970, which shocked the American public and triggered peace rallies and marches throughout the nation. For some, participating in demonstrations proved fatal. At Kent State University, Ohio National Guardsmen fired into a crowd of student protesters, killing four and wounding nine others.[8]

The next spring, an invasion of Laos, undertaken by ARVN forces with American air support, brought the antiwar movement to a dramatic crescendo. Militarily, the campaign was a disaster for the South Vietnamese, as symbolized by news footage that showed desperate ARVN troops escaping the fighting by clinging to the landing skids of American helicopters. After a while, chopper crews greased the undercarriages of their aircraft to prevent this.[9] So much for Vietnamization. But even worse for the Nixon administration, the operation in Laos, like the so-called incursion into Cambodia the year before, raised serious doubts about whether the president was acting in good faith. Nixon had promised to end the war, not widen it, and in the spring of 1971 anger on the political left reached a boiling point.

According to historian Christian Appy, "58 percent of Americans had [now] concluded that the war in Vietnam was not just a mistake, but immoral."[10] On April 24, a significant portion of this outraged public spoke out. An estimated 650,000 antiwar marchers (some say a million) poured into Washington, DC, a gargantuan expression of protest witnessed, ironically enough, by the Saigon foreign minister and the South Vietnamese senate president, who, as historian John Prados explains, happened to be visiting the capital at that precise moment.[11] What the two men saw—the clearest evidence yet that Nixon's war was politically untenable—left them shaken. How would their own regime survive if the superpower on whose support they depended was in this much turmoil?

A week later, when a contingent of fifty thousand demonstrators known as the May Day Tribe descended on the District of Columbia, the president decided that he had had enough. Police and federal authorities arrested the protesters by the thousands—in complete violation, it was later determined, of their constitutional rights. Now more than ever, the Vietnam War was tearing the nation apart. To reach this conclusion, one needed only to look at the White House, which weathered the mass protests of April and May once again surrounded by a makeshift barricade of buses parked bumper-to-bumper. This had been standard operating procedure since 1969. But now there was a new security measure: machine gun emplacements, ready for action, decorated the White House lawn.[12] The executive branch was prepared for a shooting war at home.

The first six months of 1971 also saw the conviction of Lieutenant William Calley for war crimes committed at My Lai; the publication in the *New York Times* of leaked government documents pertaining to American policy in Vietnam, known as the Pentagon Papers (these showed a pattern of dissembling throughout Lyndon Johnson's presidency); and the emergence onto the national stage of a previously little-known organization called the Vietnam Veterans Against the War (VVAW). Established in 1967, the VVAW staunchly maintained a position that many Americans, even those with misgivings about the war, found distasteful, even unthinkable: according to VVAW members, who spoke from their own personal experience, there was nothing unique about the horrific actions of Lieutenant Calley and his comrades at My Lai. On the contrary, the kind of war the United States was forced to fight in Vietnam made the casual mistreatment and indiscriminate killing of civilians both ubiquitous and inevitable. It was not a message than anyone wanted to hear, and in its early days the VVAW struggled to attract media attention. But by 1971, a year that brought one shock to the national consciousness after another, the VVAW's time had finally come. Americans—or least some Americans— were ready to listen.

In January, the organization staged what it called the Winter Soldier Investigation. In the meeting room of a Detroit Howard Johnson's hotel, panels of veterans testified to "hair-raising episodes of raw violence; standard procedures that lost, not won, 'hearts and minds'; and casual arrogance for the Vietnamese, called 'slopes' or 'gooks.'"[13] VVAW members described acts of torture, rape, and murder amid a war in which virtually every civilian was viewed as a potential enemy. The former soldiers' anguished accounts—confessions, really—did not necessarily paint the United States as an inherently evil, neoimperialistic nation (the view of some groups on the far left) or present young American men as born monsters; rather, the VVAW condemned the policies that pushed American soldiers to dehumanize the Vietnamese and to ignore their own consciences, all for dubious war aims. Outrage over the mistreatment of former soldiers in rundown Veterans Administration hospitals and the overrepresentation of veterans among the nation's unemployed and homeless, grotesque ironies given the federal funding lavished on the war (at the expense of social programs), also formed part of the organization's platform.

In the spring, the imposing-looking veterans—"dressed in their military fatigues, most with shoulder-length hair and angry eyes"—carried their message to Washington, DC, in a series of intense but nonviolent demonstrations, known as Operation Dewey Canyon III, held on the four days leading up to the gigantic April 24 rally.[14] Everything was carefully planned. During the first three days, VVAW members gave performances of so-called guerrilla theater—reenactments of search-and-destroy missions in Vietnamese hamlets, sometimes with squirming passersbys standing in for Viet Cong suspects. They visited congressional offices and met—or tried to meet—with their representatives. And, accompanied by Gold Star mothers who had lost sons in Vietnam, they marched from the Capitol to Arlington National Cemetery, which they found locked up and off-limits. Undeterred, the veterans laid their wreath at the cemetery gates.

All of this was just the lead-up to the main event on April 24, a spectacle unlike anything seen before in American history and perhaps the bitterest, most surreal moment in the entire antiwar movement. Next to a wire fence erected to keep protesters away from the Capitol, VVAW members lined up for a "medal giveback ceremony." One by one, each veteran came forward, made a few remarks, and then flung his military decorations over the barricade. Many sobbed afterward, overcome by the enormity of their public statement.

The group had originally planned to toss their medals into a body bag, which they would then present to Congress. Not surprisingly, Washington officials refused to cooperate, and as it turned out, the revised ceremony, conducted in front of a perfect symbol of the government's separation from the people, made for even better theater. Extensively covered by CBS News and other major media outlets, the event was raw and sobering. Here were young American men, many combat-wounded, some decorated for valor, rejecting—actually *throwing away*—the military's most sacred emblems of courage, service, and sacrifice. Perhaps no single scene better symbolized how far America had traveled since the confident opening days of the "splendid little war." One wonders what David Westphall would have thought had he lived to see it.

Dewey Canyon III owed much of its success to none other than future presidential candidate and secretary of state John Kerry. Although the handsome, six-foot-four former Swift Boat captain held no official title within the VVAW, his charisma, natural leadership ability, and media savvy were obvious to all. Indeed, he was the perfect front man—Yale-educated and politically ambitious, as well as a recipient of three Purple Hearts, one Silver Star, and one Bronze Star, all earned while Kerry battled the Viet Cong in the treacherous Mekong River Delta. Best of all, despite a privileged social background that separated him from the other veterans (at least at first), Kerry's anger and disgust with American policy in Vietnam were absolutely authentic; although inherently diplomatic and moderate (for a so-called radical), he passionately shared the organization's core convictions.

During the weeks leading up to Dewey Canyon III, Kerry became a "prime mover" in the organization's plans, and once the veterans arrived on the National Mall (where they camped in defiance of federal orders), he proved an effective mediator, defusing potential clashes with police, and calming troopers and fellow VVAW members alike.[15] But his biggest contribution came on April 22, when, at the invitation of Senator J. William Fulbright (who solicited testimonies from a number of VVAW members), he spoke before the Senate Foreign Relations Committee.

If Kerry's comrades in the VVAW, mostly former enlisted men naturally suspicious of officers, had any doubts about this lanky patrician's willingness to speak truth to power, those doubts evaporated within the first ten seconds of Kerry's opening statement. The speech was an uncompromising tour de force. Calmly but unequivocally, Kerry explained that Washington didn't understand the war in Vietnam—or the Vietnamese, who mostly saw American troops not as agents of democracy but as imperialists, like the French before them. Cheered on by VVAW members who packed the rear of the chamber, he also accused the US government of war crimes, underscored the patent failure of Nixon's Vietnamization program, and bemoaned the shameful neglect of Vietnam veterans at home. But the most striking passage in Kerry's statement consisted of a pair of chilling rhetorical questions: "How do you ask a man to be the last man to die in Vietnam? How do you ask a man to be the last man to die for a mistake?"[16] As historian Douglas Brinkley recounts, once Kerry uttered these words, "an eerie silence fell over the chamber."[17]

At that electrifying moment, the former Swift Boat commander became a star, at least among Americans who agreed with his dark assessment of the Vietnam War. Indeed, his widely televised testimony was almost as celebrated (and, in some circles, maligned) as the medal giveback ceremony held the next day. Kerry was now the most visible antiwar veteran in the country, and just four weeks after his explosive Senate testimony, his role as spokesman for the VVAW would carry him to an isolated high mountain valley in northern New Mexico. There he would meet Victor Westphall, an activist of a different kind, and become part of the story of America's first national Vietnam veterans memorial.

In November 1970, Victor sent out a newsletter—a regular occurrence from this point forward—to the hundreds of individuals who had donated to the chapel effort so far. With characteristic thoroughness, he gave an exact accounting of expenses to date, totaling $22,104.68, of which $1,344.12 came from contributions. When reporting on the ongoing construction, Victor found it easiest to itemize the remaining tasks, which he presented as follows:

1. Exterior stucco (The interior plastering is finished.)
2. Carillon system [This would be replaced by the high-fidelity sound equipment purchased by Walter in Okinawa.]
3. Glass in windows and door frames (presently plastic)
4. Frame complex for photos of deceased Vietnam veterans
5. Eternal Flame arrangement
6. Terrazzo floor
7. Plaques with inscriptions
8. Underground propane gas tank (heating system is in)
9. Finish installation of lighting fixtures
10. Landscaping
11. Parking area[18]

It was a lengthy list, to be sure, but considering how far the structure had come, hardly discouraging. The Westphalls could see the light at the end of tunnel at last, at least where the construction was concerned. The imminent completion of their project showed in the very design of the newsletter. Victor (or Jeanne, who helped with clerical and organizational tasks during the early years) mimeographed the text onto a dramatic background, a photograph of the chapel as viewed from the southeast. It looked then much as it does now, just starker, denuded of its white paint, and without the indigenous, almost organic quality that the uneven stucco would lend to the external walls.

A revealing milestone worth examining in some detail, issue one of the chapel newsletter also presents a brief history of the memorial, which contained the fullest description to date of Victor's views on the subject of war. A manifesto of sorts, the document makes no mention of Vietnam—at least not directly. Instead, Victor opened with his personal, eyewitness experience of armed conflict. "The history of the Chapel," he wrote, "in a sense, dates back to the years immediately following World War II."[19] He explained that "two years of observing man's inhumanity to man while

The chapel as it appeared in November 1970. Courtesy of Walter Westphall.

serving in the South Pacific" had reinforced his "conviction that peace, to be attained, must be striven for mightily and not . . . just left to grow." The "holocausts of Hiroshima and Nagasaki" vividly displayed what the human capacity for destruction could achieve, if left unchecked by direct and vigorous work on behalf of peace.[20]

Then, in a remarkable passage that displays his powers of language working at full throttle, Victor focused on the post-1945 spread of nuclear weapons and the rise of mutually assured destruction: "[Man] has lost sight of the need to correct the frightening disparity in our world between technological progress as opposed to moral, social, and behavioral growth. Rather, he looks to his atomic creations to protect himself from his invention. A collective mind dizzy with physical knowledge, blinded by greed and glutted with power, is chained to this Frankenstein, fearing it, but working overtime to make it even more fearful."[21] The chapel, its chief creator fervently hoped, would inspire visitors to "contemplate and question," to break free of this "collective mind" that legitimized violence and all but guaranteed a nuclear apocalypse.[22]

A template for many of his future pronouncements, Victor's historical sketch stressed personal revelation (anchored in his experience of the "Good War") and peace advocacy (expressed on a global scale in response to a global threat). Perhaps wisely, it steered clear of the escalating domestic war over American policy in Southeast Asia, a war that had now entered its bitterest phase, with student demonstrators recently slain at Kent State and the unprecedented spectacle of veterans hurling medals at the Capitol still to come.

But oblique criticisms of the Johnson and Nixon administrations surface nonetheless. In a section devoted to his sons' military service, Victor explained that David and Walter had shared his desire for "world unity" but nevertheless felt the need to "protect our good way of life" through enlistment.[23] Both young men, he stressed, held their country and its Defense Department to a high standard: though patriotic and committed to their military careers, neither wished to serve in an organization that had become in any way "arrogant or offensive" or that would use American might to "bully and threaten."[24] Though presented diplomatically, Victor's implication here is, of course, clear enough. Under the leadership of the White House, US forces in Vietnam *had* become arrogant and offensive. One needed only to consider the so-called strategic bombing campaign, with its wanton destruction achieved through unprecedented tonnage, or the gruesome measuring of military "progress" via body count. As for bullying and threatening, Nixon's ignoble "madman" policy epitomized both.

Victor's brief history also contains a claim that would arguably undermine the chapel's overall effectiveness as a combination of written and visual rhetoric and as a fusion of personal and public memory. According to the grieving father, David had left behind in his essays and poetry "words that might stir mankind to positive efforts toward mutual amity," hence the two inscriptions displayed inside the chapel.[25] Although understandable, this elevation of David's writings is problematic. David *was* a gifted author. But at least for most visitors—those, that is, who notice the inscriptions and read them—the two somewhat cryptic excerpts that Victor selected do not manifest the level of profundity that he claimed for them. In this instance, Victor's pride in his son, the source of so much emotive power elsewhere in the chapel's conception, perhaps blinded him to the structure's true needs as a site of public commemoration. One can't help but wish that Victor had relied upon his own considerable eloquence when crafting the textual component of his memorial. Or that he had left the chapel bare of any written explanation whatsoever.

Implicitly casting David as a spokesperson for peace was also awkward for another reason. As Patrick Hagopian notes, "the causes that Victor Westphall dignified with a father's grief were not his son's but his own."[26] In other words, the Marine lieutenant remembered at Angel Fire would have had little sympathy with the message of global "peace and brotherhood." David may, of course, have revealed a longing for world peace in private conversations with his father. We have no way of knowing for sure. But the biographical evidence points overwhelmingly in the opposite direction. For example, as we have seen in his letters from Vietnam, David issued one hawkish pronouncement after another. He longed to carry the ground war across the DMZ and into North Vietnam, saw little value in peace talks ("all communists understand is force"), and exulted in the deaths of his enemies. Given what we know of his sensibility as a committed Cold Warrior and proud combat marine, it seems likely that his thoughts on the final day of his life had little to do with peace. He was probably eager to confront an ordinarily elusive force of NVA soldiers—and annihilate them.

According to Hagopian, this apparent refashioning of David's politics illustrates that memorials are "as much—sometimes more—about those who remember as they are about the objects of remembrance."[27] True enough. But one can also look at this somewhat differently. Through its simultaneous intimacy and expansiveness—a small, family-size space located inside a vast exoskeleton—Luna's soaring design raises the personal and familial to the level of the communal. Out of private grief, this literally uplifting architecture promises, will come public good. Indeed, one might even argue that David Westphall operates as a Christ figure within the chapel's implied narrative. Like the story of Christ's crucifixion, the memory of David's sacrifice will, the chapel asserts, lead to collective redemption by ending the sin of war. Thus, Victor may well, as Hagopian asserts, have transferred his personal beliefs and attitudes onto a son who could no longer speak for himself. But it could also be argued that the commemorative logic of David's memorial demanded that transferral. In other words, the forms through which we remember others can shape—even, in some cases, distort—our memories.

Having issued his mission statement, and no longer tantalized by the mirage of support from philanthropic foundations, Victor focused his attention during the winter of 1970–1971 on the chapel's interior fixtures. By the spring, he could check off *most* of the items on the list he had shared with contributors. The most notable exception: the exterior coating of stucco, which would not be applied until the fall. Although Walter's air force duties would prevent him from attending, Victor and Jeanne decided not to wait. The time for the memorial's dedication—three years to the day since David's death—had finally come.

By this point, the steadily growing number of Vietnam veterans drawn to the Westphalls' project included Larry Rottmann, a member of the VVAW who had settled in the village of Corrales, just north of Albuquerque. As Brinkley notes, Rottmann was a striking figure—"six foot tall with shoulder-length blond hair and a beard"—whose background and talents set him apart from the VVAW's rank-and-file membership.[28] A native of Missouri, he held a bachelor's in literature and journalism from the state's flagship campus in Columbia, where he learned the skills displayed in his important contributions to American Vietnam War poetry.[29]

Rottmann's training as a journalist made him the perfect choice as a press officer for the VVAW, and during the weeks leading up to the demonstrations in Washington he had become a friend of Kerry's. Indeed, he may have played a role—at least indirectly—in Kerry's presence at the chapel dedication. Following his dramatic testimony before the Senate Foreign Relations Committee, Kerry made some television appearances and then crisscrossed the country giving lectures, sometimes sharing the stage with Rottmann, who would read poetry, or another VVAW member. In May he accepted an invitation from Victor Westphall to speak at the Vietnam Veterans Peace and Brotherhood Chapel, perhaps partly because it was so close to Rottmann's home in Corrales, where Kerry stayed during most of his visit. When Kerry arrived in New Mexico that month, Rottmann was "locked up in the Bernalillo County Jail," where he spent three days.[30] His offense: handing out antiwar leaflets. Once released, he and Kerry enjoyed a few days of leisure, a welcome reprieve from the media spotlight, before heading up to the dedication ceremony in the Moreno

Valley, which Rottmann would subsequently describe in an article for the *Saint Louis Post-Dispatch*.

According to Brinkley, Victor decided to invite Kerry after being "moved by [his] impassioned remarks" in Washington.[31] Whether Rottmann, who had become a friend of Victor's by this point, facilitated the invitation is unknown, but it seems likely since Kerry's other speaking venues that spring were mostly universities and other more established forums. In short, Victor was lucky to get the future secretary of state. At the same time, however, he must have known that Kerry was a controversial figure—a lightning rod, in fact, just as likely to draw censure as praise.

Kerry's presence gave the Westphalls an early taste of just how divisive and politicized *any* act of public commemoration could become (regardless of the intentions behind it), especially when linked to the inferno of debate over the Vietnam War. As befitted the upcoming ceremony, Victor and Jeanne had asked for a Marine color guard to be on hand, an innocuous request, one would have thought, under the circumstances. But on May 15, Walter wrote to his father with news that a Marine Corps officer in Santa Fe had contacted Jeanne with concerns about a "possible conflict" between the color guard and "the content of John Kerry's speech."[32] It was a bitter moment—one of many to come—that suddenly exposed the domestic battle lines of the Vietnam War: official military meaning, as represented by uniformed members of the corps, would not sit easily, if at all, next to the supposedly unpatriotic message offered by Kerry, a former US Navy officer supposedly gone rogue.

Since press accounts of the dedication contain no mention of formal Marine involvement, it would seem that the Westphalls failed to reassure the officer in Sante Fe, an irony for many reasons, not the least because members of the Corps would have heard relatively little that was inflammatory that day. Sometimes it was hard to hear at all. May 22, 1971, was a typically blustery day in the Moreno Valley, and as the mountain winds buffeted the semicomplete chapel, the speakers' voices—especially Victor's, which was always soft—occasionally became inaudible to the gathered crowd of approximately three hundred people. According to Rottmann, a "local minister" spoke first, followed by Luna and then by a Vietnam veteran from the area.[33] Victor came next, and while his comments, delivered with characteristic calm, were not recorded in full, we can assume that they introduced at least some of the ideas outlined in his self-published 1972 address, *Vietnam: The Hinge of Destiny*, a document to which we will turn in a moment. One remark of Victor's was widely reported: "The chapel," he announced, "is a gift to man, but I don't know what man will do with it."[34]

Kerry was the final speaker during the "brief and moving" ceremony, and by all accounts he sensed that this was not the occasion for another fiery polemic aimed at American policy in Vietnam.[35] The Marines need not have feared. In his piece for the *Saint Louis Post-Dispatch*, Rottmann reported that after "congratulat[ing] Dr. Westphall for his personal courage and dedication," Kerry emphasized the memorial's originality: "There are thousands of war memorials in our country, but the Vietnam Veterans Chapel is America's first memorial to peace."[36] Other press accounts quoted different passages from the address. For example, according to the *Kingsport Times* in Tennessee, Kerry claimed that "it was a degradation that we have come here to testify about the horror of war. I don't think the Chapel is political. It is a testament to war in general."[37] Only once, apparently, did the VVAW spokesman slip into the content of his recent Senate testimony: "When a man is dying and blood is pouring out and he looks up to you and asks 'Why?,' there's just no answer."[38]

Once Kerry finished speaking, a detachment of local New Mexico National Guardsmen fired a haunting salute to the fallen, three sharp rifle volleys, which the wind carried across the mountain valley. These soldiers, at least, saw no conflict between their commitment to service and a memorial dedicated to peace or the presence of a veteran exercising his right to criticize a war he deemed unjust.

Although Kerry's recent memoir, *Every Day Is Extra* (2018), does not mention his time in New Mexico, his visit to the Vietnam Veterans Peace and Brotherhood Chapel left a lingering impression.[39] In an interview with his biographer, Douglas Brinkley, Kerry recalled that his participation in the dedication was "quite an honor. This was the first effort to pay proper respect to the Vietnam veteran. It was—and is—a beautiful, majestic memorial. My speech talked about the need to pay homage all across America for the Vietnam soldier."[40] In 2004 Brinkley gave a book talk inside the chapel (soon to become the centerpiece of New Mexico's Vietnam Veterans State Park) and claimed that "Angel Fire is a kind of transitional moment for

Kerry."[41] During his stay at the memorial, surrounded by fellow veterans and their families, the VVAW spokesman realized for the first time that a tour of duty in Vietnam lasted a lifetime.[42] Wounds might heal, but the war in Vietnam would never loosen its grip on those who came home.

As intended, the well-publicized dedication ceremony lifted the Westphalls' project onto the national stage, and in July Luna forwarded a letter for Victor that he had received from an unexpected correspondent:

July 15, 1971
Dear Mr. Westphall,
    Recently, I read a news account describing the Chapel you built to honor the memory of your son and his twelve fellow Marines ambushed in Vietnam three years ago. Your labor of love is far more than the sheer building of a monument; it is a symbol of the love which all fathers have for their sons.
    It is written "'tis a happy thing to be the father unto many sons." You have indeed become the father of thirteen brave sons who gave their lives for their country and for freedom. In honoring their sacrifices, you honor the sacrifice of all who through the history of our Nation have died in order that we may live in peace and with liberty.
    With my best wishes,
    Sincerely,
    Richard Nixon

Ironically, Nixon's seemingly heartfelt missive may have sprung from an ulterior motive—further evidence (perhaps not surprising, given its source) of the treacherous political territory that the Westphalls had now entered. According to Kerry's FBI file (every prominent member of the VVAW has one), an agent learned of Nixon's letter to Victor, which the president presumably mailed prior to the dedication, and forwarded a copy to the bureau, together with a transcript of Kerry's speech at the chapel. The idea, apparently, was to embarrass the VVAW spokesman "by putting him on the same side of an issue with Nixon."[43]

But the file, as described in a 2004 *Los Angeles Times* article, contains an error. Nixon did not reach out to the chapel's chief founder during the same month as Kerry's address, as the FBI reported. The actual letter, contained in the David Westphall Veterans Foundation Collection at Texas Tech, is dated July 15, which means that Nixon would have known all about Kerry's dedication speech before he sent it. So did the president intend to show his support for a grieving family? Or was his letter a calculated move to discredit a new star in the antiwar movement? Or perhaps both at the same time?

For his part, Victor remained proud of the chapel's association with Kerry *and* the personal message that he had received from Nixon. As his subsequent writings would make clear, he wanted, more than anything, to somehow lift his peace crusade above politics. Despite his best efforts, however, partisan rancor over Vietnam would prove impossible to avoid.

In October 1971, Victor woke one morning to discover a piece of plywood next to one of the chapel's doors. On it someone had scrawled a brief message: "Why did you lock me out when I needed to come in?"[44] From that moment forward, the chapel remained open twenty-four hours a day—despite several instances of vandalism. Access to the memorial became a matter of sacred obligation, one of many swiftly established customs and traditions that made the Vietnam Veterans Peace and Brotherhood Chapel much more than a mere church building. The site was quickly becoming an institution, complete with its own annual rituals, ceremonial practices, and, in Victor, its own scholar-in-residence, greeter, docent, and more.

Just as the uniformed sentinels at the Tomb of the Unknowns in Arlington National Cemetery have essentially become *part* of the monument (to the point that their famous changing of the guard ceremony is now the chief attraction), Victor served from the start as an animate extension of the chapel, completely at one with his commemorative creation.[45] He was the memorial's constant ambassador and custodian, as well as an onsite healer of sorts who rendered aid, in the form of patient listening, to visitors overcome by the powerful emotions that the site typically stirred. His nickname "Doc," as he was known by the veterans he befriended, expressed more than affection or respect for Victor's PhD in American civilization: the title also acknowledged the grieving father's self-scripted role as an informal therapist constantly on the lookout for a veteran who needed a sympathetic ear. It was a role that he assumed over and over again, with thousands of veterans, over a span of thirty years. Newspaper accounts that mistakenly described him as a medical doctor—a common gaffe—were only half wrong.

Did a sense of guilt bind him to the memorial and to its visitors? Did the intensity of his devotion, which came at such personal cost, suggest that he saw the project as a kind of atonement? Perhaps. An introspective person with exacting standards of conduct, fully capable (as his letters reveal) of judging himself harshly, Victor may have concluded that by pushing David too hard, especially on the football field, he had set his son on that fatal course toward the Marine Corps and Vietnam. Had he—terrible thought—performed the role of Abraham? One can also speculate that he may have regretted not becoming a more vocal and committed peace advocate earlier in his life. Would doing so have kept David from believing in a just war? Had Victor let his heady business success and meteoric social rise distract him from what should have been his real mission in life, a mission that might have begun in 1945 when he first grasped the absurdity of armed conflict? Unfortunately, it's not hard to imagine Victor inhabiting this dark territory of what-ifs—or to imagine the pain that his grand obsession (noble and beneficial to veterans though it was) must have caused his wife, who, in effect, lost her husband so that he could become "Doc Westphall."

Whether driven by psychological demons or not, Victor's devotion to Vietnam veterans was boundless. And like the avant-garde building to which he was tied, he instantly made an impression on visitors. Lanny Tonning, who served in a US Air Force "radar detachment" near the DMZ, first encountered the memorial and its caretaker in 1972.[46] Tonning had recently moved to Albuquerque from Atlanta, and one day he accompanied a local "back country explorer" on a road trip to the high mountain town of Mora.[47] On the way back, the two decided to drive through Angel Fire, a route that Tonning had never taken before. As they entered the ski community from the south, he noticed the town's tiny airfield and, beyond that, a curious "white dart" on a distant hilltop. Tonning had to check it out. When he reached the chapel entrance, he encountered a sign: "This door will never be locked."[48] Inside, he examined the thirteen photographs mounted on the wall and read the caption beneath Lieutenant Westphall's image. David had been killed, Tonning realized, just four miles or so from his own duty station. Then Victor entered the room.

The chief founder of the Vietnam Veterans Peace and Brotherhood Chapel immediately came across as a remarkable character. He was a short man and soft-spoken, but Tonning sensed his energy and focused willpower right away. A bit Napoleonic. During conversation, he "looked you in the eye" and was "right there" as you spoke.[49] One never sensed that his attention wandered for a single second. And the more Tonning talked with this odd but likable man, who clung to his lonely memorial with a fierce and infectious sense of mission, the more he felt that Victor was the only non-Vietnam veteran he had met—in the two years since his discharge—who truly "got" the Vietnam War.[50] A friendship was born that would last thirty years.

Other Vietnam veterans had essentially the same experience. Dick Dickerson, an ex-chopper pilot who settled in the Moreno Valley and eventually became one of the directors of the David Westphall Veterans Foundation (along with Tonning), recalls that it was impossible not to open up to such an intuitive and empathetic listener: "We told Doc things we couldn't tell our own fathers. We were, in a sense, all his sons."[51] For former medic Frank Richardson, who throughout the 1990s and 2000s made a nearly annual pilgrimage to the chapel from his home in Delaware, Victor's attentive silence made all the difference: "He did not share his views about anything until you had poured out your thoughts, concerns, nightmares, fears, and worries. You shared with him because he was *listening* and you trusted him to keep your secrets and you trusted his wisdom when he gave you suggestions."[52] Richardson also fondly recalls Victor's prodigious memory, a common trait among historians. Though they met only once every year or two, Victor could always pick up the conversation exactly where it had left off.

But perhaps the most extraordinary story related to Victor's powers for good, whenever he sensed a veteran in need, is that of Ron Milam. His story dates from a later period of the memorial's history, but it speaks to interpersonal dynamics that were consistent from the start. A former "infantry advisor to Montagnard troops," Milam managed to avoid the economic hardship that befell so many veterans after their return from Southeast Asia.[53] By the mid-1980s the former first lieutenant had a good job in the Texas oil and natural gas industry, earning enough to enjoy an annual ski trip to Taos Mountain with his wife, Maxine. He had put the war behind him—or so he thought—and had zero interest in stirring up the past. Each year he would see a sign outside Taos, which read "D.A.V. Veterans Memorial—28 miles," and each year he would come up with a reason not to go: "had to catch a plane, altitude sickness, just another memorial, or just not interested."[54]

Then, in 1999, the couple finally drove the Taos Canyon Road up to Angel Fire and had the same sort of electrifying encounter with Doc Westphall—a very old man now, feeble and ailing, but still mentally sharp—that Lanny Tonning had experienced in 1972. "We fell in love," Milam would later write, "with the Chapel . . . and the Moreno Valley."[55] Like many Texans before and after them, the Milams bought a vacation home in the area, which allowed them to frequently interact with their new friend Victor.

And then something happened that Milam could never have predicted and to this day can hardly explain. As he grew closer to Victor, their conversations began to reveal a hollowness—a vague sense of missing out on something—that lurked beneath the Texan's material success. Eventually, with Victor's help, Milam concluded that what he *really* wanted to do was to become a history professor and to devote his life to the study of the Vietnam War. It was an improbable dream. Laughable, in fact. Trained in human resources, management and marketing, and political science, Milam would have to take leveling classes in history just to qualify for admission, then survive the rigors of a doctoral program *and* take his chances on a nearly nonexistent academic job market in the humanities.[56] And his fifty-some years wouldn't help: as a freshly minted PhD, he would have no choice but to apply for entry-level assistant professorships typically filled by scholars in their late twenties or early thirties. (Sadly, whatever its progress in other areas, academia remains a bastion of age-discrimination.)

Though it looked like an act of insanity, Milam took the leap. He quit his lucrative job in the oil and gas business, completed a doctorate at the University of Houston, and then, against all odds, secured an assistant professorship in military history at Texas Tech, beating out Ivy League candidates nearly half his age (perhaps, as he acknowledges, with a little help from Affirmative Action law, which gave Vietnam veterans a boost in a tight race). Books and teaching successes followed, including a groundbreaking study, *Not A Gentleman's War: An Inside View of Junior Officers in the Vietnam War* (2009), and a prestigious Fulbright in Vietnam, which led to the establishment of a summer teaching program in Southeast Asia that Milam currently directs. Eventually, he also joined the head board of the David Westphall Veterans Foundation and became the organization's resident historian. A new life. All this because of some conversations with "Doc."

In May 1972 the Westphall family decided to host an annual commemorative program, which, like the dedication ceremony the previous year, would be held on the anniversary of David's death or as close to it as possible. On Sunday, May 21, a crowd once again gathered at the hilltop memorial, which was now—at long last—complete, right down to its coating of uneven, adobe-like stucco. Only the landscaping, seating for the still empty chapel, and a few other loose ends remained.

Victor gave the main address, a remarkable jeremiad that he would subsequently self-publish. Titled *Vietnam: The Hinge of Destiny*, this speech eschewed the diplomatic tact and intentional ambiguity displayed in the Westphalls' newsletter from the previous year. Now there was no longer any question: the face of the Vietnam Veterans Peace and Brotherhood Chapel came out strongly against American actions in Southeast Asia.

However, Victor's lecture bore no resemblance whatsoever to Kerry's fiery remarks during Dewey Canyon III. Or, for that matter, the soaring rhetoric of Martin Luther King Jr., who first gave public utterance to his antiwar stance (and broke with a furious Lyndon Johnson as a result) in his famous Riverside address in 1967. Victor's assessment of the war contained no mention of American atrocities or the patently corrupt and repressive South Vietnamese regime or the kinds of deplorable governmental machinations (right here at home) revealed in the Pentagon Papers. Instead, Victor drew upon his temperament and training as a scholar to frame the Vietnam conflict, part of a larger "warlike age," within the vast span of history.[57] His audience that day suddenly found themselves embarked upon a trip through three thousand years of human development.

War, Victor declared, was not man's natural state, and to support this claim he cited evidence that supposedly primitive *Homo sapiens* had, in fact, lived together in peace. In this regard, prehistoric man was superior to his descendants. Ironically, the very civilization of which modern human beings boasted gave birth to armed conflict—or, rather, the "desires stimulated by civilization"; namely, acquisitiveness and the urge to dominate, both of which modern societies concealed behind sacrosanct military traditions and the false glamor of martial heroism.[58] To see past these omnipresent disguises required mental discipline and, above all else, adherence to reason: "War is produced primarily by the mind and will of man. It is up to man; he must find his guiding genius within himself."[59]

Having established reason as the antidote for pernicious cultural fictions built up over thousands of years, Victor proceeded to dissect America's war in Vietnam, which he framed as an especially irrational and wasteful conflict, one biting statistic at a time. Moral indignation rarely surfaced in his words. Here, at least, he preferred to characterize the war as a monstrous offense against common sense (and fiscal responsibility), rather than human decency. Perhaps the most devastating part of his critique came when he addressed the bombing campaign against the North from a cost-benefit perspective: "The average B-52 strike in Vietnam costs some $40 million. If we consider 300 killed in each strike, we are spending approximately $133,333 for each enemy killed, or enough to set each one up with a regional franchise for McDonald's over here."[60] Applying the same logic to the war effort as a whole, whose total cost he calculated at $240 billion (or $343,000 per enemy fatality), Victor concluded it would have been cheaper "to buy each pro-communist soldier killed the finest country estate and a lifetime annuity than to kill him."[61]

One hears echoes in this address of the statistics-wielding logician who once argued (unsuccessfully) with David's football coaches. Victor moves with assurance from figure to figure, confident that once his audience has viewed the war from a great enough distance, and with enough statistical information in hand, they will come to accept his point of view. Compared with other notable antiwar speeches from the era, his seems almost clinical. However, his address also reflected his academic immersion in American history and literature, especially in its second half. Indeed, as signaled by its portentous title, *Vietnam: The Hinge of Destiny* tapped into the deep American preoccupation with all things apocalyptic. More than just a statistician, Victor came to assume the role of prophet in this address, warning of approaching end times lest the nation fail the test of self-examination presented by Vietnam. "The hard fact," he declared, "is that we can no longer afford to waste our precious resources on the expensive frivolity of war; too much is at stake in the world."[62]

Victor then outlined the threat of environmental collapse—"depletion of natural resources, increase of pollution levels, crowding, and inadequate food supplies"—that made the problem of ending war more pressing than ever.[63] And here his speech reflected a central cultural anxiety during the early 1970s; namely, fear that industrial civilization was destroying the planet—a fear that global warming may yet realize. In 1970, two years before Victor's address and eight years after the publication of Rachel Carson's *Silent Spring* (1962), which effectively inaugurated the American environmental movement, public pressure led the Nixon administration (not exactly remembered for its progressivism) to establish the Environmental Protection Agency. The Clean Air and Clean Water Acts date from the same period, along with the first official Earth Day, and the iconic Keep America Beautiful ad on television, which depicted a Native American (played by an Italian American actor) weeping at the sight of modern Americans defiling the natural world.[64] Meanwhile, Hollywood picked up on the greening of the popular imagination in films such as *Silent Running* (1972) and *Soylent Green* (1973), both depictions of ecological catastrophe. In short, Victor's approach to the issue of peace—via environmental alarm—could not have been timelier. And the physical setting for his lecture, a chapel nestled in the heart of a stunningly beautiful wilderness area, only amplified his message.

As Walter has remarked of his father's later book, *The People's Revolution for Peace* (1984), Victor "was trained as a historian, not as an economist or geographer. Consequently, his notions are not well developed." The same could be said of this address from 1972, which covers so much ground that it must have left its audience dizzy and exhausted. Nevertheless, *Vietnam: The Hinge of Destiny* stands among Victor Westphall's more interesting and multilayered writings, notable both for its emotional restraint and its dual focus on war and looming environmental disaster. Within just a couple of months, however, a much briefer and more emotive public statement would come to overshadow Victor's impressive rhetorical performance on May 21.

During the early summer of 1972, Victor received a visit from *New York Times* reporter Gloria Emerson, who had recently returned to the United

140   Chapter 4

States after two long years of covering the Vietnam War. Emerson was an accomplished journalist known for her outspokenness. In 1969 she had conducted a legendarily combative on-camera interview with John Lennon and Yoko Ono at Apple Records headquarters in London. Having already reported on violence in Northern Ireland and Nigeria, Emerson shared the couple's desire for world peace, but she found their protest movement ridiculous, and said so. The rock star and his wife were not pleased—especially after the exasperated reporter cut the interview short and stormed out of the room.

In Vietnam, Emerson was just as bold. To understand the war from every angle, she talked with everyone she could, including and especially South Vietnamese troops and civilians, the people who would bear the full brunt of the fighting once Vietnamization was complete. When reporting from combat zones, she routinely broke away from the regular press corps, often at great personal risk, and drove her bureau chief to distraction with worry.[65]

Once back in the USA, Emerson found public apathy toward the suffering of the Vietnamese (on both sides of the DMZ) intolerable, famously remarking that Americans' deepest emotions "are wired to baseball players."[66] Given the harshness of some of her comments, it seems likely that the reporter was traumatized by her homecoming, by the surreal contrast, so often noted by returning servicemen and servicewomen, between the world of violence and death in Vietnam and the complacent consumer culture back in the United States. If so, her meeting with Victor must have been particularly electric. Here were two people—both writers—who relied upon their attention to craft to carry them through emotionally overwhelming experiences. Indeed, Emerson's resulting article in the *Times*, titled "Chapel, A Father's Memorial Honors More than Vietnam Dead," includes a quotation in which Victor reflected on the emotional coping mechanism offered by his academic writing and peace scholarship: "My wife is more bitter than I am about David's death. She just cannot have the objectivity that I have. I am a historian and it's futile to just crawl into a shell. I do what I can because I must."[67]

Victor proudly showed the journalist around the memorial, which had already begun to extend beyond the walls of the chapel, a development that would intensify and accelerate during later decades. Emerson noted thirty-six circular cement stepping-stones leading to the chapel entrance and to a cluster of outdoor benches located to the side. Each step bore the name of an American killed in Vietnam. "There is room for 250," Victor told her.[68] Inside the chapel, benches had yet to be installed, which led the war correspondent, no fan of the American public at the moment, to note some unflattering behavior on the part of visitors. Emerson looked on as a "middle-aged woman with three children" rudely complained that "there's no place to sit down." Others who stopped to see the interior of the chapel seemed "uneasy," not knowing how to behave in such a strange and personal space. And some even went so far as to ask Victor, who patiently greeted each guest (no matter how boorish), "How much did it cost you?"[69] Oddly, in her eagerness to present the chapel as a proverbial case of pearls before swine, Emerson made no mention in her article of the Vietnam veterans who sought out this lonely spot in the Sangre de Cristos and who typically responded to the Westphalls' project with gratitude and understanding.

Emerson was more perceptive when it came to the visual and aural details of the memorial. Her practiced eye took in the thirteen photographs on the wall, along with the thirteen-star Betsy Ross flag, which flew outside, and the tubular thirteen-foot-tall crucifix next to the chapel's only window. (Victor's numerological fixation was hard to miss.) From the top of the cross burned an eternal gas flame, a feature that the Westphalls would eventually discontinue because of smoke damage to the chapel ceiling. She also studied Walter's sound system, with its "24 speakers inside the Chapel and on the grounds," and took note of the performers—"Joan Baez and Bob Dylan and Peter, Paul, and Mary"—whose songs incongruously broke "the silence of the lonely hill."[70] "The music of the young," Victor called it.[71]

Then, as Victor answered the journalist's questions about the meaning and scope of his memorial, he made a proclamation so extraordinary that it subsequently served as the centerpiece of Emerson's article and the inspiration for its title. The chapel, he asserted, did "not honor Americans alone": "'There seems to be some commotion today—of protest—when you say peace and brotherhood,' Dr. Westphall said. 'If I found out that the person who had killed my son . . . in turn had been killed, I would put his photo in the Chapel.'"[72]

The interior of the chapel, circa late 1970s–early 1980s. Courtesy of Walter Westphall.

Although Victor went on to offer a mild qualification—"I am not singling out the North Vietnamese, but I am not excluding them"—readers of Emerson's article, which appeared on June 15, must have been stunned, some even outraged.[73] How could an American citizen, the father of a combat fatality, no less, even consider memorializing the *enemy*? Readers still supportive of the war effort probably concluded that either the homebuilder had spoken off the cuff in a moment of anguish, without realizing the implications of his words, or he had joined the far left's embrace of the North Vietnamese.[74]

Of course, neither was the case. Victor had, in fact, come up with the idea of honoring the dead of both sides in 1969, when he wrote a letter to Ho Chi Minh requesting photographs of deceased NVA soldiers. This remarkable document appears in Albert Reising's foreword to *Vietnam: The Hinge of Destiny*, and at a glance one can see that Victor had hardly chosen the side of the North Vietnamese.[75] In fact, he made no mention of causes or war aims at all. Instead, he adopted the same long view of armed conflict presented in his recent address. Once again, Victor stressed that when it comes to international relations today's enemies invariably become tomorrow's friends (and vice versa), a conclusion he had first reached in 1945. And he implicitly treated *all* who had died in Vietnam as actors in the same tragedy and therefore worthy of the same recognition. Since the letter remains controversial today (for reasons that we will consider shortly), it is worth quoting in full:

> Doctor Victor Westphall, Secretary
> Vietnam Veterans Peace and
> Brotherhood Chapel, Inc.
> Post Office Box 666
> Springer, New Mexico

September 3, 1969
His Excellency Ho Chi Minh
President of North Vietnam
Hanoi, North Vietnam
Excellency:
    While your country and mine are at war, if the lessons of history are a valid indication, they will not always be so. We have lost a son

in that war. As a result of that loss, and as a testimonial of faith in the ultimate goodness of man, we are building the Vietnam Veterans Peace and Brotherhood Chapel.

Photos of deceased veterans of the war in Vietnam will be therein presented to view, and they will be changed each month. Also on view will be two inscriptions—enclosed—from the writings of our son.

We invite your people to send photos of their deceased veterans. If at all possible they should be in color, and they must be eight inches by ten inches in size.

Very respectfully,
Victor Westphall[76]

Ho Chi Minh never saw this invitation. Ironically, Victor wrote on the day after Ho died, and, in any event, it is unlikely that Secretary of State William P. Rogers, whom Victor addressed in a cover letter, would have actually forwarded the message to Hanoi.[77] The two nations were, after all, at war.

But it's interesting to speculate on how the North Vietnamese leader would have reacted if he had received Victor's appeal. Would he have encouraged his countrymen to send photographs to New Mexico? It seems doubtful. Just as David Westphall was a true believer in the crusade against communism, Ho devoted his entire life to the cause of Vietnamese nationalism. And behind his kindly, avuncular persona was a ruthless strategist, undeterred by the millions of deaths that the reunification and full independence of Vietnam would ultimately require. One suspects that he would have resisted any commemorative scheme proposed from abroad, especially a display in which American and North Vietnamese fatalities carried the same meaning, a meaning over which the Vietnamese themselves would have no control. After all, the communist regime in Vietnam had—and has—its own war memorials. For example, each of the nation's ubiquitous war cemeteries features a central monument, which, as historian and novelist Viet Thanh Nguyen notes, treats the fallen as martyrs and bears the nationalistic inscription "The Fatherland Remembers Your Sacrifice."[78] A war is memorialized differently by its victors.

In 2018, forty-nine years after Victor wrote to Ho Chi Minh, the Vietnam veterans on the board of directors of the David Westphall Veterans Foundation found themselves in disagreement over whether or not to acknowledge Victor's attempted communication with an enemy leader. A new documentary about the Angel Fire memorial was in the works, and the board members faced the difficult task of determining which details—drawn from a complex story spanning a half century—should be included in a film with a running time of just under one hour.

Walter felt the documentary should at least acknowledge the Ho Chi Minh letter, but wearied by decades of controversy and debate, he didn't push too hard. The rest of the board split, predictably enough, along political and ideological lines. At least one member, who viewed America's war in Vietnam as a mistake from the start, regarded the letter's potential omission as a disservice to history. Others believed that Victor's memory would be dishonored by dwelling on a gesture that went nowhere and that had little to with what they saw as his greatest accomplishment—the creation of a sanctuary where veterans of an unpopular American war had received welcome and understanding.

Emails went back and forth, and both sides provided compelling arguments. In the end, the letter remained in the script, but without dramatic emphasis—a compromise of sorts. Indeed, the filmmakers decided to focus at least equal attention on the memorial's UH-1 Huey helicopter, an evocative artifact to which almost *any* Vietnam veteran could relate. Though conducted amiably, the discussion revealed old, familiar divisions, as did the reception of Ken Burns's eagerly anticipated documentary *The Vietnam War*, which debuted around the same time and inspired a similarly (and predictably) polarized response within the Vietnam veteran community. Even forty-three years after the fall of Saigon, the wounds of Vietnam remained raw.

However, the lack of a consensus among the board members on how to weigh the historical and biographical importance of Victor's letter to Ho also spoke to divisions within Victor himself, as well as ideological instability within the memorial he created. The scholar and historian who solemnly characterized the Vietnam War as an apocalyptic "hinge of destiny" was, in many respects, a different man from the genial Doc Westphall who greeted visitors. As an intellectual, Victor condemned the war that had taken his son, but when interacting with veterans (in whom he *saw* his son), he remained nonjudgmental and reached out to former soldiers of all political and ideological stripes. As Tonning, who knew Victor as well as anyone, put it, "Doc was the antithesis of agenda-driven."[79] In a way, the question of whether or not to include the Ho Chi Minh letter came down to which Victor Westphall the board and the filmmakers wished to foreground.

Just as a tension existed within Victor between the scholar, who stood for world peace, and the memorial caretaker, committed to the healing and relief of American veterans (regardless of their views), the Vietnam Veterans Peace and Brotherhood Chapel straddled a metaphorical fault line. The structure's very title pointed to its ideological instability. Did this title refer to global peace and brotherhood, the aim of Victor's scholarly writings, or peace and brotherhood among American Vietnam veterans, the outcome that drove Victor's day-to-day interactions with former soldiers? The chief founder of the chapel believed that these two goals were compatible. As subsequent events would demonstrate, however, the site could not support both objectives. This would become especially clear as a determined legislative and grassroots movement sought official recognition of the chapel's standing as a national memorial.

5

A National Memorial

> Any ultimate justice which may be granted to
> those who died in Vietnam, or to those who
> were maimed in body or spirit, will not be of this
> world. Nevertheless, imperfect human beings
> and seemingly inadequate human institutions
> can achieve a measure of justice by choosing to
> memorialize the valor, the effort, and the sacrifices
> of all Vietnam veterans. If we, as a nation, fail to do
> at least that, we will have managed to add but one
> more tragic chapter to the Vietnam chronology.
> –*Walter Westphall*, Vietnam Veterans Chapel
> Bulletin *(March 1975)*

Among the visitors who made the lonely trek to the Westphalls' memorial during its first decade was the New York–based writer Corinne Browne, the nom de plume for Corinne de Laittre Browne. Vietnam haunted the author, who had participated in antiwar protests during the Johnson administration, and became the focus of her work throughout the 1970s. Published in 1973, her first book, *Body Shop: Recuperating from Vietnam*, tells the stories of amputees at the Letterman Army Medical Center in San Francisco. Drawn to the Moreno Valley by a newspaper article on the chapel, Browne decided to focus her next project on a different kind of amputation and prosthesis—the Westphalls' loss of David and their creation of his memorial. Over the next eight years or so, she visited the chapel repeatedly; interviewed Victor, Jeanne, and Walter;

and collected her impressions of the New Mexico landscape and its peoples, a strange and even forbidding world in many respects, as it remains for outsiders today.

The result was an odd book, now long out of print. Titled *Casualty: A Memoir of Love & War* (1981), Browne's account offered an uneasy blend of autobiography, Westphall family history, romance (part of the narrative details Browne's brief relationship, mostly imagined, with a Vietnam veteran who worked on the Val Verde Ranch), and ruminations on masculinity and war. For their part, Victor and Walter were deeply dissatisfied with the book, a perhaps inevitable response given the writer's eccentric, genre-defying approach. What stands out in *Casualty* almost forty years later are Browne's often startling metaphors and similes—lit up at night, the chapel "gleam[ed] like a crooked phantom finger over the black valley"—and her evocation of the memorial's isolation and eeriness, the sound of the cord on the chapel's "bare flagpole" as it twanged in the unceasing wind (while Bob Dylan played in the background, courtesy of Walter's sound system), the spectral headlights of a truck on the two-lane highway at the base of the hill, passing late at night.[1] The book is, in part, a prose-poem about a place of palpable energy. But whether that energy was ultimately positive or negative, the writer could never quite decide.

Victor had his own ideas about the memorial's relationship with its physical and cultural setting. And with the uncanny. In a short essay composed sometime in the mid-1970s, titled "The Chapel Stucco and Aboriginal Tradition: A Sacred Element," he explained that the chapel's outer texture intentionally evoked the look and feel of "hand applied plaster," an essential ingredient in the architecture of "ancient people."[2] For him, this was a mystical as well as historical connection. The chapel, he explained, stood on land recognized as sacred by local Native Americans, and the sensations of "unaccountable spirituality" experienced by visitors to the site were no accident: a line of spiritual energy, or "force," he posited, flowed from the summit of Mount Wheeler to the Blue Lake and then on to the prominence occupied by the Val Verde Ranch.[3]

In this way, Victor not only revealed his attraction to mysticism (as first seen, decades earlier, through his induction into the Order of the Magi), he also added yet another layer of meaning to an already complex and multidimensional site of memory. As philosopher Edward S. Casey notes, the

The chapel at night. Photograph by Richard Dickerson.

German language, which is far more precise than English when it comes to the vocabulary of commemoration, distinguishes among three different types of public memorials: "a *Denkmal*, a monument meant to memorialize a person or event, a *Mahnmal* (a public reminder that acts as warning), and a *Gedenkstätte* (a place in which momentous events can be mediated)."[4] From the beginning, the Vietnam Veterans Peace and Brotherhood Chapel fit all of these definitions at once, one reason, among many, for the structure's extraordinary impact on visitors. Temporally, the chapel's meaning ran in three directions or, if you will, on three different clocks—one set to 1968, one running on regular time, and one speeding into the future. By honoring David's life specifically, along with those of all Americans lost in Vietnam, the memorial sought to preserve the past, and thus performed the function of a *Denkmal*. At the same time, the chapel offered a beacon of "peace and brotherhood" for living veterans and their families, a safe space, one might say, for reflection and recovery in the present, and thus a *Gedenkstätte*. And, finally, through the inclusion of David's apocalyptic verse, which Victor regarded as prophetic, the structure served as a *Mahnmal*, a warning of the nuclear Armageddon that would result if America ignored the "hinge of destiny" represented by Vietnam.[5] In a remarkable intertwining of future and past, the ultimate Cold War anxiety played a role in the Westphalls' one-of-a-kind remembrance project.

However, Victor's thoughts in "The Chapel Stucco and Aboriginal Tradition" also invite a different, perhaps equally useful distinction, one that may further help to explain the memorial's power. Many public monuments—perhaps most—have a somewhat perfunctory relationship with their surroundings. For example, community war memorials, those that don't take the shape of buildings or parks, typically appear in public spaces selected on the basis of visibility and tradition. Soldier statues from the late nineteenth or early twentieth century stand at attention (or at parade rest) before courthouses or city halls because *that's where they go*. In this case, there is nothing particularly complicated or meaningful about a monument's relationship to its setting—until, that is, a city government decides to move the object elsewhere (often to a more obscure location), a fate visited upon far more public memorials than one would think.[6]

But some commemorative structures draw energy from their physical location. Battlefield memorials, for instance, have—or can have, depending on the success of their design and the status of a given conflict in collective memory—exceptional commemorative power. Consider the armies of stone and bronze at Gettysburg, where nearly two thousand markers and memorials cover the landscape.[7] Even individuals who have ceased to notice public statuary in their own community (and that's most people) will likely be impressed by the battlefield's commemorative legions, especially in the early morning, when the half-perceptible monuments emerge from the darkness like a host of phantoms. In this instance, place is everything: the impact of Gettysburg's monuments depends entirely upon the visitor's awareness that the statues stand where actual soldiers were once positioned. Flesh has become stone—the Pygmalion myth in reverse.

Ground marked as sacred confers intensity and importance to memorials, whether that ground is a battlefield, the scene of a massive disaster or tragedy (such as the Flight 93 crash site or the Twin Towers location in lower Manhattan), or the National Mall in Washington, DC. The latter, a commemorative setting like no other, is absolutely supercharged with meaning. Here a memorial's message goes well beyond what it can produce on its own. Where a monument stands, whether it can be seen from others, whether they can be seen from it—everything signifies. Such factors play a particularly fascinating role in the way that visitors experience the National Vietnam Veterans Memorial, the only monument on the Mall that is practically invisible upon approach, the only one to occupy space *below* ground—funerary characteristics that the informal title "the Wall" barely acknowledges. In this case, the monument's visual isolation from other national memorials that share the same sacred space contributes enormously to its meaning, suggesting a place of anguished, half-hidden memory. By the same token, the decision to place the National World War II Memorial above ground and, as Barbara Biesecker remarks, "at the very center of the Capitol" says volumes about the way in which Americans collectively remember the so-called Good War.[8]

Thus, one doesn't have to accept Victor's supernatural explanation to see that a line of energy or "force" leading in and out of the chapel makes a kind of sense, at least metaphorically. The Westphalls' memorial, like its better-known cousin on the Mall, carries meanings shaped, in part, by the specifics of its location, meanings that would be entirely different if the chapel were situated elsewhere or constructed with a different relationship to its surroundings. Some of these meanings, such as the eerie correspondences between the Val Verde Ranch and the setting of *Wings for Per*, operated on a deeply personal level and were shared primarily among David's surviving family members. But others carried into the public realm. We have already noted, for example, that Ted Luna's design, with its soaring glacial peak, visually fuses the memorial with the Sangre de Cristo mountains, blurring the line between the natural and the manmade. This creates a sense of timelessness, reminding visitors that the desire for peace, like the problem of war, stretches far into antiquity.

Victor's reference to the Blue Lake, the "sacred place of the Taos Pueblo Indians," suggests another important line of connection, you could say, between the chapel and its physical and cultural environment.[9] Due west of the memorial, on the other side of a mountain pass, stands the Taos Pueblo, one of the oldest continually inhabited structures in North America and a true living memorial (like the ancient mesa-top community of Acoma farther west) to the indigenous peoples of New Mexico. The home of the chapel's nearest Native American neighbors is, of course, constructed of adobe. Thus, by asserting a kinship between the memorial and examples of ancient architecture like the Taos Pueblo, Victor's essay on the chapel stucco implicitly (and somewhat ironically) aligned his neo-modern memorial with the premodern, even the pre-Columbian. As a historian and a student of art history, Victor would have understood the implications here: if, both visually and *tactually*, his memorial expressed the aesthetics of ancient cultures, then it was tied, at least in part, to an alternative narrative of American history, one that did not move on the east-west axis of Manifest Destiny.

Additional lines of energy flowed from twentieth-century painting and literature. Luna's revolutionary design for the chapel, with its organic contours and disorienting break from ecclesiastical convention (nothing about the building could even remotely be described as Romanesque or Gothic), took its place among a host of iconoclastic artworks associated with New Mexico. The Taos area, in particular, enjoys a well-earned reputation as a hub for the avant-garde and features a number of pilgrimage destinations for aficionados of modernist visual art and literature. For example, south of the Taos Pueblo, several miles below the turnoff for the Taos Canyon Road, stands the San Francisco de Asis Mission Church in Ranchos de Taos, which the celebrated painter Georgia O'Keeffe depicted in a series of semiabstract canvases. To the north of Taos, a winding dirt road leads to the D. H. Lawrence Ranch, a literary memorial, overseen by the University of New Mexico, where the visionary English novelist is buried. And within Taos proper, visitors can stay in the former home of Mabel Dodge Luhan, a wealthy patron of the arts whose regular guests in the 1920s included Willa Cather, whose creative roots ran deep in the region as well. In *Death Comes for the Archbishop* (1927), Cather created perhaps the most evocative novel about New Mexico ever written, but in a plotless, episodic style that is almost as experimental, in its quiet way, as Luna's bold design for the Vietnam Veterans Peace and Brotherhood Chapel.[10]

In short, the Westphalls' memorial tapped into a wealth of local associations and influences, all of which contributed to its multiple layers of meaning. Think of it, if you will, as existing within a grid or matrix created by connecting all of the various locations mentioned above, a web of commemorative energy constantly transferred from point to point. And when combined with the site's aesthetic appeal and poignant origin story, this rich physical and cultural milieu helped make the chapel one of the most distinctive memorials in the nation, a point often made in the mountain of praise-laden cards and letters that the Westphalls received. Many who made the journey to Angel Fire and then shared their impressions with Victor described an encounter with the Romantic sublime. Attuned to the chapel's complex relationship with place, a visitor from College Park, Maryland, put her response in regional terms: "The spirit of New Mexico and the spirit of love are strong there."[11] After driving to the memorial from Albuquerque, another traveler reported that she "almost went off the highway" when she "spotted 'wings' sprouting from a hill."[12] And for a grateful pilgrim from Colby, Kansas, the chapel was "a magnificent structure which appears to be God made rather than man made."[13]

Ever the historian and archivist, Victor carefully cataloged each and every written reaction that he received, as well as remarks overheard in the chapel or on the grounds nearby. Such responses formed a compelling record of the site's impact as a *Denkmal*, *Gedenkstätte*, and *Mahnmal* all rolled into one. Thus, Walter included several dozen of the more striking examples in a pair of information sheets, titled "Excerpts from Letters" and "Comments Heard at the Chapel by Dr. Westphall," part of a promotional packet that he prepared three years or so after the chapel's dedication.

Remarkably, while testimonials from visitors abound in these documents, many of the letters he cited came from individuals who had never been to the Moreno Valley. Simply reading about the Westphalls' Herculean enterprise—or learning about it by word of mouth—was enough to inspire putting pen to paper. For example, a correspondent from Monterey Park, California, wrote to say that she had "just read of & saw the picture of the beautiful Chapel built as a gesture of love—how wonderful to make us all stop & think."[14] A college-bound Vietnam veteran sent a request for more information, one of many such inquiries. "Before going back to school," he wanted to find a "retreat" where he could "spend some time with [his] thoughts."[15] The chapel sounded like just the thing. And there were even words of praise, penned before the ceasefire in 1973, sent by American soldiers in Vietnam. Rarely have those fighting a war been able to comment at the same time on its commemoration at home. For instance, in his letter from Southeast Asia, one serviceman mentioned that he had just learned about the memorial from an article in the *Stars and Stripes*: "I feel that the Chapel will be about the greatest contribution to all Vietnam veterans by one man."[16]

Politically, the missives selected by Walter ran the gamut from declarations of ongoing support for the South Vietnamese regime (albeit a minority view) to expressions of uncompromising pacifism. On duty in Vietnam, a major in the US Air Force used the language of official military commemoration in his note, which refused to characterize American fatalities in an unpopular war as victims: "Their sacrifice for their country makes the rest of us realize how dear we must hold true to those things they gave their lives for. Thank you for helping us remember their sacrifice."[17] In contrast, a more pacifically minded visitor from Santa Fe wrote to praise not only the chapel but also Victor's proposal for a national secretary of peace, a notion he had first floated in *Vietnam: The Hinge of Destiny*: "What an ideal to set up for a nation obsessed with military ambition and lacking the humility and dignity to acknowledge a critical error! For so long I have prayed for leadership toward moral rather than military strength."[18] A "civilian secretary" in Vietnam offered a view that perhaps fell halfway between these two poles: "If [our soldiers'] sacrifices are to be remembered, then what you are doing in their honor seems to me to be deeply fitting. If what you are doing will make people stop and think, will bring tears to their eyes and their hearts, then perhaps the next war will not happen so easily."[19]

Discordant notes sometimes sounded as well. But Victor recorded them just the same. For example, on one occasion, an "elderly lady from Springer" (obviously not one of Jeanne's friends there) gazed at the memorial and "disdainfully" asked, "Where's the Chapel?"[20] Victor also sometimes encountered the annoying question, "Is this all there is to it?"[21] However, his imperturbability and good manners were perhaps most put to the test when a particularly oblivious visitor wanted to know whether "the slope of the roof was symbolic of the ski areas in the vicinity."[22]

And amid the flood of appreciative letters, expressions of annoyance—even anger—occasionally appeared in connection with the chapel's antiwar message. One particularly fiery specimen dates to 1979, when *Parade* magazine featured a widely read story on the Westphalls and their memorial.

The letter writer, a member of the US Army in World War II and later the merchant marines during Korea and Vietnam, did not like what he saw in *Parade*, and he did not mince words: "This memorial should be dedicated to All veterans, not just those of the Vietnam War. I think that is ridiculous. . . . We had the Korean War won and the Vietnam War won, but the commies, fellow travelers, pinkos, etc., in Washington DC wouldn't allow it. . . . The showdown between the free world (what is left of it) and communism has to come. It's one or the other."[23]

Such reactions were, however, exceedingly rare, perhaps surprisingly so given the raw emotions stirred by Vietnam. Far more common were statements that highlighted the Westphalls' personal loss, as well as the courage and strength it had taken to transform personal tragedy into a remembrance effort relevant to all. For many who shared their thoughts about the chapel in the 1970s, the family story behind the memorial mattered more than anything else, a response that would have significant implications later. Writing from Vietnam, one soldier expressed admiration for Victor personally: "I was moved by the way you reacted to your son's death, not in despair nor hate nor political action, but in going back to the very essence of man's fate on this earth."[24] Yet another serviceman in Southeast Asia put his thoughts more succinctly: "It is for you, and your ideas and ideals, that I am proud of being an American."[25]

By 1974 it had become clear that without necessarily setting out to do so, the Westphalls had created a de facto national memorial to American veterans of the Vietnam War. Thus, Victor and Walter set their sights on a new goal: transferring the chapel ownership to the federal government.

Walter would lead the effort. Though still energetic, Victor was beginning to feel the strain of the family's colossal remembrance project. After all, he had done much of the construction work on the chapel himself and, true to his nature, had lived for months at a time in a state of near-constant frustration and anxiety provoked by the family's darkening financial outlook, as well as the usual problems and delays associated with contractors. His calm, soft-spoken manner usually masked this inner angst, but there was no hiding the oxygen tank that he kept by his side (except when jogging, of course) at the insistence of his physician. Now, with Walter finally released from his air force responsibilities, Victor was ready to at least partially surrender the most wearisome part of the entire endeavor—the incessant quest for funding—and to pursue some activities outside his role as the chapel's principal caretaker. To secure some much-needed income, he took a job with the developer who now owned the Val Verde Ranch, ironically completing construction tasks on the property that he had once owned and planned to develop himself. And he devoted a bit more of his time to his scholarly writings on New Mexico history, as well as the quest for global peace.

After his discharge from the air force in 1973, Walter seemed, for a period, unable to take hold of anything except the unending task of securing funding for the chapel. He was, as he later explained, "uncertain what to do or where to go."[26] David's death, combined with the disillusionment he had felt with the nation's military and political leadership, had left him feeling utterly directionless. When not staying at his parents' house in Springer, he drifted through a string of technical schools and universities, moving from institution to institution whenever he became bored or restless. He was also admitted to schools "from California to Florida" that he never attended.[27] His only serious ambition—short-lived, as it turned out—was to become a commercial airline pilot, a position for which his service aboard KC-135s fully qualified him. But the Arab oil embargo had hit the American airline industry hard, and there were no jobs for ex-military aviators. Walter seemed on his way to becoming a lost soul—or at least as close as a member of the innately self-disciplined, goal-oriented Westphall clan could come to that doleful description.

In the fall of 1975 he regained his bearings. He enrolled in the MBA program at the University of Denver and received his degree the next year, eventually landing a position with the Federal Home Loan Bank Board (later amusingly titled the Office of Thrift Supervision). A solitary man, soft-spoken like his father and reserved, Walter was perhaps most in his element when working with numbers and details. He dreaded public speaking or being the center of attention, and to those who knew him in the 1970s he must have come across as an unlikely crusader. But beneath his placid manner lurked great passion—a barely contained rage toward the policy makers, the supposed "best and brightest," who had blunderingly committed the United States to an unwinnable war in Southeast

Asia, combined with a fierce determination to see that Americans who served in Vietnam (the living and the dead) were appropriately honored and remembered.

And as he became more involved with the writing of the chapel bulletin, as well as other promotional materials related to the memorial, a shift in the tone and focus of these documents became apparent. Victor wrote eloquently about the quest for universal peace and brotherhood. Although he shared that lofty goal (at least to a point), Walter was more likely to critique the fatal flaws of politicians and military leaders during the Vietnam era, as well as the foolhardy strategies and tactics developed for US forces and the advantages held by the North Vietnamese, advantages that American war planners had stubbornly refused to see.

An issue of the chapel bulletin from November 1978 provides a representative sample of Walter's rhetoric and thematic preoccupations throughout this period of the memorial's history. Here he offered "a few personal thoughts about the nature and meaning of the Vietnam War," mostly excoriating criticisms of the political and military establishment.[28] Echoing David's assessment in 1968, he maintained, for instance, that the Pentagon ignored important lessons that should have been drawn from the French experience in Southeast Asia: "The American government . . . put troops into Vietnam without adequately developing a counter insurgency doctrine [and] without adequately considering the lessons of previous counter insurgency efforts [i.e., the French war against the Viet Minh]."[29] Walter reserved his harshest judgments, however, for the individuals at the top, the people who—in his view, at least—had used patriotic soldiers like David as disposable pawns for their own ends. "All too often," he wrote, "higher level military commanders permitted an obsessively careerist orientation to have priority above the safety of their troops . . . and above the truth about the morality and efficacy of American strategy and tactics."[30] A scalding verdict straightforwardly expressed.

As passages like this one make clear, *both* sons in the Westphall family carried the wordsmith gene. Walter did not necessarily write in a rhetorically forceful or dramatic way, and his prose perhaps lacked the gracefulness that characterized his brother's essays and letters. However, his measured style—characterized by the same precision and logic that he applied to his regulatory duties at the Federal Home Loan Bank Board—

was the perfect one for a battle with Washington bureaucrats. And, sadly, that's exactly what the Westphalls' effort to transfer their memorial to the US government became.

On the surface, achieving federal recognition for the Vietnam Veterans Chapel (as the memorial was now known) seemed a reasonable objective. One year after the ceasefire that ended the nation's involvement in Vietnam, the more than 2.7 million Americans who had served there had no federally designated monument. And there was no talk of creating one. Jan Scruggs's grassroots effort to establish a national Vietnam veterans memorial in Washington, DC (about which we will hear more later), was still years away, and none of the two dozen or so local Vietnam War memorials established elsewhere in the country by 1974 enjoyed anything like the chapel's devoted following. The Westphalls could argue with good reason that the thousands of Vietnam veterans drawn to their memorial since 1971 had already made their case for them. Surely a site that had attracted so many visitors—and, by this point, so many newspaper articles and favorable testimonials—could lay claim to the word "national."

But there were formidable obstacles that the Westphalls, still new to the political dimensions of public memory, underestimated. For one thing, no group of American veterans from *any* war had, by this point, received their own federally designated national memorial. A visitor to the National Mall in 2020 might be forgiven for assuming that America's epicenter of commemoration has always showcased war monuments. In fact, however, the transformation of the Mall into a space for political *and* military remembrance is a fairly recent development, and it has played out, oddly enough, in reverse chronological order.[31]

Completed in 1982, the oldest such structure honors the veterans of the Vietnam War, the most recent conflict represented on the Mall. The National Korean War Veterans Memorial came next in 1995, followed by the memorial to American World War II veterans, the most imposing monument of them all, in 2004. In short, the specific federal designation that the Westphalls sought didn't exist yet. As of the mid-1970s there were no traditions or standard practices to warrant what they proposed.[32] Thus, they would have to argue on two fronts, asserting both the need for a national memorial to honor Vietnam veterans (a hard sell given the cultural silence that quickly settled over the conflict after 1973) *and* making the case for the chapel as the appropriate vehicle for governmentally sanctioned remembrance.

Other impediments would soon present themselves as well. There was, for example, no denying the chapel's physical remoteness. From Albuquerque, New Mexico's only real metropolis (or the closest thing to it), it took three hours to reach the Moreno Valley. Santa Fe at this time was less a city than a large town with just forty thousand residents and a tiny municipal airport.[33] In addition, the specific aesthetic, cultural, and mystical qualities that Victor attributed to the chapel, qualities that anchored the chapel in its Southwestern environment and gave it its peculiar energy, also created problems. Was the memorial in this sense too exotic—too New Mexican—to serve as a symbol for the entire country?

But the biggest difficulty of them all stemmed from the autonomy that the Westphalls had enjoyed when creating their chapel, autonomy that would cease to exist once they entered any sort of partnership with the federal government. Built on their own land, privately funded, and subject to no one's approval but their own, the family's memorial exemplified, as historian Deborah Kidwell points out in her in-depth study of the site, *vernacular* remembrance.[34] Kidwell's analysis draws upon the work of fellow historian John Bodnar, who distinguishes between official remembrance, which is identified with the interests of the state and characterized (at least in the United States) by a lofty rhetoric of idealized concepts such as "sacrifice" and "duty," and the vernacular variety, which grows from the bottom up and expresses the views of individuals directly affected by the events they have chosen to commemorate.[35]

Official and vernacular remembrance are not, of course, mutually exclusive, as the complicated history behind almost any public memorial reveals. An often-protracted process of negotiation and accommodation usually reconciles the two; this would, in fact, later become the case at Angel Fire. But in the mid-1970s, the Westphalls' memorial was, quite simply, about as vernacular as you can get.

Nothing about the structure—from its otherworldly visual design to its uneven, adobe-like texture to its display of thirteen photographs and wall-mounted passages of cryptic verse—resulted from compromise or negotiation of any kind. Victor and Walter had done everything *their* way, including the creation of a one-of-a-kind commemorative soundtrack that, as Gloria Emerson and Corinne Browne both noted, mingled with the booming of the ceaseless high mountain winds to eerie effect. Walter selected the playlist, which eschewed Vietnam-era acid rock in favor of top-forty, AM radio hits such as "Walk Away Renée," by the Left Banke; "The First Time Ever I Saw Your Face," by Roberta Flack, "Yesterday When I Was Young," by Roy Clark; "What the World Needs Now," by Jackie DeShannon; and "Galveston," by Glen Campbell. Meant to evoke the themes of "youth, adolescence, love, war, and inspiration," the music played nonstop throughout the day and evening, and visitors often praised the high-fidelity sound produced by the deluxe reel-to-reel system that Walter obtained in Okinawa, an unexpected feature of a thoroughly idiosyncratic sacred space.[36]

In 1982, when the Westphalls transferred ownership of the chapel to the Disabled American Veterans (DAV), this aural accompaniment to the dramatic visual rhetoric created by Ted Luna was, of course, one of first things to go—a vernacular casualty, one could say, that did not survive the site's transition to a more official mode of remembrance. And, as we will see later in this chapter, the DAV introduced other changes to the chapel as well, none of which pleased its founders. But in 1974, as Victor and Walter embarked upon what would become an eight-year struggle to find a stable financial home for the memorial, the notion that anyone would have the nerve to alter their creation seemed utterly inconceivable. Both men innocently believed that they could secure long-term funding from a larger organization, governmental or otherwise, while maintaining control over a fiercely vernacular structure, replete with commemorative oddities (such as the passages from David's poetry) that not everyone would necessarily understand or appreciate. Unfortunately, as subsequent events would demonstrate, the politics of public memory simply don't work that way.

To launch their quest for formal recognition of the chapel's standing as a national memorial, the Westphalls reached out to New Mexico senator Pete V. Domenici, who would prove a determined and reliable ally, as well as US Representative Manuel Lujan Jr. Apparently, neither politician required much convincing—at least not according to Victor's copious records. A pall of silence may have descended upon the Vietnam War on the national level, but these New Mexico congressmen had little difficulty perceiving the advantages of securing such a prestigious designation (as well as the stream of federal dollars that would go with it), and in January 1975, at the opening of the 94th Session of Congress, they swung into action. Domenici teamed up with fellow New Mexico senator Joseph M. Montoya to cosponsor bill S. 171, which, if approved, would authorize "a feasibility study to determine if there was justification for the establishment of the Vietnam Veterans Chapel as a memorial within the National Park Service."[37] Meanwhile, Lujan introduced H.R. 2909, a parallel proposal, in the House of Representatives.

If the Westphalls were a bit naïve when it came to the dynamics of state-sanctioned remembrance versus the vernacular variety, they had no illusions about Washington politics. Written in this case by Walter, the chapel bulletin for March 1975 reflects an in-depth understanding of the legislative process and its many perils. "No one," wrote Walter, "should assume that the obvious merits of S. 171 and H.R. 2909 will guarantee that they will receive a prompt and fair hearing."[38] By this point, both bills had been referred to committee, where, as Walter realized, they might very well die. The Domenici-Montoya bill was now in the hands of the Senate Committee on Interior and Insular Affairs; Lujan's rested with the House version of the same committee. Neither committee had scheduled a hearing to discuss the Westphalls' proposal, which prompted Walter to strike a note of alarm and to offer a quick civics lesson: "It should be realized by all persons interested in the Chapel that the fact of referral to a committee by no means ensures a hearing by the committee. Many thousands of bills are introduced in Congress during each session; many of these bills are never considered during committee hearings, and only a relatively small number are actually enacted into law."[39] He then urged all supporters to use the only leverage at their disposal by writing to the "key legislators" on both committees.[40]

In October, the Westphalls learned that the effort had failed. There would be no hearing. Both bills were moribund. As copies of documents reached them, forwarded by Domenici and Lujan (who had tried their best), Victor and Walter learned why. Asked to weigh in on S. 171 and H.R. 2909, the federal advisory board on National Parks, Historic Sites, Buildings and Monuments had made it clear that the National Park

Service (NPS) wanted nothing to do with the proposed feasibility study. And in a memo addressed to the secretary of the interior, the chairman of the advisory board, Steven L. Rose, had basically nailed the door shut, citing two central objections to any legislation that might potentially make the chapel the NPS's responsibility.

Predictably enough, the first objection involved a matter of precedent: "The Board notes that the National Park Service presently administers no war memorials outside the National Capital area, other than those located in historic battlefield parks."[41] The second was guaranteed to infuriate the family that had worked so hard—and given up so much—in order to sustain their one-of-a-kind memorial: "The Board concludes that the Vietnam Veterans Chapel does not possess national significance under the provisions of the Historic Sites Act of August 21, 1935, and is, therefore, not eligible for Registered National Historic Landmark status."[42]

The Vietnam Veterans Chapel does not possess national significance—no sooner had the sting of these bitter words worn off than Walter began work on a lengthy and eloquent rebuttal, which he ultimately included in a large packet of materials designed to help Domenici and other supporters in Washington make the case. They would need all the ammunition they could get. Not easily deterred, Domenici planned to put forward a new bill, with the same objective as S. 171, during the very next session of Congress (scheduled to begin January 3, 1977), knowing full well that it would come up against the same congressional committee as before, as well as the tender mercies of the NPS. Meanwhile, the Westphalls settled in for a long fight.

Walter's response to the advisory board's decision addressed the two objections outlined in Rose's memo, along with a third, which Walter only discovered in a roundabout way. In early 1977, a chapel supporter named Toni Currin appealed directly to President Jimmy Carter, whose office forwarded her letter to the headquarters of the NPS. The Westphalls eventually received a copy of the NPS's reply, which, in the midst of a summary of the advisory board's position, introduced an objection that had not appeared in the earlier memo penned by Rose. And this one was enough to make Victor's and Walter's blood boil: "The Advisory Board also considered it inappropriate for the National Park Service to administer an active church facility."[43]

In his rebuttal, Walter pointed out that the description of the chapel as an "active church facility" was absurd. While various church groups from Taos and the Moreno Valley had held services there from time to time, there was no regular program of religious observances. The chapel had neither a formal congregation nor formal clergy; for most visitors, it was a place for quiet reflection and the experience of a kind of spirituality that had nothing to do with organized religion. Moreover, if the NPS objected to the periodic use of the site by formal religious denominations, it would be easy enough to put a stop to the practice once the chapel became a national monument. In the case of this objection, in particular, Walter believed (perhaps a bit unfairly) that he was dealing not with a reasonable and appropriate argument, but with a rationalization put forth to spare NPS bureaucrats additional trouble and expense, no matter how warranted the proposal under consideration. An anger, born of years of frustration, sometimes broke through the calm surface of Walter's prose: "Is it not possible," he wrote, "that the Advisory Board was merely looking for an excuse to bolster an essentially weak case for rejecting S. 171/H.R. 2909?"[44]

As for the board's other two claims—that the chapel fell outside the NPS's purview (because of its location) and that it lacked "national significance"—Walter tried his best to dismantle them both. He pointed out, for example, that the NPS *did* administer at least two memorial sites that were not located in Washington, DC, or on national battlefields; namely, the monument to Admiral Perry on the shore of Lake Erie and the Andersonville National Historic Site in Georgia. If the federal government could live with these exceptions to a general rule, why not do the same in the case of the Vietnam Veterans Chapel?

To counter the argument about significance, Walter looked for national historic sites whose importance was debatable when set beside a memorial built to honor the fifty-eight thousand Americans who died during the nation's then longest war. In other words, he wanted to show that the NPS did not consistently apply the standard it had cited as an objection to S. 171 and H.R. 2909.

Unfortunately, the chief example upon which he based his case—perhaps not the best one he could have selected—was the Chalmette battlefield park in Louisiana, which marks the site of Andrew Jackson's celebrated victory over the British in the Battle of New Orleans in 1815. What, in Walter's view, disqualified the famous Battle of New Orleans from any claim of national importance? Simple chronology. Walter explained that Jackson's triumph occurred more than two weeks after the Treaty of Ghent ended the War of 1812. Thus, the battle achieved "nothing... which had not already been accomplished by treaty."[45] According to Walter's line of deductive reasoning, the timing of Jackson's victory made its historical importance a "clouded issue" and therefore placed the Chalmette battlefield below the stated threshold for eligibility as a national historical site.

In this instance, Walter's logic was, as usual, impeccable; his understanding of how societies make sense of history though the anything-*but*-logical vehicle of cultural myth, somewhat less so. Indeed, in his eagerness to catch the NPS in an inconsistency, he overlooked the role of collective memory in federal decision making related to commemoration. For most Americans, the site of the Battle of New Orleans represented sacred ground, but not because of the battlefield's historical importance, which was indeed questionable (depending on one's perspective). What mattered was the battlefield's place in national myth. At Chalmette, a future president of the United States had triumphed over a vastly superior British force and done so with a ragtag army that even included pirates. As a story of victorious American underdogs, the episode was irresistible, and it remained so during the mid-twentieth century when rockabilly singer Johnny Horton celebrated the American victory in his hit song "The Battle of New Orleans" (1959), and Hollywood cast Charlton Heston as Jackson (alongside Yul Brynner as Jean Lafitte) in the inevitable big-screen version of the battle, *The Buccaneer* (1958). In short, whatever the NPS's policies and standards, it would have been utterly inconceivable for the agency *not* to have administered the battlefield park at Chalmette.

Viewed from a distance of more than forty years, the NPS's stated objections to S. 171/H.R. 2909 actually don't seem that unreasonable, especially given the eccentric nature of the site under consideration. Vernacular to the core, constructed as a place of worship (though, as Walter persuasively argued, hardly a "church facility"), and located far from Washington, DC, the Westphalls' iconoclastic memorial perhaps inevitably fell outside the criteria for federal recognition. But another factor, never articulated explicitly in any of the explanations offered by the NPS, probably played a role as well: the controversial nature of America's war in Vietnam and its wounds to the nation's collective psyche.

In April 1975, three months after Domenici, Montoya, and Lujan submitted their bills, North Vietnamese tanks rolled into Saigon. Up to this point, it was still possible to believe (albeit naively) that the Nixon administration's policy of Vietnamization had actually worked and that the South Vietnamese could successfully defend their own country. Now, as the bottom fell out in Southeast Asia, the nation knew the truth: at the cost of fifty-eight thousand American lives, the United States had lost a war for the first time. Thus, of all the possible times for the NPS to wade into the treacherous subject of Vietnam, this was arguably the worst. And then there was the vexing question of just how this particular arm of the federal government, charged with preserving *and* interpreting historic sites, would handle the memorial's complex multiple layers of meaning. How, without alienating a significant number of veterans or betraying the chapel's integrity as a vernacular memorial rooted in family history, would the NPS negotiate the tangle of competing messages that the Westphalls had woven into their commemorative creation?

Whether such issues lurked in the background or not, Domenici's second attempt to secure a "feasibility study" met, predictably enough, with the same fate as his first. And once again, it was the NPS's advisory board that delivered the death blow, citing reasons identical to those offered before. But the New Mexico senator wasn't giving up just yet. As Kidwell notes, "the fate of the memorial as a national monument continued to be at issue" as late as 1979, when Domenici introduced a new bill (S. 1431) designed to outflank the advisory board.[46] Walter shared the details of this promising maneuver with readers of the chapel bulletin: S. 1431, he noted, "was written in such a way that if the Congress passes it, the Secretary of the Interior would be directed to proceed with acquisition of the Chapel and would be required to develop a management plan. In other words,"—and here was the key point—"the Advisory Board for the NPS would not necessarily have an input into the decision."[47]

Although S. 1431 enjoyed bipartisan sponsorship in the Senate—two Republicans, John Warner (Virginia) and Howard Baker (Tennessee), and one Democrat, future presidential candidate Gary Hart (Colorado), joined forces with Domenici—the effort went nowhere. The reason: a rival bill, calling for the erection of what would ultimately become the Vietnam Veterans Memorial (aka the Wall) near the Lincoln Memorial, suddenly drew all the attention away from the Westphalls' proposal. Bad timing had struck again. Overnight, it seemed, congressional indifference toward the idea of honoring Vietnam veterans with a physical monument gave way to a widely shared conviction that any such memorial *must* be located in the nation's capital. For the Westphalls and their allies in Washington, who had been ahead of the times, it was the final bitter blow, the end to a quixotic legislative effort that had dragged on for four years.

But the push for a Vietnam veterans memorial on the National Mall also carried potential benefits for the chapel—provided that the Westphalls could find a way to piggyback funding for their own memorial on this soon-to-be-successful campaign. Led by Scruggs, the Vietnam Veterans Memorial Fund, Inc. (VVMF), the tenacious grassroots organization responsible for the pressure on Congress (and on President Ronald Reagan) that resulted in the establishment of the Wall, would play a little-known role in the history of the Chapel at Angel Fire. At the same time, another organization committed to remembrance, the Disabled American Veterans, would finally bring the Westphall family the financial relief they so desperately sought, though at great cost to Victor's vernacular conception of the memorial and its meaning.

In November 1979, as Victor and Walter anxiously followed the progress (or lack thereof) of Domenici's latest efforts on their behalf, their memorial enjoyed a publicity coup that surpassed all others up this point. That month, *Parade* magazine, a compact arts-and-culture weekly inserted into Sunday editions of newspapers from coast to coast (and thus read by millions), included an article titled "One Man's Shrine to All Who Fell in Vietnam." It was the piece's subtitle, however, that was guaranteed to draw attention: "Without help from government Marine's father builds chapel to honor the dead of both sides."[48] Once again, Victor's controversial attitude toward the North Vietnamese was highlighted.

While Walter's ongoing historical analysis of the origins and conduct of America's war in Vietnam had become an increasingly prominent feature of the chapel bulletin, Victor's quoted voice dominated the *Parade* article almost entirely. The author, Michael Satchell, made no mention of Victor's youngest son (a fact for which the self-effacing and media-wary Walter was probably grateful), and he included just a single quotation from Jeanne, never once hinting at the suffering and isolation she had endured as an indirect result of David's commemoration. The latter was a part of the saga simply not told by anyone.

In short, like most press reports sympathetic to the Westphalls' project, this well-written article streamlines the chapel's complicated history into the dramatic tale of a father's heroic struggle in isolation, a narrative that Victor had long decided he could live with since it captured the public's imagination and served the interests of the memorial. In fact, it had become his preferred version of the story.

Satchell emphasized that Victor had worked "almost singlehandedly" on his creation for eleven years (no reference to Vedeler and his crew) and that he had used "mostly his own money," which was sadly true enough.[49] The obstacles he had faced were immense—"lack of funding, public apathy, government indifference, and skepticism about his motives."[50] And he had overcome them all, though Satchell noted, with appropriate alarm, that the memorial's future was by no means certain: "Westphall has neither the financial resource nor the years ahead of him to assure its continued existence. Despite attempts by the New Mexico Congressional delegation to introduce legislation to have the National Parks Service take over the memorial, and repeated approaches to various foundations, help is nowhere in sight."[51]

The two photographs that accompanied the article, both taken by Satchell, reinforced this account of one man's epic quest to commemorate by putting Victor literally at the center of each frame. Both images feature him alone. In the first, he sits perched on the Westphalls' hilltop, strong and limber-looking for his sixty-five years, gazing purposefully into the distance, the white hair on the sides of his otherwise bald head blown back in the wind. His expression has an almost mystic quality, like that of a divinely inspired seer or prophet. The chapel is lined up directly behind him, as if having magically materialized from his thoughts. In the second image, shot inside the memorial, Victor looks small and feeble, as though crushed by the weight of the photographs of soldiers killed in action displayed on the back wall. Here his eyes look vacant, his face expressionless.

Victor in front of the chapel, Parade, *November 1979. Photograph by Michael Satchell.*

Victor inside the chapel, Parade, November 1979. Photograph by Michael Satchell.

Without the captions, one might have difficulty realizing that these are two portraits of the same man. The first shows an individual inspired and energized by loss. The second captures the results of an utterly annihilating grief.

As promised by its provocative subtitle, "One Man's Shrine" also addresses Victor's stance toward America's former enemy in Southeast Asia and includes a statement from the memorial's chief founder almost identical to the one that appeared in Emerson's article seven years earlier. Once again, Victor offered a concrete and specific example—one that must have caused some readers to gasp—of his philosophy of peace of brotherhood in action: "If there were any way to learn the identity of the Vietnamese who killed my son, and if he too died and it were possible to get a photograph of him, I would display it right alongside David's picture. This memorial is for all Vietnam veterans, of any nationality."[52]

When Victor spoke along these lines in 1972, no one paid any attention. Walter does not recall learning of any negative reactions to Emerson's article in the *New York Times*—or even any notice of his father's potentially inflammatory statement. This time, it would be a different story, in part because the Westphalls were inching their vernacular memorial toward the realm of official commemoration on two different paths.

The first of these paths opened in 1977, two years before the *Parade* article appeared, when the chapel received a promise of partial financial support from the Disabled American Veterans, a federally chartered organization that provides assistance to combat-wounded Americans, as well as congressional lobbying on their behalf. With "apparently few strings attached," the Westphalls received a commitment of $10,000 per year for the next ten years, the first significant monetary contribution to the memorial by any institution, governmental or otherwise.[53] Not surprisingly, Victor and Walter dreamed of a day when the organization might go even further and assume ownership of the chapel. The second avenue, which we will consider in a moment, involved a tricky political maneuver, one that proved too tricky in the end; that is, ensuring that the VVMF include as part of its legislative push for a Washington, DC–based national memorial a provision that would guarantee long-term funding for the Vietnam Veterans chapel.

The kind of ground war Americans had endured in Vietnam helps explain the DAV's interest in the Westphalls' memorial. While enemy mines and booby traps routinely produced ghastly injuries, severing limbs or emasculating their victims in the blink of an eye, medevac helicopter flights, which could be summoned by radio, greatly improved an injured soldier's odds of survival. As a result, the total number of Americans physically wounded in Vietnam comes to more than 303,000, almost six times the number killed, the highest such ratio seen in any American war up to that point.[54] The US military's experience in World War I, fifty years earlier, provides an illuminating contrast. In that war, fought before the widespread adoption of antibiotics and characterized by huge muddy battlefields where it typically took hours to transport severely wounded men to field hospitals, an injury sustained in combat was far more likely to be lethal. The number of American KIAs in World War I was about the same as Vietnam; however, the number of wounded (just over 200,000) came in much lower.[55]

Once home, disabled Vietnam veterans joined the DAV in the tens of thousands, anxious to secure what benefit they could from a time-tested charity and political lobby. They even came to occupy some of the leadership positions within the organization. Thus, it is not surprising that the DAV chose to support the chapel, the most prominent Vietnam veterans memorial at the time, when other ex-servicemen's organizations such as the American Legion (still dominated politically by veterans of World War I and II) did not. However, tension between the Westphalls' idiosyncratic commemorative agenda, which accommodated both patriotic tribute and peace aspiration, and the DAV's more conventional ethos of patriotic service and sacrifice emerged early on. And, not surprisingly, Victor's comments about hypothetically displaying the portrait of a North Vietnamese soldier within a sacred *American* space served as the trigger.

In the December 1979 issue of the chapel bulletin, Walter reported that the article in *Parade* magazine had generated an estimated "$2,000 in contributions," as well as "considerable mail."[56] Unfortunately, a significant portion of the latter consisted of "adverse reactions" to the notion of honoring the dead of both sides.[57] And some of the letters even scolded the DAV for supporting a memorial where such heretical commemoration was contemplated.

Whether this stack of negative correspondence included missives from DAV members themselves is unknown, but it seems likely given Walter's vigorous backpedaling. Clearly in damage-control mode, he first reassured his readers that "as a practical matter, the Chapel is, and in all probability shall continue to be, a commemoration of our own Vietnam veterans only. . . . [W]e always strive to ensure that the Chapel is patriotic in the most meaningful sense of the word."[58] Then, in an adroit rhetorical move, he praised the DAV—especially its assistant national adjutant for public relations, Richard M. Wilson, the man most responsible for the organization's monetary commitment to the chapel—for remaining resolute in the face of criticism. Walter encouraged bulletin readers to write to Wilson and express their satisfaction with "this most noble of institutions."[59]

Victor's controversial statement would also apparently play a role in the unraveling of the relationship between the Westphall family and the

VVMF, perhaps the bitterest chapter yet in a history already filled with false starts and disappointments. As Kidwell notes, prior to becoming the formal president of the VVMF, Scruggs was "initially receptive" to the notion of attaching funding for the chapel to his proposal for a national Vietnam veterans memorial in the nation's capital.[60] In fact, an early fundraising brochure produced by Scruggs and his followers "featured a description of the Chapel and noted plans to support it with a 'substantial' contribution of $100,000."[61]

However, as the VVMF's grassroots campaign grew into a congressional juggernaut in 1980, this commitment became increasingly tenuous. In May of that year, Walter updated readers of the chapel bulletin with a report bristling with indignation and alarm. Certain to be passed, the bill calling for a memorial on the National Mall (SJ Res 119) no longer contained any mention of a specific dollar amount set aside for the Westphalls' memorial in New Mexico. Instead, SJ Res 119 carried two chapel-related provisions that Walter regarded (accurately, as it turned out) as "vague, tenuous, and contingent" and possibly holding "no genuine significance."[62] Both were, in fact, laughable. The first stated that any surplus private monies raised for the construction of the national memorial could go to the chapel, a dubious outcome, to say the least. The second promised an even more unlikely windfall: if the secretary of the interior concluded that funds raised to *maintain* the new memorial in DC were in excess of the amount actually needed, the chapel could receive the balance. Since the Wall would presumably require upkeep as long as the United States existed, it wasn't difficult to see that this commitment, like the first, would yield absolutely nothing.

Without pressure from the steadfast Domenici and fellow New Mexico senator Harrison H. Schmitt, even these two pitiful provisions might never have appeared in the proposed legislation. In its final push to gain governmental approval of a national memorial, the VVMF had obviously forgotten all about the Westphalls' chapel. Thus, in December, Walter took the bold step of disavowing Scruggs's organization altogether. His bulletin that month blasted the VVMF, which had added insult to injury by claiming that no "significant Vietnam war memorial effort" predated the current campaign in Washington, DC.[63] Failure to follow through on promises of monetary support was bad enough; now it seemed to Walter as if the VVMF sought to deny the very existence of a site that had, in fact, served as a de facto national memorial for nearly a decade and at a terrible cost (financial and otherwise) to its founders. "Under the circumstances," he wrote, "I cannot continue to endorse the VVMF until such time as they demonstrate a meaningful commitment to the Chapel and until they refrain from representing their effort as the first and only significant memorial effort on behalf of Vietnam veterans."[64]

Once the official National Vietnam Veterans Memorial became a reality—without any of the money raised on its behalf ever going to New Mexico—Walter's grudge against the VVMF grew deeper still. In the early 1980s, word reached him that Scruggs had supposedly justified dropping the chapel from his plans because of Victor's controversial comments in the *Parade* article: according to the chapel's onetime ally, a memorial that would honor the dead of both sides did not fit the VVMF's charter mission to bring honor and recognition to American Vietnam veterans.[65]

To Victor and Walter, this explanation, though logical, seemed like a cheap shot. After all, since writing his note to Ho Chi Minh in 1969, a dead letter to a dead leader that probably made it no further than the US secretary of state's office, Victor had never reached out to the communist regime in Vietnam. Moreover, no photographs of North Vietnamese soldiers had ever appeared inside the chapel—or were likely to appear there in the future. Thus, as far as the Westphalls were concerned, Scruggs had used Victor's description of a purely hypothetical situation not only to disqualify the chapel for funding consideration but also to cast unwarranted aspersions on their patriotism. It was an affront (whether intended or not) that the family would never forget or forgive, one that marked the sad end to a little-known partnership between the Westphalls and the movement that resulted in the establishment of the Wall.

While the VVMF proved an unreliable ally, thereby joining a discouragingly long list of individuals and organizations that had failed the chapel in some way, the DAV's appreciation for the Westphalls' commemorative achievement only seemed to grow, and in September 1981 Walter sent out an important announcement in place of the usual bulletin: on October 16, he declared, eight DAV officials, led by former national commander

Stan Peeler, would tour the Westphalls' hilltop property in order to determine "the feasibility of DAV ownership of the Chapel."[66] Salvation, it appeared, had finally come. Although the committee's site visit fell on a weekday, Walter urged supporters to drop whatever they were doing and to make their way to Angel Fire in order to meet with Peeler and his team. "This may," he wrote, "be the best opportunity we will ever have to achieve Chapel perpetuation."[67]

Thirteen years earlier—surely, Victor must have noted the numerical coincidence—a pair of marines in immaculate dress uniforms drove from Santa Fe to the Westphalls' home in the Blood of Christ Mountains, carrying the shattering news of David's death. Now a delegation of veterans, representing an organization filled with men bearing the scars of war, traveled the same road to the same destination, though the Westphalls' property, five acres of windswept grass and pinons surrounding a strange and otherworldly white structure, no longer bore any resemblance to the golf-course-community-in-the-making encountered by the Marine officers in 1968. The tragedy of war—and the desire for peace—had changed this lonely corner of New Mexico into something profoundly different from what the Westphalls, who once seemed to personify the American dream, had originally intended.

The meeting went well. Like most people visiting the chapel for the first time, the DAV delegation, which included at least two veterans of the war in Southeast Asia, must have felt overwhelmed by the majesty of Luna's soaring design, the splendor of the surrounding valley and mountains, and, perhaps, that unaccountable spiritual power that linked the site (according to Victor's mystic conception) to the sacred Blue Lake and the distant crag of Wheeler Peak. From the Westphalls' perspective, the conversations held on this momentous day, which included talk of a future visitors center (something Victor and Walter had wanted for years), raised few, if any, red flags. After all, the DAV had been the family's one and only institutional backer for the last four years, a true friend in need whose annual contribution of $10,000 had kept the chapel from closing. "It would not be surprising," Walter later recalled, "if one had some hesitation about a takeover, [but] the prospect of relief through support from a major organization would have overcome some degree of trepidation—if it did exist."[68]

On September 6, 1982, the agreement became official. The DAV received the title to the chapel and its surrounding acres at no cost. In exchange, the organization agreed to build a visitors center on the site (with a tiny apartment in back); to purchase a large tract of land beyond the Westphalls' property line (so that no future development would block the view of the valley from the chapel); and to retain Victor, at a modest salary, as the "memorial director," a position whose scope and responsibilities would soon become a matter of contention.[69] The transfer also resulted in name changes: what was once known as the Vietnam Veterans Peace and Brotherhood Chapel (followed by Vietnam Veterans Chapel) now became the Vietnam Veterans Memorial Chapel, a title superseded in 1986 by a much more official-sounding moniker—the DAV Vietnam Veterans National Memorial. As scholars who study war remembrance know, alterations to the title of a memorial usually signal some kind of conflict or internal politics churning somewhere in the background. This would certainly prove to be the case in this instance.

Although the DAV ultimately made good on all of its promises—the chapel visitors center, for example, opened in 1986—friction between the Westphalls and their saviors soon erupted, a perhaps inevitable outcome of Victor's inability to relinquish control of a building that was, in fact, no longer *his*, combined with a failure of imagination on the part of the chapel's new owners. Together, these flaws on both sides created a volatile cocktail.

Over the next few years, disputes involving the memorial's chief founder, who increasingly felt besieged within his stucco castle, and DAV officials, who understandably had their own ideas about how best to maximize the chapel's appeal, occurred with sad regularity. In horror, Victor watched as work crews replaced the chapel's circular light fixtures, an integral component of Luna's organic design, with square units. Other, more serious desecrations followed. Someone determined that the chapel's crucifix was inappropriate to a memorial open to all faiths, and so it was removed. David's photograph and the other twelve images of American fatalities soon met with the same fate, as did the thirteen-star Betsy Ross flag. And the program of popular music that Walter had selected to evoke the experiences of the Vietnam generation. And the intentionally uneven, hand-applied texturing on the chapel's interior and exterior walls.[70]

176   Chapter 5

Victor howled at every defilement, as he saw it, of the memorial's original conception, and he made no secret of his dissatisfaction in the press. After a while, his protest also took the form of a silent gesture more powerful than any public pronouncement he could have made: he would walk visitors to the entrance of the chapel and then go no further.[71] He now refused to enter the memorial he had struggled for two and a half years to build, and to which he had devoted himself entirely (at the cost of his health, marriage, and nearly his sanity) since 1968. In short, if DAV officials had taken a wrecking ball to the Westphalls' creation, they could scarcely have caused either Victor or his surviving son more consternation or pain. In his capacity as the family's semiofficial rhetorician, Walter blasted each alteration in a five-page memo sent to the board of directors in 1986: "Numerous unnecessary changes," he wrote, "have made the chapel's interior a vacant, spiritless and uninspiring place instead of the cherished shrine it once was."[72]

In fairness, the changes introduced to the chapel were not as capricious or cruel as they may seem and they served a not-unreasonable goal—transforming a somewhat eccentric structure, defined by the peculiar tastes of one family, into a more standardized facility that no veteran would find strange or objectionable. Indeed, the DAV probably felt an obligation in this regard. In retrospect, however, the organization would have been wise to leave the chapel as it had appeared during that fateful preliminary meeting in 1981. For as Kidwell observes, the Westphalls were not the only individuals offended by the DAV's well-meaning alterations.[73] Many veterans who had visited and supported the chapel before the DAV takeover shared the family's outrage.[74] For them—no less than for Victor, Jeanne, and Walter—the memorial had become a sacred edifice whose significance was enhanced, not limited, by its omnipresent reminders of vernacular origin. Ironically, removing these reminders (in the name of "improvement") shifted the chapel away from the origin story that gave the building its power and actually lessened its appeal, a lesson that would not be lost on the Westphalls' future commemorative partners.

One would have thought that a "memorial director" could have put a stop to any changes that he found offensive. But this was the other problem. Over time, Victor's role in the day-to-day operations of the DAV memorial became essentially titular. Or, as Victor explained to one of his lawyers, he had started out as a "director" and then been downgraded to the status of "other employee," a clear violation, in his view, of the terms agreed upon by the DAV and the Westphall family in 1982.[75]

Steady resistance and protest from Victor, combined with an avalanche of negative letters from chapel supporters (many of them DAV members), led to the restoration in 1987 of the crucifix, along with the photo display of soldiers killed in action, and most of the other commemorative features previously stripped from the memorial. Even the light fixtures were returned to their original appearance. In a David vs. Goliath bout, the vernacular had beaten the official. But bad blood between Victor and what Walter had once called "that most noble of institutions" remained. Fed up with the elderly father's nagging and opposition, some administrators on the board of directors for the site wanted him out.[76] Victor refused to budge. He would not, he made clear, give up his claim to the apartment at the back of the visitors center or be bullied into relinquishing the authority promised by his original title.

In May 1992, Victor's attorneys, James McKay and David Greer (both Vietnam veterans), filed a lawsuit against the DAV and the memorial's administrators, citing breach of contract.[77] The chapel's board of directors, they claimed, had stripped Victor of his rightful powers as permanent memorial director, slashed his promised salary of $20,000, eliminated his health insurance policy (a matter of particular concern to a man now nearly eighty years old), and threatened to evict him from a residential space that had been built specifically *for him*.

The DAV's response, offered by memorial president Dennis A. Joyner (also a Vietnam veteran), was conciliatory. No one, he explained, was out to get Victor: as a nonprofit, the DAV simply could not promise a lifetime appointment to anyone in any capacity (no matter what the agreement from 1982 stated), and budget deficits, not malice, had led to Victor's reduced salary and imperiled living quarters. As for the aging founder's health benefits, Joyner announced that in an apparent effort to make amends the board had "approved reimbursement of medical insurance premiums for Westphall and his wife."[78]

However, the optics, as they say, of the situation worked entirely in Victor's favor. Here was an embattled veteran of the Second World War, the father of a soldier killed in Vietnam, fighting to retain control of a celebrated memorial that he had all but singlehandedly created. No one pitted against such a plaintiff would want a trial. Thus, the situation was resolved amicably with an out-of-court settlement that gave Victor most of what he asked for, including "unspecified monetary damages," a "renewable contract," and free access (for the rest of his life) to the apartment on the memorial grounds.[79]

Six years later, the DAV pulled out, leaving everything to the David Westphall Veterans Foundation, the latest incarnation of the nonprofit corporation that the Westphall family had established back in 1968. Just why this happened remains somewhat unclear. Some of the DAV administrators at Angel Fire had surely had enough of Victor by now, but the main reasons for the DAV's withdrawal probably had more to do with other factors. For example, the "budget deficits" mentioned by Joyner suggest that the high-maintenance, high-altitude memorial had become a financial burden for the DAV, just as it had for the Westphalls. At the same time, the impractical distance between the chapel and the DAV's headquarters in Cold Spring, Kentucky, may have figured into the decision, along with concerns (particularly among the organization's World War II veterans) over the controversial peace message that had once been so prominent at the site.[80]

Despite its conflict with the Westphalls, the DAV made an earnest effort to broaden the chapel's appeal, and its stewardship of the memorial from 1982 to 1998, however controversial, had at least some lasting results. Most notably, the chapel visitors center, which today houses exhibits that tell the story of David Westphall and his remembrance, artifacts from the Vietnam War, and the memorial's vast collection of KIA photographs, owes its existence to the board of directors with which Victor butted heads. No matter how acrimonious the situation at Angel Fire became, the DAV never wavered in its commitment to build this spacious (and expensive) structure. Likewise, the organization made good on its promise to purchase additional acreage adjacent to the memorial. Thus, visitors today have the DAV to thank for the site's breathtaking, unspoiled view of the Moreno Valley.

And, finally, the organization added an element of crowd-pleasing spectacle to the annual Veterans Day and Memorial Day observances held at the chapel, a tradition that endures to this day. Dramatic military flyovers and flag marches became the norm, along with speeches by celebrity guests, including some, such as General William Westmoreland, whom the Westphalls would not exactly have welcomed earlier in the memorial's history. (In fact, the general wasn't universally welcome when he spoke at the memorial on Memorial Day, 1992.[81] Chuck Hasford, a Vietnam-War-era veteran and member of the David Westphall Veterans Foundation of directors, recalled that a number of bikers revved their engines in the board parking lot in order drown out Westmoreland's words.[82])

In the end, however, the DAV did not see an adequate return on its investments at Angel Fire, and the chapel never quite clicked as a national shrine to Americans disabled during the Vietnam War. The memorial's expensive upkeep, isolation, murky ideological history, and vernacular oddity (fiercely defended by Victor) perhaps all made it a poor fit as an *institutional* symbol.

A case of "be careful what you wish for" if ever there was one, the DAV's acquisition of the chapel in 1982 hardly turned out as either party would have liked. Nevertheless, this moment of transition, which coincided with the unveiling of the official National Vietnam Veterans Memorial in Washington, DC, marked the end of an era for Victor and his family. For most of the chapel's subsequent history, the Westphalls would no longer go it alone; organizational affiliations of one kind or another would be the norm.

And with these affiliations would come a streamlining of the chapel's complexly layered and, from the start, conflicted meaning as a memorial to David *and* to all Americans who served in the Vietnam War *and* to the cause of world peace. Although Victor continued, as an intellectual, to ponder the origins of violence and to seek a means of curbing humankind's worst appetites, his peace scholarship soon became detached from the public image of the chapel. He perhaps had little choice in this regard. After all, his comments in *Parade* magazine, where he had committed the ultimate heresy by describing a gesture of conciliatory remembrance that equated North Vietnamese lives with those of Americans, apparently led to the VVMF's withdrawal of its support for the Westphalls' memorial. And without some deft political maneuvering on Walter's part, the same thing might have happened with the DAV. As Victor discovered once he began to court institutional backers, there was little room for the word *peace* or, for that matter, *forgiveness* in America's official commemoration of a lost war.[83]

From 1982 onward, the chapel would also fall into relative obscurity (despite the best efforts of the DAV and other organizations that partnered with the Westphalls), its history and significance increasingly unknown to Americans outside of New Mexico. A wall—namely, *the* Wall—hid the chapel from view. As the VVMF prevailed and architect Maya Lin's brilliant creation became one of the most talked-about and widely imitated memorials of the twentieth century, Americans began to forget that a grieving family in New Mexico had, more than a decade earlier, created the *first* national Vietnam veterans memorial, a story of public and private remembrance like no other in American history.

Epilogue
Phantoms of Peace and War

> The Chapel is a gift to man, but I don't know what man will do with it.
> —Victor Westphall, dedication address at the Vietnam Veterans Peace and Brotherhood Chapel, May 22, 1971

Once the David Westphall Veterans Foundation (DWVF) assumed control of the chapel in 1998, financial woes descended on the site like a band of vengeful furies. The Westphalls were finally free of a benefactor that had ultimately become an adversary, but no one could say just how their operation would survive on its own. According to the Disabled American Veterans (DAV), the chapel was now self-sufficient. However, Walter quickly learned otherwise, and in a memo to supporters he described a dire situation. "Contributions at the Memorial are," he wrote, "historically far short of the amount needed to operate the Memorial," and it would take time to access those funds that the DAV had managed to collect on the chapel's behalf.[1] This money now resided in the organization's Kentucky headquarters. How would the memorial get by in the meantime?

This was just the start to a new funding nightmare that dragged on for years. As a result, nothing from the Westphalls' earlier experience with the administrative side of public memory, not even their battles with the DAV, would quite match the turbulence of this period in the chapel's history. It was arguably the memorial's nadir. Unable to deal with the incessant financial pressures, directors came and went. Three in just four years. Meanwhile, the foundation board, unstable due to turnover and often embroiled in personality conflicts, floated one increasingly desperate fundraising idea after another.

One of the most striking of these involved a partnership with a local chapter of the American Veterans (AmVets), which offered to help support the cash-strapped memorial by peddling a unique local brand of drinking water: the label on each bottle of "Freedom Pure Water" would feature the photograph of a deceased "American Hero," along with a brief obituary that listed details about his or her death in battle.[2] Part of the proceeds would go to what was now officially titled—with a defiant nod to Jan Scruggs and company—the First Vietnam Veterans National Memorial.

Lieutenant Westphall's photograph was scheduled to appear on the initial batch of bottles, which, according to an article in the April 14, 2002, issue of the *Santa Fe Journal*, would land on grocery and convenience store shelves within a month.[3] (Here, surely, was the strangest form of commemoration ever to invoke David's memory.) But "Freedom Pure Water" never got off the ground. As Walter recalls, "there was another interested party that claimed it should be the company [to] market 'Memorial' water" and the entire project (like so many others during this painful period) degenerated into "conflict, threatened legal actions, arguments, and tension."[4]

By 2003, and for the umpteenth time in its tumultuous history, the chapel once again faced the threat of imminent closure. But deliverance, this time from an organization more amenable to the preservation of the site's unique features as a historical landmark (and as an expression of vernacular commemoration), was at hand. That year, the DWVF board of directors began petitioning officials in Santa Fe, including newly elected governor Bill Richardson, to incorporate the First Vietnam Veterans National Memorial into the New Mexico State Parks (NMSP) system. The effort paid off, and on Veterans Day, 2005, the transfer became official. Per one of the more felicitous name changes in the chapel's history, the Westphalls' five acres, plus all the additional land acquired by the DAV, became Vietnam Veterans Memorial State Park, the only state park in the entire country specifically devoted to Vietnam War commemoration.

Sign at the base of the hill during the memorial's status as a New Mexico state park (2005–2017). Photograph by Robert Rook.

Now led by a more stable and committed board of directors, the DWVF stayed in place as a full partner with the NMSP, and while there were tensions (as always happens with the messy business of public commemoration), relations between the two bodies remained remarkably cordial. According to Walter, the director of the NMSP, Christy Tafoya, "literally loved the memorial and its mission," and the leadership of the DWVF could not have been happier with the committed park officials who operated the chapel and visitors center.[5] The only significant point of disagreement: whether or not to charge admission at the site, a requirement at all thirty-two of the other state parks in New Mexico. Representing the interests of a chronically underfunded branch of state government (in New Mexico and elsewhere), some NMSP officials stressed the necessity of this vital revenue stream at Angel Fire. But the DWVF stood firmly against it. *Requiring* any kind of payment—donations, of course, had always been welcome—violated the tradition of 24/7, free access to the chapel, a tradition that the memorial's founders had resolutely maintained despite multiple instances of vandalism. Reluctantly, the proponents of a park fee backed off.

Big plans, rather than any discontent with the NMSP, eventually put the memorial on the path toward a new home within the state government. Throughout the 2010s, board members like Chuck Howe, a retired US Army lieutenant colonel and Vietnam veteran, dreamed of establishing a state veterans cemetery adjacent to the chapel, as well as a facility for the treatment of former servicemen and servicewomen who suffered from PTSD as a result of America's twenty-first-century wars. In an interview in 2013, Howe summed up his ambitions for the memorial in three words: "Make it relevant!"[6]

This shift in objectives—from what we might call pure memorialization to an array of services for veterans and their families—carried the facility well beyond the mission of the NMSP. Thus, on July 3, 2017, the memorial changed hands yet again, becoming the property of the New Mexico Department of Veterans Services, which operates the chapel and visitors center in partnership (just as the NMSP did) with the DWVF. Around the same time, approval finally came through—after years of DWVF lobbying in Santa Fe—for a state veterans cemetery located on some of the windswept acreage overlooked by the chapel, land generously donated by a local Vietnam veteran, Harry Patterson. A $3.2 million grant from the federal Veterans Administration, received by the State of New Mexico on September 12, 2018, will cover the construction costs, with the first burials scheduled for the spring of 2020.[7]

Two grave markers, unrelated to the cemetery project, already stand near the memorial. Victor Westphall did not live to see his chapel become the focal point of a state park and enter a phase of unprecedented security and stability. On July 22, 2003, cardiovascular disease, first signaled by a minor heart attack in 1968, the terrible year of David's death, finally caught up with the octogenarian. At his request, the eighty-nine-year-old was buried in a small plot just a few yards from the chapel. Jeanne joined him there almost thirteen months later, traveling posthumously all the way from Wichita, where she had spent her final year—one of her happiest—close to Walter and his family, visited regularly by her beloved granddaughter,

Kimberly. Death, which had driven the husband and wife apart when they were alive, now brought them together for good.

The old couple received simple, side-by-side headstones befitting their humble Midwestern origins. In addition, a stone veteran's marker honors Victor's military service as a "Lt US Navy/World War II." The austere white rectangle is the standard size and shape, but a brief personalized inscription appears above the bottom edge. It comes from the Vietnam veterans—Ron Milam, Dick Dickerson, Lanny Tonning, Larry Rottmann, Frank Richardson, and thousands more—he befriended over the years: "DOC THANKS FOR EASING OUR BURDENS."

In a published tribute, Walter noted that his father had died hard, wracked by physical pain and full of anxiety and doubts. His body, once a monument to athletic brawn, betrayed him cruelly during his last decade of life. Severely arthritic, the former bodybuilder became a hunched, shrunken figure with knotted, twig-like limbs, sometimes requiring "45 minutes of painful maneuvering just to get out of bed."[8] Loss of vision (an especially terrible thing for a compulsive writer and voracious reader) tormented him, along with poor hearing and shortness of breath. Despite these physical maladies, his fierce bond with the memorial—and the veterans it attracted—remained intact to the end. Over the years, as the familiar equipment of advanced old age became necessary and he moved from cane to walker to wheelchair, he never stopped greeting visitors or connecting, through his unerring gift for rapport, with those who needed his attention.

His fight with the DAV, Walter reported, had left deep mental and emotional scars. However, what disturbed Victor most at the close of his long life was the chapel's uncertain future. What would happen to his "gift to man"? Ironically, he left his embattled creation as its darkest hour struck, as the onetime memorial to peace and brotherhood, seemingly caught in a financial doom spiral, became a backdrop for clashing egos and power grabs among some of its administrators. And this time there was no outside organization, such as the DAV, to blame. Even to a man of Victor's granite resolve and emotional resilience, the situation must have been heartbreaking. Perhaps literally heartbreaking.

But there was one extraordinary event from Victor's final decade that brought him a measure of peace. In the spring of 1994, at the age of eighty, he traveled to Vietnam to visit the ambush site where David had been killed twenty-six years earlier. He did not make the formidable journey alone. Three Vietnam veterans accompanied him on the pilgrimage—Gerry Schooler, the owner of a tour company that organized trips to Southeast Asia for former servicemen; Jim Goss, a close family friend, registered nurse, and former navy corpsman who served in Vietnam; and, of course, Walter Westphall.

By this point, the latter, now fifty-four years old, was no longer the solitary, emotionally closed-off man he had once been. He had become an unlikely paterfamilias. In 1982, his field work for the Federal Home Loan Bank Board brought him to the district office in Topeka, where he met and fell in love with Dorothy Wilson, an outgoing typist his junior by nearly two decades.[9] Three years later, the two married. Children followed, first daughter Kimberly, who became so close to Jeanne, and then a son, David, named after the lost uncle he never knew. In his quiet way, Walter reveled in his family life, savoring a happiness that had seemed impossible to imagine during the bleak years immediately following David's death.

As their journey to the ambush site drew near, Victor and his son braced themselves for an emotional confrontation with the past. But first the aging father had to endure the fourteen-hour flight from Los Angeles to Taipei, which his already advanced arthritis made excruciating. Despite his pain, the gleaming ocean thirty thousand feet below his cabin window brought back memories of his deployment in the Pacific decades earlier, and "he marveled at the idea of crossing that vast body of water in a matter of hours instead of days."[10] In Taipei, the four men caught a flight to Ho Chi Minh City (formerly Saigon), where they spent the night and tried to sleep. Vietnam, they immediately noticed, was a sea of young faces, the site of a population explosion that had already left Vietnamese veterans of the "American War" vastly outnumbered by countrymen with no memory of the conflict. Ironically, here the war seemed to matter less than it did at home.

In the morning, Victor and his companions flew to Da Nang, the coastal city where David, incoming from Okinawa, Rocky Wirsching at his side, had first set eyes on Vietnam in 1967. Twenty-four hours later, they hired a car and pressed on to Hue. Victor ignored his arthritis and jet lag, and somehow kept up with the whirlwind pace of a trip that would have utterly

Walter with his family in 2013. Photograph taken in the visitors center at Vietnam Veterans Memorial State Park. Courtesy of Walter Westphall.

exhausted a much younger traveler. By the very next day, in fact, he was ready to see the ground where Bravo Company had met with disaster. The group drove from Hue to Dong Ha, the best jumping-off point for an expedition to the ambush site. But it was Sunday, and no one could locate the police official who had agreed to accompany them into the countryside. As an alternative, Schooler proposed a trip to Con Thien.[11]

Led by a local interpreter, the four Americans climbed to the top of the Hill of Angels, Victor pressing forward with his cane. There they discovered all that remained of the once extensive stronghold—a single bunker, preserved for American tourists.[12] A quarter century earlier, the very same spot, a magnet for NVA artillery and rockets, had looked out on the DMZ and formed one of the four corners of Leatherneck Square, some of the most contested real estate in all of Vietnam. It was at Con Thien that David had laughed off that close call with an enemy artillery shell that seemed to be aimed at the sandbag full of beer and cigars he was carrying. Now all was quiet and peaceful.

On day four they returned to Dong Ha and met up with one Mr. Chin, the chief of police for the province and a former wartime interpreter who had served, at one point, with marines in B/1/4. With Chin's help, and

Walter and Victor near the ambush site. Photograph by Jim Goss.

with the aid of the battalion journal from David's unit, the group pinpointed their destination as precisely as possible on a map. Then they drove—and subsequently walked—until they reached a particular rubber plantation. As best they could determine, this was the ambush site—utterly transformed from its appearance in 1968.[13] Victor later described the scene: the plantation consisted of "row on stately row" of rubber trees laid out with "an orderliness that [belied] the chaotic confusion of the battlefield it once had been. . . . It was good to see green, living growth coming from the earth where so much blood had been spilled."[14]

As planned, Victor scattered a handful of dirt he had brought all the way from Angel Fire. Then he scooped up some red clay from the plantation floor, noting its similarity to the soil in the Moreno Valley. This he subsequently carried back to New Mexico and scattered near the chapel. A year later, during the annual Memorial Day observance, the Westphalls unveiled a plaque that marked the location of the Vietnamese earth and told the poignant story of Victor's pilgrimage to the other side of the world, to the spot where his son died.

That story, like the soil exchange, suggested symmetry—a trip from Angel Fire to the Hill of Angels—and closure, and there is no doubt that Victor found the experience extremely meaningful, as did Walter. But the fog of war that had always enshrouded David's death stubbornly refused to dissipate. It even clung to the obscure corner of Vietnam that Victor and his son had traveled so far to find.

According to at least one observer among the group of Americans that day, Victor "felt strongly that we were at the precise site" of the ambush.[15] However, in their unpublished biography of Victor, Pat Mendoza and Joe Haukebo wrote that Victor almost immediately had doubts. As the party walked back toward Dong Ha, "Victor was upset because he had not explored the road behind him that led to a rise in the terrain some one third of a mile away."[16] He fought against a nagging suspicion that the collision between B/1/4 and members of the North Vietnamese 320th Division—an event that he had seen in dreams and imagined for decades—had occurred there, not on the ground now covered by the orderly columns of rubber trees. Walter subsequently wondered the same thing. In his view, the area the group identified as the ambush site was probably too far south of the Trace, that zone of cleared ground (mockingly referred to as the

McNamara Line) from which David and his comrades had advanced toward the NVA.[17]

To a different group of pilgrims, none of this might have mattered. Wasn't it enough to perform the soil exchange in the general vicinity of the ambush site? Surely, to the dead, it made no difference. But Victor was a historian, as well as a man driven by the belief that specific places and events harbored mystic significance, and his surviving son, a details person, liked to get things right.

What both men discovered that afternoon in central Vietnam is that history pushes back against commemoration. Victor and Walter had traveled several thousand miles to impose order—through their ceremony—on a painful past (both personal and national), the same impulse, essentially, that had driven them to create their memorial back in New Mexico. However, the historical exactitude they sought, as the basis for their ritual, proved impossible. Despite maps and documents that promised to clear away the chaos of war, no one could say for certain just where Bravo Company's desperate firefight had occurred.

The past had even set up defenses against Victor and his companions. Mendoza and Haukebo's account of the pilgrimage contains a richly metaphorical detail: at one point in the expedition, prior to the discovery of the rubber plantation, Schooler wandered off the dirt road to explore some ground that looked like a promising location for the ambush. Chin "loudly and emphatically" advised him to go no further.[18] Some of the reddish soil near the Hill of Angels still contained land mines.

Just as the Westphalls' trip to Vietnam, cathartic though it was, underscored the sense of mystery that still surrounded David's death, by the early 2000s the Westphalls' chapel had become half enveloped in what we might call the fog of war commemoration. Over time, various monuments and commemorative artifacts had sprung up adjacent to the original building, turning the five-acre site into a veritable memorial complex. No longer an isolated structure, the chapel now served as the focal point for an assemblage of objects whose various and often competing meanings *almost* concealed the memorial's original peace mission.

The Viking Surprise with the chapel garden in the foreground. Photograph by Richard Dickerson.

A self-guided-tour brochure created in the mid-to-late 2000s by Kate German, the heritage educator (and later superintendent) at Vietnam Veterans Memorial State Park, describes multiple monuments at the site, all of which remain in place today. German began the tour with the park's stunningly beautiful garden, a horticultural war memorial created by the Angel Fire Garden Club as a "tribute to the Armed Forces of America."[19] Next came the addition that was hardest to miss—the Huey UH-1 helicopter mounted on steel columns. As German explained, this particular aircraft, nicknamed the Viking Surprise and given to the DWVF by the New Mexico National Guard in 1999, has an extraordinary history. On March 19, 1967, the Viking Surprise provided smoke cover for a rescue operation in the Mekong Delta, swooping in at tree-top level thirteen times in order to conceal a besieged landing zone, all the while taking ground fire. Afterward, the damaged smokeship required a complete rebuilding in Corpus

Christi, where mechanics counted 135 bullet holes in the craft, including six in the pilot's compartment.[20]

After describing this remarkable relic of battle, the brochure points visitors to the stone-and-bronze marker erected in honor of Victor's trip to Vietnam in 1994, as well as the legions of commemorative bricks (a standard feature at most American war memorials by the 2000s), each inscribed with the name of an individual serviceman or servicewoman, which now lined the walkways in the park. A special section of four bricks honored the Westphall family (Victor, Jeanne, David, and Walter). Another section, containing sixteen bricks (later expanded to seventeen), recognized fatalities from the May 22 ambush.

The next two stops on the tour were the visitors center and the chapel. The former, the brochure announces, contained "a gift shop, media room showing the HBO documentary *Dear America: Letters Home from Vietnam*, research room and library."[21] As for the latter, German's description of the park's central memorial did not skip over the antiwar message that still formed an acknowledged (if fading) component of the building's visual rhetoric. In addition to describing the memorial's chief founder as a "man ahead of his time," presumably because of his vision of international peace and brotherhood, the brochure even includes Victor's statement about displaying the photograph of the NVA soldier who had killed his son.[22]

From the chapel, the self-guided tour directs visitors to the graves of Victor and Jeanne, enclosed within a small wrought-iron fence, and then on to the final stop, a statue titled *Dear Mom and Dad* by Taos artist Doug Scott. A gift from the artist to the DWVF, this bronze figure was dedicated in 2003. In the words of the brochure, the statue depicts an American infantryman "faced with the dilemma of writing home to his family. What can he say about what he's doing that they will understand?"[23]

Each of these additions to the Westphalls' original conception subtly— and, in some cases, not so subtly—altered the meaning of the site. For example, the commemorative bricks, which memorialize men and women who served in conflicts ranging from World War I to the Iraq War, form a composite and essentially ahistorical narrative of duty and sacrifice. Here all veterans and all wars (including Vietnam) become one, hardly what the chapel's founders (led by a historian) originally had in mind. Lovingly in-

Dear Mom and Dad *by Doug Scott. Photograph by Robert Rook.*

scribed by family members, and thus symbolizing a fusion of personal and public memory, the bricks collectively signify a sacred military tradition that transcends the specific rights and wrongs of any individual conflict.

In contrast, the Huey UH-1 helicopter, so dramatically positioned that it almost commands as much attention as the chapel, is a beloved talisman central to Vietnam War remembrance. Associated with deliverance in the midst of battle (through its use as a medevac vehicle), this storied aircraft pushes the site's meaning away from the universalism represented by the bricks. It hovers over the memorial's thirty acres as if to declare the space a landing zone for Vietnam veterans only.

The statue *Dear Mom and Dad* sends a similar message. The bewildered correspondent cast in bronze holds a blank page, a letter that will perhaps never be written. He cannot describe what he has seen or connect his experience to the mosaic of miniature memorials that line the sidewalk in front of him. In this case, the meaning of America's war in Vietnam is both specific and ineffable; only someone who has *been there* can grasp it, a theme that clashes both with the educational mission of the visitors center, with its film loop of soldiers' letters from Vietnam (one of which is

David's), and the ambitions of the memorial's founders, who believed that out of an especially traumatic national episode could come shared wisdom and liberation from the false promises of war.[24]

Personalized bricks, military hardware, and statuary—the array of conventional commemoration added to the chapel over time (an "encrustation," in the words of one scholar)—also reflects a shift in the way that Americans have thought about the Vietnam War from the 1980s onward.[25] Throughout this period, public debate over the morality of the conflict, once so intense that it threatened to tear the country apart, gave way to a ubiquitous rhetoric (both verbal and visual) of national healing.

Thus, in the state- and community-level memorials to Vietnam veterans that spread across the country during the 1980s and 1990s, many of them copycat designs based on Maya Lin's initially controversial monument in Washington, DC, historian Patrick Hagopian has identified more forgetting than remembering. With their rosters of names, usually unaccompanied by any explicit assessment of the war itself, such memorials typically offer little context for the sacrifices they record. In other words, they carefully sidestep the big questions that were once central to any discussion of the war: Should the United States have been in Vietnam? Did Americans die there in vain? And what lessons does the war hold for future generations?[26]

At Angel Fire, these questions have become an increasingly faint echo, a considerable irony given the energy and eloquence with which Victor once analyzed the Vietnam War as an apocalyptic "hinge of destiny" (to say nothing of Walter's excoriating critiques of the "best and brightest" and their foolhardy strategies). But the seeds of what the memorial has become today—a patriotic shrine, by and large, to wartime service—were there from the start. Honoring Americans who served in an unpopular conflict formed part of the Westphalls' mission long before the wave of Vietnam War commemoration inspired by the Wall. This very goal was, in fact, present in 1968, formed just hours after Jeanne's moment of inspiration, already sitting uneasily next to the memorial's message of world peace. And perhaps because Victor saw no contradiction between these two aims, he ultimately became content—or at least resigned—to see one thrive without the other.

Yet for all the conventionality seen in its encrustation, the memorial at Angel Fire remains on many levels as iconoclastic as ever. The site is hardly, to use the words of one critic, just "another American memorial touting American exceptionalism."[27] Photographs of NVA soldiers will likely never appear inside the chapel. Nevertheless, the DWVF has steered the memorial away from explicit displays of militarism and at least partially preserved the radical vision of its creators. For example, when the New Mexico National Guard offered—free of charge—a Cobra attack helicopter for display next to the Viking Surprise, the foundation declined: an attack helicopter, Walter and his fellow board members explained, was synonymous with military aggression, something the foundation most certainly did *not* endorse.[28] (The Huey, on the other hand, often performed a humanitarian mission by lifting wounded soldiers from the battlefield and thus belonged next to the chapel.) Few other remembrance organizations, one suspects, would have been so scrupulous when presented with such an attention-getting piece of military hardware.

And in an even more notable instance of principled action, the board has overseen the installation of commemorative bricks inscribed with the names of South Vietnamese soldiers, members of the once frequently reviled Army of the Republic of Vietnam (ARVN), and welcomed formal delegations of Vietnamese Americans to Memorial Day events.[29] These gestures, as bold in their way as Victor's letter to Ho Chi Minh nearly forty years earlier, recognize that the Vietnam War was an international human catastrophe signifying much more than lost American lives and lost American innocence. Arguably no other Vietnam War memorial in the nation has gone so far in this direction, a development that would likely have pleased Doc Westphall to no end.

Still, despite the board's audacity on a number of commemorative fronts, it's hard not to think of the Viking Surprise as a metaphor: perhaps, hovering atop its steel mooring, the aircraft operates as a smokeship still, helping to lay down a cloud of ideological camouflage that largely obscures the memorial's original mission of inspiring a global crusade against war. Such is arguably the function, whether intended or not, of nearly every commemorative item added to the site since 1982.

Make no mistake: nothing at Angel Fire today celebrates warfare or glorifies violence—far from it. Thanks to the dedication and vision of the DWVF and its partners in the New Mexico Department of Veterans Services, this out-of-the-way site in the Sangre de Cristos remains a place of

ARVN remembrance bricks at Angel Fire. Leduc Hua, the soldier represented on the top brick in the center, was an NVA defector who served with American troops as an interpreter. Photograph by Daniel Rogers.

solemn reflection, therapeutic quiet, and (despite its consolatory patriotic trappings) overwhelming and cathartic sadness. Historian James M. Mayo has offered perhaps the best description of the memorial's persistently mournful effect: "The visitor leaves with a feeling that more was lost in Vietnam than battles; a great wealth of human potential was lost."[30] But one can still argue that the site's robust and admirable commitment to remembering America's warriors has largely obscured the question of whether there should be warriors at all, especially during an age of nuclear weapons and (per a contemporary trend in armed conflict that Victor would have found especially repugnant) increased suffering and loss of life among *civilians*, the true heart of war in the twenty-first century.

The chapel at dawn. Photograph by Robert Rook.

Recognizing and celebrating military service in wartime is not an ignoble purpose for an American memorial, especially one focused on Vietnam veterans, many of whom were treated abominably upon their return, treated as if they, and not their leaders, were responsible for a disastrous national episode. However, the Chapel at Angel Fire was originally built to do much more—namely, to see that this service would never be demanded of anyone again. Of course, it's easy to dismiss this grandiose goal, which was absurdly unrealistic, born of near-madness (brought on by grief), and, ironically enough, out of keeping with the values of David Westphall, a contented field officer and resolute Cold Warrior who *wanted* to be in Vietnam.

But the yearning for an end to war, all war, haunts the memorial still, along with the ghosts that reportedly reside in the visitors center and the chapel. The sound of a woman weeping inconsolably has occasionally startled staff members late at night, when there are no visitors. And sometimes, again when the buildings are empty, a strange murmur of voices can be heard coming from somewhere, the words indistinct.[31] Perhaps these spectral sounds perform a kind of memorial function of their own, reminding us of unfinished business and an unrealized dream, of peace and brotherhood yet to be attained.

Notes

Introduction

1. Unattributed Source, letter to Victor Westphall, December 18, 1982, Scotch Pines, NJ, David Westphall Veterans Foundation Collection. Name of letter writer withheld because author could not be contacted to give consent.
2. Corinne Browne, *Casualty: A Memoir of Love and War* (New York: Norton, 1981), 14–15.
3. Patrick Hagopian, *The Vietnam War in American Memory: Veterans, Memorials, and the Politics of Healing* (Amherst: University of Massachusetts Press, 2009), 2.
4. Christina Nealson, *New Mexico's Sanctuaries, Retreats, and Sacred Places* (Boulder, CO: Westcliffe, 2001), 38.
5. Victor Westphall, *David's Story: A Casualty of Vietnam* (Springer, NM: Center for the Advancement of Human Dignity, 1981), 136.
6. For an excellent study of the memorial's impact on visitors—via the objects they leave behind as commemorative gestures—see Kristin Ann Hass, *Carried to the Wall: American Memory and the Vietnam Veterans Memorial* (Berkeley: University of California Press, 1998).
7. John Bodnar, *Remaking America: Public Memory, Commemoration, and Patriotism in the Twentieth Century* (Princeton, NJ: Princeton University Press, 1992).
8. For an astute discussion of horizontality and its meaning in twentieth- and twenty-first-century war memorials, including the Wall, see Jay Winter, *War Beyond Words: Languages of Remembrance from the Great War to the Present* (Cambridge: Cambridge University Press, 2017), 143–172.
9. Winter, 139.
10. Chis Hedges, "Celebrating Slaughter: War and Collective Amnesia," *Truthdig.com*, October 5, 2009, accessed June 2012, https://www.truthdig.com/articles/celebrating-slaughter-war-and-collective-amnesia/.

Chapter 1. Father and Son

1. "*Sun Trails* Home of the Month," *New Mexico Sun Trails*, November 1952, 1.
2. "*Sun Trails* Home of the Month," 4.
3. Pat Mendoza and Joe Haukebo, "A Hero's Trail: Dr. Victor Walter Westphall," 32, unpublished typescript, Walter Westphall Collection.
4. Mendoza and Haukebo, 35.
5. Mendoza and Haukebo, 42.
6. Mendoza and Haukebo, 68.

7. Mendoza and Haukebo, 68.
8. Mendoza and Haukebo, 84.
9. Mendoza and Haukebo, 92.
10. Mendoza and Haukebo, 98.
11. Mendoza and Haukebo, 99.
12. Thomas J. Cutler, *The Battle of Leyte Gulf: 23–26 October 1944* (New York: HarperCollins, 1994), 285.
13. Victor Westphall, *David's Story: A Casualty of Vietnam* (Springer, NM: Center for the Advancement of Human Dignity, 1981), 19.
14. Westphall, 21.
15. Westphall, 21.
16. Westphall, 17.
17. Westphall, 16.
18. Ingri d'Aulaire and Edgar Parin d'Aulaire, *Wings for Per* (Garden City, NY: Doubleday, Doran, 1944), n.p.
19. Westphall, *David's Story*, 16.
20. D'Aulaire and d'Aulaire, *Wings for Per*, n.p.
21. Philip Caputo, *A Rumor of War* (New York: Henry Holt, 1996), 6.
22. Jim Brown, *Impact Zone: The Battle of the DMZ in Vietnam, 1967–1968* (Tuscaloosa: University of Alabama Press, 2004), 3.
23. John Bodnar, *The "Good War" in American Memory* (Baltimore, MD: Johns Hopkins University Press, 2010), 139.
24. D'Aulaire and d'Aulaire, *Wings for Per*, n.p.
25. Mendoza and Haukebo, "Hero's Trail," 105.
26. Mendoza and Haukebo, 105.
27. Walter Westphall, email message to author, May 31, 2015. Such an attitude perhaps had much to do with the war—the *First* World War—that overshadowed Victor's early childhood and its subsequent construction in American collective memory. After all, it was the issue of unrestricted submarine warfare that pulled the United States into that particular conflict in 1917, and for some time afterward German U-boats enjoyed a place in the popular imagination as mysterious weapons of terror. For more on the way submarines were depicted during Victor's childhood, see Chris Dubbs, *America's U-Boats: Terror Trophies of World War I* (Lincoln: University of Nebraska Press, 2014).
28. Mendoza and Haukebo, "Hero's Trail," 95.
29. Mendoza and Haukebo, 95.
30. Westphall, *David's Story*, 140.
31. Walter Westphall, email message to author, May 31, 2015.
32. Westphall.
33. David Kammer, "Post-War Suburban Expansion 1945–1959," Albuquerque 1945–1959, New Mexico History.org, February 14, 2014, accessed on July 20, 2015, http://newmexicohistory.org/2014/02/14/albuquerque-1945-1959/.
34. Kammer.
35. Westphall, *David's Story*, 10.
36. Fidel L. Baca, letter to Victor Westphall, January 31, 2002, New Mexico, Walter Westphall Collection.
37. Baca.

38. Walter Westphall, email message to author, March 6, 2015.
39. Walter Westphall, email message to author, March 13, 2015.
40. Westphall, *David's Story*, 28.
41. Westphall, 29.
42. Westphall, 39.
43. Westphall, 47.
44. Westphall, 48.
45. Westphall, 48.
46. Westphall, 53.
47. Westphall, 27.
48. Westphall, 27.
49. Westphall, 40.
50. David Westphall, "Planning Paper," July 16, 1964, Walter Westphall Collection.
51. David Westphall, "Autobiography," July 16, 1964, Walter Westphall Collection.
52. Westphall, *David's Story*, 58.
53. Westphall, 60.
54. Westphall, 63.
55. Walter Westphall, email message to author, October 8, 2015.
56. Westphall, *David's Story*, 63.
57. Westphall, 68.
58. Westphall, 73.
59. David Westphall, letter to Jeanne and Victor Westphall, June 7, 1965, Missoula, Montana, Walter Westphall Collection.
60. Walter Westphall, email message to author, October 8, 2015.
61. David Westphall, letter to Jeanne and Victor Westphall, June 7, 1965, Missoula, Montana, Walter Westphall Collection.
62. David Westphall, "Autobiography—The Basic School," n.d., Walter Westphall Collection.
63. See, for example, Irene de la Rosa Fuentes's letter from October 10, 1966: "I consider our relationship very special, like an illusion, a beautiful dream, where one person meets another, where you love and understand, and there are no faults only love and in the end like a beautiful poem [sic]." Irene de la Rosa, letter to David Westphall, June 7, 1965, Mexico, Walter Westphall Collection.
64. Henry W. Blake, letter to Medical Department Representative, US Marine Corps Recruiting Station, Building #5, Fort Douglas, Salt Lake City, Utah, May 19, 1966, Albuquerque, New Mexico, Walter Westphall Collection.
65. Commandant of the Marine Corps, Officer Candidate Assignment to Active Duty Orders for Cpl. Victor D. Westphall, November 1, 1966, Walter Westphall Collection.
66. Westphall, "Autobiography—The Basic School."
67. Caputo, *Rumor of War*, 2.
68. List of Basic School Courses, United States Marine Corps, Walter Westphall Collection.
69. Officer Fitness Report—US Marine Corps for David Westphall, August 22, 1967, Walter Westphall Collection.
70. Permanent Change of Station orders issued to David Westphall, July 24, 1967, Walter Westphall Collection.

71. Walter Westphall, email message to author, October 8, 2015.
72. Westphall.
73. Westphall.
74. Westphall, *David's Story*, 82.

Chapter 2. A Casualty of Vietnam

1. Ron Milam, *Not a Gentleman's War: An Inside View of Junior Officers in the Vietnam War* (Chapel Hill: University of North Carolina Press, 2009), 4.
2. Jim Brown, *Impact Zone: The Battle of the DMZ in Vietnam, 1967-1968* (Tuscaloosa: University of Alabama Press, 2004), 17.
3. Brown, 18-19.
4. Otto J. Lehrack, *No Shining Armor: The Marines at War in Vietnam, An Oral History* (Lawrence: University Press of Kansas, 1992), 241.
5. Brown, *Impact Zone*, 88-89.
6. For an especially vivid account of daily life at a marine base under siege, see James P. Coan's outstanding memoir, *Time in the Barrel: A Marine's Account of the Battle for Con Thien* (Tuscaloosa: University of Alabama Press, 2018).
7. Brown describes the relationship between risk and location along the DMZ as follows: "If you were at a major base such as Dong Ha or Camp Carroll, there was a certain amount of incoming, but these bases had substantial fortifications and large numbers of personnel that reduced the chance of ground attack. Lesser positions, however, such as Gio Linh, Con Thien, and the Rockpile, also had ground attacks with which to contend. Of course, other positions with even smaller contingents were even more vulnerable to any kind of attack. They included such places as Ca Lu, C-2 Bridge, Hill 881, Lang Vei, and many others." Brown, *Impact Zone*, 152.
8. Brown, 116.
9. Jack McLean, *Loon: A Marine Story* (New York: Ballantine, 2009), 69.
10. David Westphall, letter to Jeanne and Victor Westphall, November 16, 1967, South Vietnam, Walter Westphall Collection.
11. David Westphall, letter to Walter Westphall, November 26, 1967, South Vietnam, Walter Westphall Collection.
12. Westphall, letter to Jeanne and Victor Westphall, November 16, 1967.
13. Westphall.
14. Westphall.
15. Westphall, letter to Jeanne and Victor Westphall, November 26, 1967.
16. Westphall.
17. Westphall, letter to Walter Westphall, November 26, 1967.
18. Westphall, letter to Jeanne and Victor Westphall, November 26, 1967.
19. Walter Westphall email message to author, October 8, 2015.
20. Westphall, letter to Jeanne and Victor Westphall, November 26, 1967.
21. Westphall.
22. Westphall.
23. Westphall.
24. Westphall.

25. Westphall.
26. Westphall.
27. David Westphall, letter to Jeanne and Victor Westphall, December 4, 1967, South Vietnam, Walter Westphall Collection.
28. Andre J. Ognibene and O'Neill Barrett Jr., eds., *Internal Medicine in Vietnam*, vol. 2, *Infectious Diseases* (Washington, DC: Office of the Surgeon General and Center of Military History United States Army, 1982), 264.
29. Ognibene and Barrett, 264.
30. David Westphall, letter to Jeanne and Victor Westphall, December 8, 1967, South Vietnam, Walter Westphall Collection.
31. David Westphall, letter to Jeanne and Victor Westphall, December 28, 1967, South Vietnam, Walter Westphall Collection.
32. David Westphall, letter to Jeanne and Victor Westphall, February 3, 1968, South Vietnam, Walter Westphall Collection.
33. Westphall.
34. David Westphall, letter to Jeanne and Victor Westphall, February 19, 1968, South Vietnam, Walter Westphall Collection.
35. Westphall.
36. Westphall.
37. David Westphall, letter to Jeanne and Victor Westphall, Feburary 28, 1968, South Vietnam, Walter Westphall Collection.
38. David's assessment anticipated that of later historians. For a parallel discussion of the McNamara Wall and the strategy imposed on the Marines from above, see James P. Coan, *Con Thien: The Hill of Angels* (Tuscaloosa: University of Alabama Press, 2004), 28. "Westmoreland and McNamara," Coan writes, "had created a set-piece strategy that robbed the Marines of their mobility and valuable resources for bringing the war to the NVA. Strongpoints required troops to protect them from attack, thus reducing the numbers available for maneuver."
39. Westphall, letter to Walter Westphall, November 26, 1967.
40. David Westphall, letter to Jeanne and Victor Westphall, December 28, 1968, South Vietnam, Walter Westphall Collection.
41. David Westphall, letter to Walter Westphall, February 20, 1968, South Vietnam, Walter Westphall Collection.
42. David Westphall, letter to Jeanne and Victor Westphall, February 22, 1968, South Vietnam, Walter Westphall Collection.
43. David Westphall, letter to Jeanne and Victor Westphall, March 28, 1968, South Vietnam, Walter Westphall Collection.
44. David Westphall, letter to Walter Westphall, January 18, 1968, South Vietnam, Walter Westphall Collection.
45. Westphall.
46. Officer Fitness Report—U.S. Marine Corps, December 31, 1967, evaluation of David Westphall, Walter Westphall Collection.
47. Officer Fitness Report—U.S. Marine Corps, April 25, 1968, evaluation of David Westphall, Walter Westphall Collection.
48. David Westphall, letter to Jeanne and Victor Westphall, April 22, 1968, South Vietnam, Walter Westphall Collection.

49. Westphall, letter to Walter Westphall, January 18, 1968.
50. Terry Middleton, letter to Victor Westphall, April 26, 1982, David Westphall Veterans Foundation Collection.
51. David Westphall, letter to Jeanne and Victor Westphall, May 9, 1968, South Vietnam, Walter Westphall Collection.
52. Westphall, letter to Jeanne and Victor Westphall, November 16, 1967.
53. Westphall, letter to Jeanne and Victor Westphall, December 28, 1967.
54. David Westphall, letter to Walter Westphall, February 3, 1968, South Vietnam, Walter Westphall Collection.
55. Westphall, letter to Jeanne and Victor Westphall, December 4, 1967.
56. Westphall, letter to Walter Westphall, January 18, 1968.
57. Westphall, letter to Walter Westphall, February 20, 1968.
58. David Westphall, letter to Walter Westphall, May 15, 1968, South Vietnam, Walter Westphall Collection.
59. Westphall, letter to Jeanne and Victor Westphall, November 26, 1967.
60. Westphall, letter to Jeanne and Victor Westphall, February 3, 1968.
61. David Westphall, letter to Jeanne and Victor Westphall, November 1, 1967, South Vietnam, Walter Westphall Collection.
62. Westphall, letter to Jeanne and Victor Westphall, November 26, 1967.
63. Westphall, letter to Jeanne and Victor Westphall, February 22, 1968.
64. David Westphall, letter to Jeanne and Victor Westphall, February 28, 1968, South Vietnam, Walter Westphall Collection.
65. Westphall, letter to Walter Westphall, May 15, 1968.
66. David Westphall, letter to Jeanne Westphall, May 12, 1968, South Vietnam, Walter Westphall Collection.
67. Westphall.
68. Westphall.
69. Coan, *Con Thien*, 297–298.
70. Coan, 297–298.
71. Philip Caputo, *A Rumor of War* (New York: Henry Holt, 1996), 71.
72. Walter Westphall, "Details of the 1st Battalion, 4th Marines battles near Con Thien, 22 May and 23 May, 1968," 5, typescript, updated June 4, 2015, Walter Westphall Collection.
73. Westphall, 5.
74. Coan, *Con Thien*, 299.
75. Westphall, "Details of the 1st Battalion," 7.
76. Westphall, 9.
77. Westphall, 15.
78. Westphall, 16.
79. Westphall, 19–20.
80. Westphall, 20.
81. Westphall, 16.
82. Westphall, 22.
83. Westphall, 17.
84. Coan, *Con Thien*, 301–302.
85. Kyle Longley, *The Morenci Marines: A Tale of Small Town America and the Vietnam War* (Lawrence: University Press of Kansas, 2013), 65.

86. Longley, 60.
87. Longley, 281.

Chapter 3. Terrible News in a Beautiful Place

1. Kyle Longley, *The Morenci Marines: A Tale of Small Town America and the Vietnam War* (Lawrence: University Press of Kansas, 2013), 146.
2. Victor Westphall, *David's Story: A Casualty of Vietnam* (Springer, NM: Center for the Advancement of Human Dignity, 1981), 1.
3. Westphall, 1.
4. Victor Westphall, "Twenty-Fifth Anniversary Address, DAV Vietnam Veterans Memorial," 1, David Westphall Veterans Foundation Collection.
5. Westphall, 1.
6. Westphall, 2.
7. Westphall, 2.
8. Westphall, 3.
9. Westphall, *David's Story*, 141.
10. Westphall, 5.
11. Westphall, 6.
12. David Westphall, "The Prophets and their Times," paper for Religion 320, University of Montana, June 1, 1965, Walter Westphall Collection.
13. Walter Westphall, "The Vietnam Veterans Memorial at Angel Fire," in *The Vietnam War in Popular Culture*, vol. 2, *After the War*, ed. Ron Milam (Santa Barbara, CA: Praeger, 2017), 340.
14. This information on the location of David's grave and its inscription was obtained during the author's visit to the Sante Fe National Cemetery, May 29, 2016.
15. Walter Westphall, email message to author, June 20, 2015. The Congregationalist church attended by the Westphalls in the late 1940s still stands today, but bears a new name: United Church of Christ. It is located at 2801 Lomas Boulevard NE in Albuquerque.
16. Westphall, email message to author, June 20, 2015.
17. Ingri D'Aulaire and Edgar Parin D'Aulaire, *Wings for Per* (Garden City, NY: Doubleday, Doran, 1944), n.p.
18. Westphall, "Vietnam Veterans Memorial at Angel Fire," 328.
19. Westphall, *David's Story*, 136.
20. Westphall, 326–327.
21. Westphall, 325.
22. Walter Westphall, "Description," Vietnam Veterans Peace and Brotherhood Chapel Information Sheets, November, 1974, Walter Westphall Collection.
23. Westphall.
24. Westphall, *David's Story*, 137.
25. Kate Ruland Thorne, *Upon this Rock: Marguerite Brunswig Staude and Her Sedona Chapel* (Phoenix, AZ: Amor Deus, 2016), 1.
26. Robert Allen Nauman, *On the Wings of Modernism: The United States Air Force Academy* (Urbana: University of Illinois Press, 2004), 5.
27. Ted Luna, "Architect's Statement," n.d., Walter Westphall Collection.

28. Luna.
29. Estimate sheet filled out by Ted Luna, August 31, 1968, Walter Westphall Collection.
30. Walter Westphall email message to author, September 24, 2018. The calculated buying power of $32,669 in 2018 is provided by dollartimes.com, accessed September 4, 2018, https://www.dollartimes.com/inflation/inflation.php?amount=1&year=1968.
31. Walter Westphall, "Construction History," Vietnam Veterans Peace and Brotherhood Chapel Information Sheets, November 1974, Walter Westphall Collection.
32. Quoted in Walter Westphall, email message to author, August 22, 2018.
33. Westphall, "Vietnam Veterans Memorial at Angel Fire," 325.
34. Westphall, 327.
35. Victor Westphall, letter to Georg Vedeler, August 11, 1969, Springer, New Mexico, Walter Westphall Collection.
36. Victor Westphall, letter to Ted Luna, November 10, 1968, Walter Westphall Collection.
37. Victor Westphall, letter to Ted Luna, November 20, 1968, Walter Westphall Collection.
38. Westphall.
39. Westphall, "Construction History."
40. Victor Westphall, letter to Ted Luna, January 9, 1969, Walter Westphall Collection.
41. Walter Westphall, email message to author, March 10, 2016.
42. Westphall, letter to Vedeler, August 11, 1969.
43. Walter Westphall, "Recollections about My Mom," attachment to Walter Westphall, email message to author, April 8, 2016.
44. Westphall, 1.
45. Westphall, 1.
46. Westphall, 2.
47. Westphall, *David's Story*, 137–138.
48. Walter Westphall, email message to author, March 10, 2016.
49. Westphall.
50. Walter Westphall, email message to author, August 29, 2018.
51. Westphall.
52. Westphall, *David's Story*, 138.
53. Westphall, "Recollections about My Mom," 1.
54. Walter Westphall, email message to author, June 5, 2012.
55. Westphall.
56. Westphall, "Recollections about My Mom," 1.
57. Kimberly Westphall, "Grandma Westphall Anecdotes," attachment to Walter Westphall, email message to author, March 18, 2016.
58. Westphall.
59. Westphall.
60. Westphall.
61. Victor Westphall, letter to Ted Luna, December 5, 1968, Val Verde Ranch, Walter Westphall Collection.
62. Westphall.

63. Walter Westphall, email message to author, September 27, 2018.
64. Walter Westphall, email message to author, September 18, 2018.
65. Victor Westphall, Summary of Letters, Chapter 4: 1969–1977, 20, Walter Westphall Collection.
66. Victor Westphall, letter to Ted Luna, August 26, 1969, Walter Westphall Collection.
67. Westphall.
68. Westphall.
69. Walter Westphall, "Administrative History," Vietnam Veterans Peace and Brotherhood Chapel Information Sheets, November 1974, Walter Westphall Collection.
70. Westphall, *David's Story*, 142.
71. Westphall, 142.
72. Westphall, 142.
73. Victor Westphall, letter to Ted Luna, March 28, 1969, Walter Westphall Collection.
74. Westphall, *David's Story*, 143.
75. Westphall, 144.
76. Westphall, letter to Luna, March 28, 1969.
77. Walter Westphall, email message to author, September 11, 2018.
78. Walter Westphall, "Details of the 1st Battalion, 4th Marines battles near Con Thien, 22 May and 23 May, 1968," 5, typescript, updated June 4, 2015, Walter Westphall Collection.
79. Westphall, *David's Story*, 138.
80. Walter Westphall, email message to author, January 26, 2015.
81. Westphall.
82. Westphall.
83. "Tankers at War: Air Refueling in Southeast Asia," National Museum of the US Air Force, May 18, 2015, accessed September 11, 2018, https://www.nationalmuseum.af.mil/Visit/Museum-Exhibits/Fact-Sheets/Display/Article/196003/tankers-at-war-air-refueling-in-southeast-asia/.
84. Westphall, "Vietnam Veterans Memorial at Angel Fire," 329.
85. Walter Westphall, email message to author, March 10, 2016.
86. Westphall, letter to Luna, August 26, 1969.
87. Westphall, "Construction History."
88. Westphall, "Administrative History."
89. Westphall, "Construction History."

Chapter 4. Peace and Brotherhood

1. Jerry Lembcke, *The Spitting Image: Myth, Memory, and the Legacy of Vietnam* (New York: New York University Press, 1998), 94.
2. As historian Rhodri Jeffreys-Jones points out, secretary of defense Melvin Laird "coined the word *Vietnamization* to replace *de-Americanization*, implying a positive strategy rather than a flight before . . . public opinion." Jeffreys-Jones, *Peace Now!: American Society and the Ending of the Vietnam War* (New Haven, CT: Yale University Press, 1999), 83.

3. John Prados, *Vietnam: The History of an Unwinnable War, 1945–1975* (Lawrence: University Press of Kansas, 2009), 405.

4. Prados, 418.

5. Marilyn B. Young, *The Vietnam Wars, 1945–1990* (New York: Harper Perennial, 1991), 238.

6. Henry Grabar, "What the Bombing of Cambodia Tells Us about Obama's Drone Campaign," *Atlantic Monthly*, February 14, 2013, accessed September 23, 2018, https://www.theatlantic.com/international/archive/2013/02/what-the-us-bombing-of-cambodia-tells-us-about-obamas-drone-campaign/273142/.

7. Young, *Vietnam Wars*, 235.

8. Ten days after the shooting at Kent State, police gunned down two students of color at Jackson State, a historically black university located in the Mississippi capital. However, while often mentioned in the same breath with Kent State, the tragic violence at Jackson State was not directly tied to Vietnam War protest.

9. Young, *Vietnam Wars*, 253.

10. Christian G. Appy, *American Reckoning: The Vietnam War and Our National Identity* (New York: Viking, 2015), xvi.

11. Prados, *Vietnam*, 427.

12. Prados, 427.

13. Prados, 423–424. These testimonials subsequently appeared in book form. See Vietnam Veterans Against the War, *The Winter Soldier Investigation: An Inquiry into American War Crimes* (Boston: Beacon Press, 1972).

14. Douglas Brinkley, *Tour of Duty: John Kerry and the Vietnam War* (New York: HarperCollins, 2004), 3. The title "Dewey Canyon III" referred to the code names for military incursions into Laos.

15. Prados, *Vietnam*, 424.

16. Brinkley, *Tour of Duty*, 11.

17. Brinkley, 11.

18. Victor Westphall, letter to contributors, November 16, 1970, Springer, New Mexico, Walter Westphall Collection.

19. Victor Westphall, "The Vietnam Veterans Peace and Brotherhood Chapel," November 16, 1970, Walter Westphall Collection.

20. Westphall.

21. Westphall.

22. Westphall.

23. Westphall.

24. Westphall.

25. Westphall.

26. Patrick Hagopian, *The Vietnam War in American Memory: Veterans, Memorials, and the Politics of Healing* (Amherst: University of Massachusetts Press, 2009), 7.

27. Hagopian, *Vietnam War in American Memory*, 7.

28. Brinkley, *Tour of Duty*, 355.

29. In 1973, together with Jan Berry, the founder of the VVAW, and Basil T. Paquet, Rottman would edit *Winning Hearts and Minds: War Poems by Vietnam Veterans*, the first collection of its kind and a foundational moment in the history of American Vietnam War literature. The volume contains several of Rottman's own pieces, including the wry

"What Kind of War?," which showcases his keen ear for language, dark sense of humor, and sensitivity to the paradoxes of war experience. In this short poem, the speaker considers "what kind of war it is" when American ground troops silently "cheer" as a USAF jet is shot down by the enemy. See Larry Rottmann, "What Kind of War?," in *Winning Hearts and Minds: War Poems by Vietnam Veterans*, ed. Larry Rottman, Jan Barry, and Basil T. Paquet (New York: 1st Casualty Press, 1972), 97.

30. Brinkley, *Tour of Duty*, 404.
31. Brinkley, 405.
32. Victor Westphall, Summary of Letters, Chapter 4: 1969–1977, 22, Walter Westphall Collection.
33. Larry Rottmann, "Builds Memorial to Vietnam Dead," *Saint Louis Post-Dispatch*, June 8, 1971, 33.
34. Patrick Lamb, "Viet Veterans Peace Chapel Dedicated in New Mexico," *Albuquerque Journal*, May 23, 1971, 4.
35. Rottmann, "Builds Memorial to Vietnam Dead," 33.
36. Rottmann, 33.
37. "He Built It, But What Now?," *Kingsport Times*, May 25, 1971, 17.
38. Lamb, "Viet Veterans Peace Chapel," 4.
39. *Every Day Is Extra* offers a disappointingly brief summary of Kerry's activities following his testimony in Washington: "For a number of months after the Washington protests, I gave speeches around the country, drawing a small salary and donating money raised from the speeches to the VVAW. I was booked for speaking engagements as far from home as Norman, Oklahoma, to standing-room-only crowds. As the fall of 1971 turned toward winter, I began to pull back a bit." John Kerry, *Every Day Is Extra* (New York: Simon & Schuster, 2018), 133.
40. Brinkley, *Tour of Duty*, 405.
41. Quoted in Patrick Miller, "Kerry Had Epiphany at Angel Fire," *Albuquerque Journal*, February 4, 2004, 49.
42. Miller, "Kerry Had Epiphany," 49.
43. Gerald Nicosia, "Veteran in Conflict," *Los Angeles Times*, May 23, 2004, accessed October 11, 2018, http://www.latimes.com/style/la-tm-kerry21amay23-story.html.
44. Victor Westphall, *David's Story: A Casualty of Vietnam* (Springer, NM: Center for the Advancement of Human Dignity, 1981), 150.
45. For more on the evolution of the Tomb of the Unknown Soldier, especially the introduction of the Tomb Guards, see Steven Trout, *On the Battlefield of Memory: The First World War and American Remembrance, 1919–1941* (Tuscaloosa: University of Alabama Press, 2010), 153–156.
46. Lanny Tonning, email message to author, October 20, 2018.
47. Lanny Tonning, interview by the author, October 24, 2018.
48. Tonning.
49. Tonning.
50. Tonning.
51. Richard Dickerson, interview by the author, July 30, 2013.
52. Frank Richardson, email message to author, June 10, 2016.
53. Ron Milam, *Not a Gentleman's War: An Inside View of Junior Officers in the Vietnam War* (Chapel Hill: University of North Carolina Press, 2009), 2.

54. Ron Milam, "Comments Regarding Doc Westphall," unpublished manuscript, last modified July 2, 2017.
55. Milam.
56. Ron Milam, email message to author, November 19, 2018.
57. Victor Westphall, *Vietnam: The Hinge of Destiny* (Springer, NM: Vietnam Veterans Peace and Brotherhood Chapel, 1972), 6.
58. Westphall, 3.
59. Westphall, 4.
60. Westphall, 6.
61. Westphall, 6.
62. Westphall, 6.
63. Westphall, 6–7.
64. According to environmental historian Finis Dunaway, the famous Crying Indian ad, which debuted in 1971, was duplicitous on many levels. The Indian was played not by a true Native American, but by Iron Eyes Cody, "an Italian American who played Indians in both his life and on screen." Nor was the Make America Beautiful campaign what it seemed. Can and bottle manufacturers created the campaign with their own anything-but-environmentally-friendly interests in mind. See Finis Dunaway, "The 'Crying Indian' Ad that Fooled the Environmental Movement," *Chicago Tribune*, November 21, 2017, accessed October 16, 2018, http://www.chicagotribune.com/news/opinion/commentary/ct-perspec-indian-crying-environment-ads-pollution-1123-20171113-story.html. For more on the Nixon administration's landmark environmental reforms, as well as the establishment of Earth Day, see Ted Steinberg's superb *Down to Earth: Nature's Role in American History*, 3rd ed. (Oxford: Oxford University Press, 2012), 250–253.
65. Harold Jackson, obituary for Gloria Emerson, *Guardian*, August 7, 2004, accessed October 17, 2018, https://www.theguardian.com/news/2004/aug/07/guardianobituaries.haroldjackson.
66. Quoted in Jackson.
67. Gloria Emerson, "Chapel, a Father's Memorial, Honors More than Vietnam Dead," *New York Times*, June 15, 1972, 22.
68. Emerson, 22.
69. Emerson, 22.
70. Emerson, 22.
71. Emerson, 22.
72. Emerson, 22.
73. Emerson, 22.
74. As *New York Times* journalist David Halberstam notes in *Ho* (1971), a brief biography of Ho Chi Minh that Victor Westphall may well have read, American antiwar protesters in 1970 often took up the cry "Ho, Ho, Ho Chi Minh." North Vietnamese flags and other expressions of solidarity with the cause of Vietnamese independence and nationalism sometimes appeared at rallies. David Halberstam, *Ho* (New York: Knopf, 1971), 117.
75. A copy of the original typed letter resides in the David Westphall Veterans Foundation Collection at Texas Tech.
76. Victor Westphall, letter to Ho Chi Minh, September 3, 1969, Springer, New Mexico, David Westphall Veterans Foundation Collection.

77. Victor Westphall, letter to William P. Rogers, September 3, 1971, Springer, New Mexico, David Westphall Veterans Foundation Collection.
78. Viet Thanh Nguyen, *Nothing Ever Dies: Vietnam and the Memory of War* (Cambridge, MA: Harvard University Press, 2016), 26. For another valuable study of war memorials within Vietnam, see Christina Schwenkel, *The American War in Contemporary Vietnam: Transnational Remembrance and Representation* (Bloomington: Indiana University Press, 2009).
79. Tonning, interview by the author, October 24, 2018.

Chapter 5. A National Memorial

1. Corinne Browne, *Casualty: A Memoir of Love and War* (New York: Norton, 1981), 17, 44.
2. Victor Westphall, "The Chapel Stucco and Aboriginal Tradition: A Sacred Element," Walter Westphall Collection.
3. Westphall.
4. Edward S. Casey, "Public Memory in Place and Time," in *Framing Public Memory*, ed. Kendall R. Phillips (Tuscaloosa: University of Alabama Press, 2004), 42.
5. The program for the 1972 commemorative ceremony at the chapel, the occasion of Victor's address titled "Vietnam: The Hinge of Destiny," further drove home this point by including some additional lines from David's poem "The Ultimate Curse." According to Victor, his son's poem "sets forth the hard reality that man may be trapped beyond the point of reason by his nuclear creation":

> Man would take Prometheus'gift?
> Ah, the skies did not show sloth,
> But the gods were quick to claim Vengeance.
> And to make the blow complete,
> To cut off possible retreat
> They fashioned sealed hope within the jars.
> That was no lame vengeance.

Commemorative Program, Vietnam Veterans Peace and Brotherhood Chapel, May 21, 1972, David Westphall Veterans Foundation Collection.
6. The recent removal of Confederate memorials from positions of prominence in many Southern communities is merely the most notable manifestation of this phenomenon. Regardless of the conflict it commemorates, a community memorial can be moved for a host of reasons, including street expansion, additions to nearby buildings, damage to the memorial left unrepaired, and so forth. Sometimes the move also suggests fading relevance. For example, as Olathe, Kansas, a Kansas City area suburb, expanded rapidly in the late twentieth century, it chose to move its World War I memorial from a centralized location downtown to the city cemetery. See Steven Trout, "Forgotten Reminders: Kansas World War I Memorials," *Kansas History* 29 (Autumn 2006): 214.
7. Edward Linenthal, *Sacred Ground: Americans and Their Battlefields* (Urbana: University of Illinois Press, 1993).

8. Barbara Biesecker, "Renovating the National Imaginary: A Prolegomenon on Contemporary Paregoric Rhetoric," in *Framing Public Memory*, ed. Kendall R. Phillips (Tuscaloosa: University of Alabama Press, 2004), 216.

9. Westphall, "Chapel Stucco."

10. Willa Cather, *Death Comes for the Archbishop* (New York: Knopf, 1927).

11. Walter Westphall, "Excerpts from Letters," 5, Center for the Advancement of Human Dignity Information Sheets, n.d., Walter Westphall Collection.

12. Westphall, 3.

13. Westphall, 3.

14. Westphall, 1.

15. Westphall, 2.

16. Westphall, 3.

17. Westphall, 3.

18. Westphall, 5.

19. Westphall, 5.

20. Walter Westphall, "Comments Heard at the Chapel by Dr. Westphall," 1, Center for the Advancement of Human Dignity Information Sheets, n.d., Walter Westphall Collection.

21. Westphall.

22. Westphall.

23. Unattributed source, letter to Victor Westphall, November 12, 1979, Fargo, ND, David Westphall Veterans Foundation Collection. Name of letter writer withheld because author could not be contacted to give consent. Victor didn't necessarily disagree with this belligerent writer's final point. He simply found the notion of all-out war between superpowers intolerable. In his one and only work of fiction, *Trial by Combat*, he imagined an alternative—an arranged duel between a Russian scholar and his elderly American counterpart (a character clearly based on Victor himself), each representing his respective nation. Marooned on Easter Island, the two men fight to the death to determine the outcome of an international crisis, thereby sparing the world a nuclear conflagration. See Victor Westphall [David White, pseud.], *Trial by Combat* ([Springer, NM]: Center for the Advancement of Human Dignity, 1978).

24. Walter Westphall, "Excerpts from Letters," 4.

25. Westphall, 4.

26. Walter Westphall, email message to author, December 19, 2018.

27. Westphall.

28. *Vietnam Veterans Chapel Bulletin*, November 1978, 1.

29. *Vietnam Veterans Chapel Bulletin*, November 1978, 1.

30. *Vietnam Veterans Chapel Bulletin*, November 1978, 2.

31. For a superb examination of the National Mall and the heated politics that have accompanied each new memorial placed there, see Kirk Savage, *Monument Wars: Washington, DC, the National Mall, and the Transformation of the Memorial Landscape* (Berkeley: University of California Press, 2009).

32. Though proposed for Pershing Park (an area near the White House), not the National Mall, a National World War I Memorial may soon add to the pattern of federal commemoration in reverse chronological order. A recent appeal for donations to support the construction of the memorial, sent by the United States World War I

Centennial Commission, vividly reflects the contrast between the tradition of military commemoration operative in the nation's capital today and the situation faced by the Westphalls in the mid-1970s: "The United States honors the American veterans of every major conflict of the 20th Century with a national memorial in Washington, DC— except the veterans of World War I. With your help, that can change." "Every Veteran Deserves to be Remembered," United States World War I Centennial Commission email message to the author, December 30, 2018.

33. "Population of Sante Fe," Population.us, accessed January 1, 2019, https://population.us/nm/santa-fe/.

34. Deborah Colene Kidwell, "Remembering and Forgetting War: Vietnam Memorials and Public Memory" (PhD diss., University of Kansas, 2006), 64–103.

35. John Bodnar, *Remaking America: Public Memory, Commemoration, and Patriotism in the Twentieth Century* (Princeton, NJ: Princeton University Press, 1992).

36. Walter Westphall, email message to author, August 20, 2018.

37. Walter Westphall, "National Memorial Proposal," n.d., 20, Walter Westphall Collection.

38. *Vietnam Veterans Chapel Bulletin*, March 1975, 1.

39. *Vietnam Veterans Chapel Bulletin*, March 1975, 1.

40. *Vietnam Veterans Chapel Bulletin*, March 1975, 1.

41. Steven L. Rose, chairman, Advisory Board on National Parks, Historic Sites, Buildings and Monuments, memorandum to the Secretary of the Interior, October 8, 1975, Walter Westphall Collection.

42. Rose.

43. Richard C. Curry, chief, Office of Legislation, National Park Service, letter to Toni Currin, April 5, 1977, Walter Westphall Collection.

44. Walter Westphall, "National Memorial Proposal," 24.

45. Westphall, 21.

46. Kidwell, "Remembering and Forgetting War," 74.

47. *Vietnam Veterans Chapel Bulletin*, December 1979, 1.

48. Michael Satchell, "One Man's Shrine to All Who Fell in Vietnam," *Parade*, November 4, 1979, 19.

49. Satchell, 19.

50. Satchell, 19.

51. Satchell, 19.

52. Satchell, 19.

53. Kidwell, "Remembering and Forgetting War," 78.

54. John Prados, *Vietnam: The History of an Unwinnable War, 1945–1975* (Lawrence: University Press of Kansas, 2009), 531.

55. Laurence Stallings, *The Doughboys: The Story of the AEF, 1917–1918* (New York: Harper & Row, 1963), 376.

56. *Vietnam Veterans Chapel Bulletin*, December 1979, 1.

57. *Vietnam Veterans Chapel Bulletin*, December 1979, 1.

58. *Vietnam Veterans Chapel Bulletin*, December 1979, 1.

59. *Vietnam Veterans Chapel Bulletin*, December 1979, 1.

60. Kidwell, "Remembering and Forgetting War," 75.

61. Kidwell, 75.

62. *Vietnam Veterans Chapel Bulletin*, May 1980, 1.
63. *Vietnam Veterans Chapel Bulletin*, December 1980, 1.
64. *Vietnam Veterans Chapel Bulletin*, December 1980, 1.
65. Kidwell, "Remembering and Forgetting War," 76.
66. *Vietnam Veterans Chapel Announcement*, September 15, 1981, 1.
67. *Vietnam Veterans Chapel Announcement*, September 15, 1981, 1.
68. Walter Westphall, email message to author, February 1, 2019.
69. Kidwell, "Remembering and Forgetting War," 81.
70. Kidwell, 81.
71. Pat Mendoza and Joe Haukebo, "A Hero's Trail: Dr. Victor Walter Westphall," 145, unpublished typescript, Walter Westphall Collection.
72. Quoted in Mendoza and Haukebo, 144.
73. Kidwell, "Remembering and Forgetting War," 83–85.
74. The following veteran's reaction is typical: "I am flabbergasted, disappointed, and sick about what I saw last weekend at the DAV Vietnam Veterans Memorial in Angel Fire, NM. The board members in charge of the memorial should have their collective heads examined and then replaced." Chet Krone, letter to DAV National Commander, May 27, 1986, David Westphall Veterans Foundation Collection.
75. Krone.
76. Krone.
77. Joseph Haukebo, "Memorial Founder Sues National DAV," *Sangre de Cristo Chronicle*, May 21, 1992, 8. For assistance with his legal expenses, Victor actually placed an appeal in several New Mexico newspapers. See Victor Westphall, "To My Fellow New Mexicans" [clipping], n.p., n.d., David Westphall Veterans Foundation Collection.
78. Victor Westphall, "To My Fellow New Mexicans."
79. Kidwell, "Remembering and Forgetting War," 90.
80. Mendoza and Haukebo, "Hero's Trail," 146; Kidwell, "Remembering and Forgetting War," 92.
81. In his brief speech, Westmoreland stressed that "Americans who served in Southeast Asia and in other wars this century have made the world safer for freedom and democracy." Then, citing the recent Los Angeles riots and the "decline of family values," he called for America to "turn its attention inward." Thom Cole, "Hundreds to Brave Rain to Honor New Mexico Vets," *Albuquerque Journal*, May 26, 1992, A1.
82. Chuck Hasford, interview with the author, July 31, 2013.
83. One can trace the near-disappearance of the memorial's peace message in its official, public presentation by looking at articles published in the late 1970s through the 1980s. Victor's mission to end war is highlighted in "A Plea for Eternal Peace: The Vietnam Veterans Peace and Brotherhood Chapel" [offprint], *DAV* (July 1977), n.p., and "The DAV Vietnam Veterans Memorial" [offprint], *DAV* (February 1983), n.p.; it receives no mention in "The DAV Vietnam Veterans National Memorial: A Mountain Valley's Place of Destiny . . . and a Nation's Honor" [offprint], *DAV* (July 1984), n.p.; "A Timeless Message of Dignity" [offprint], *DAV* (June 1985), n.p.; and "Where Eagles Soar . . . a Vietnam Reunion," *DAV* (July 1986), 14–18. Not surprisingly, an article on the chapel in *The Retired Officer* did not include Victor's philosophy of peace and brotherhood either. See Shanti K. Khalsa, "Where Eagles Soar," *Retired Officer*, August 1987, n.p.

Epilogue: Phantoms of Peace and War

1. Walter D. Westphall, memorandum to board members, David Westphall Veterans Foundation, February 24, 1999, David Westphall Veterans Foundation Collection.
2. "Veterans find unique way to raise funds for Angel Fire Memorial" [Main title missing from clipping], *Santa Fe Journal*, April 4, 2002, David Westphall Veterans Foundation Collection.
3. "Veterans find unique way."
4. Walter Westphall email message to author, February 10, 2019.
5. Walter Westphall email message to author, February 11, 2019.
6. Chuck Howe, interview with the author, July 28, 2013.
7. Walter Westphall, "Angel Fire State Veterans Cemetery," October 30, 2018.
8. Walter Westphall, "A Son's Thoughts on His Father's Legacy" [clipping], *Sangre de Cristo Chronicle*, n.d., n.p.
9. Walter Westphall, email message to author, March 3, 2019.
10. Pat Mendoza and Joe Haukebo, "A Hero's Trail: Dr. Victor Walter Westphall," 149, unpublished typescript, Walter Westphall Collection.
11. Mendoza and Haukebo, 149.
12. Mendoza and Haukebo, 149.
13. Mendoza and Haukebo, 151.
14. Victor Westphall, "Soil Plaque Dedication," Memorial Day, 1995, David Westphall Veterans Foundation Collection.
15. Walter Westphall, email message to author, February 10, 2019.
16. Mendoza and Haukebo, "Hero's Trail," 151.
17. Walter Westphall, email message to author, February 10, 2019.
18. Mendoza and Haukebo, "Hero's Trail," 151.
19. Kate German, "Self-Guided Tour, Vietnam Veterans Memorial State Park," Vietnam Veterans Memorial State Park, n.d.
20. Kate German, "UH-1D 64-13670 Huey Helicopter," "Park Features," David Westphall Veterans Foundation, accessed March 9, 2019, https://www.vietnamveteransmemorial.org/memorials-features/huey-helicopter/.
21. German, "Self-Guided Tour."
22. German.
23. German.
24. The HBO documentary *Dear America: Letters Home from Vietnam* (1987) features David's letter to his parents dated November 16, 1967. For reflections on the myth of war's ineffability, and the damage this myth does to both veterans and their families, see Phil Klay's powerful essay, "After War: A Failure of Imagination," *New York Times*, February 8, 2014, accessed March 21, 2019, https://www.nytimes.com/2014/02/09/opinion/sunday/after-war-a-failure-of-the-imagination.html.
25. My thanks to Michael Panhorst for offering this apt description of the memorial's post-1982 additions.
26. A fuller summary of Hagopian's important argument in *The Vietnam War in American Memory* runs as follows: by sidestepping issues of morality, American Vietnam War memorials refuse, by and large, to participate openly in historical interpretation or judgment. These are walls indeed. And by focusing exclusively on American losses and/

or veterans, they treat the Vietnam War as something that simply "happened" to the United States—and to the United States alone. Hidden from view is the active decision making, on the part of the nation's leaders, that carried tragic consequences for millions of Vietnamese—and for neighboring countries like Cambodia and Laos. Therefore, in Hagopian's view, the "healing" these memorials supposedly provide is not healing at all but a form of selective amnesia. Lost in the shiny granite surfaces are once urgent issues that the nation no longer wishes to face.

Moreover, Hagopian observes that recognizing what many American memorials to the Vietnam War refuse to record and remember is made all the more difficult by the irresistible messages that they *do* contain. Restoring the confidence and unity lost during America's most internally divisive twentieth-century conflict has often required that public sites identified with the war give the appearance of being entirely neutral spaces where controversy and rancor are held at bay—hence the nonthreatening emphasis on service and sacrifice (treated as noble ends unto themselves) that characterizes these monuments. Right or wrong, such memorials tell us, Americans served in Vietnam. They performed their duty and should not be forgotten. Here are their names. Honor their service.

Hagopian's magisterial volume is the densest, most thoroughly researched study to date of American Vietnam War remembrance. However, much of the moral self-examination that Hagopian finds lacking in physical monuments occurred in American literary and cinematic responses to the war. Useful supplements to *The Vietnam War and American Memory* include Robert D. Schulzinger, *A Time for Peace: The Legacy of the Vietnam War* (New York: Oxford University Press, 2006); Mark Taylor, *The Vietnam War in History, Literature and Film* (Tuscaloosa: University of Alabama Press, 2003); and Fred Turner, *Echoes of Combat: Trauma, Memory, and the Vietnam War* (Minneapolis: University of Minnesota Press, 2001).

27. Thomas Brinson, "Militarizing Angel Fire," *In the Mind Field*, July 13, 2011, accessed June 7, 2012, URL no longer available. Brinson's negative assessment of changes that had occurred at the memorial since Victor Westphall's death received a response from park superintendent Tom Turnbull, who argued that the writer's perspective was "clouded by prejudices." Turnbull, "Response to 'Militarizing Angel Fire' by Thomas Brinson," *In the Mind Field*, August 1, 2011, accessed June 12, 2012, URL no longer available.

28. Walter Westphall, email message to author, September 28, 2012.

29. Vietnamese members of the Asian American Association in Albuquerque first made a "pilgrimage" to the memorial in 2000. Six years later they presented a wreath during the annual Memorial Day ceremony, where the South Vietnamese flag was flown. Press Release, "First Memorial Day as a State Park for the Vietnam Veterans Memorial in Angel Fire, Vietnamese-American Group to Present Wreath of Unity; 1.8 million in park improvements planned for 2006–2007," New Mexico State Parks, May 22, 2006, Walter Westphall Collection.

30. James M. Mayo, *War Memorials as Political Landscapes: The American Experience and Beyond* (New York: Praeger, 1988), 201.

31. Kate German, interview with the author, July 31, 2013.

Bibliography

Archival Collections

David Westphall Veterans Foundation Collection. Vietnam Center and Archive, Texas Tech University, Lubbock, TX. (*DWVFC*)
Walter Westphall Collection. Westphall residence. Andover, Kansas. (*WWC*)

Personal Interviews

Dickerson, Richard. Interview by the author, July 30, 2013.
German, Kate. Interview by the author, July 31, 2013.
Hasford, Chuck. Interview by the author, July 31, 2013.
Howe, Chuck. Interview by the author, July 28, 2013.
Tonning, Lanny. Interview by the author, October 24, 2018.

Emails

Milam, Ron. Email to the author, November 19, 2018.
Richardson, Frank. Email to the author, June 10, 2016.
Tonning, Lanny. Email to the author, October 20, 2018.
United States World War I Centennial Commission. "Every Veteran Deserves to be Remembered." Email to the author (fundraising message). December 30, 2018.
Westphall, Walter. Email to the author, June 5, 2012.
———. Email to the author, September 28, 2012.
———. Email to the author, January 26, 2015.
———. Email to the author, March 6, 2015.
———. Email to the author, March 13, 2015.
———. Email to the author, May 31, 2015.
———. Email to the author, June 20, 2015.
———. Email to the author, October 8, 2015.
———. Email to the author, March 10, 2016.
———. Email to the author, March 18, 2016.
———. Email to the author, April 8, 2016.
———. Email to the author, August 20, 2018.
———. Email to the author, August 22, 2018.

———. Email to the author, August 29, 2018.
———. Email to the author, September 11, 2018.
———. Email to the author, September 18, 2018.
———. Email to the author, September 24, 2018.
———. Email to the author, September 27, 2018.
———. Email to the author, December 19, 2018.
———. Email to the author, February 1, 2019.
———. Email to the author, February 10, 2019.
———. Email to the author, February 11, 2019.
———. Email to the author, March 3, 2019.

Letters and Memoranda

Baca, Fidel L. Letter to Victor Westphall, January 31, 2002, NM. WWC.
Blake, Henry W. Letter to Medical Department Representative, US Marine Corps Recruiting Station. May 19, 1966. Albuquerque, NM. WWC.
Curry, Richard C. Letter to Toni Currin. April 5, 1977. Washington, DC. WWC.
Fuentes, Irene de la Rosa. Letter to David Westphall. October 10, 1966, Mexico. WWC.
Krone, Chet. Letter to DAV National Commander. May 27, 1986, Guymon, OK. DWVFC.
Middleton, Terry. Letter to Victor Westphall, April 26, 1982. DWVFC.
Nixon, Richard. Letter to Victor Westphall, July 15, 1971, San Clemente, California. DWVFC.
Rose, Steven L. Letter to the Secretary of the Interior. October 8, 1975. Washington, DC. WWC.
Unattributed Source. Letter to Victor Westphall, December 18, 1982. DWVFC.
Unattributed Source. Letter to Victor Westphall. November 12, 1979, Fargo, ND, DWVFC.
Westphall, David. Letter to Jeanne Westphall, May 12, 1968, South Vietnam. WWC.
———. Letter to Jeanne and Victor Westphall, June 7, 1965, Missoula, MT. WWC.
———. Letter to Jeanne and Victor Westphall, November 1, 1967, South Vietnam. WWC.
———. Letter to Jeanne and Victor Westphall, November 16, 1967, South Vietnam. WWC.
———. Letter to Jeanne and Victor Westphall, November 26, 1967, South Vietnam. WWC.
———. Letter to Jeanne and Victor Westphall, December 4, 1967, South Vietnam. WWC.
———. Letter to Jeanne and Victor Westphall, December 8, 1967, South Vietnam. WWC.
———. Letter to Jeanne and Victor Westphall, December 28, 1967, South Vietnam. WWC.
———. Letter to Jeanne and Victor Westphall, February 3, 1968, South Vietnam. WWC.
———. Letter to Jeanne and Victor Westphall, February 19, 1968, South Vietnam. WWC.
———. Letter to Jeanne and Victor Westphall, February 22, 1968, South Vietnam. WWC.
———. Letter to Jeanne and Victor Westphall, February 28, 1968, South Vietnam. WWC.
———. Letter to Jeanne and Victor Westphall, March 28, 1968, South Vietnam. WWC.
———. Letter to Jeanne and Victor Westphall, April 6, 1968, South Vietnam. WWC.

Bibliography 219

———. Letter to Jeanne and Victor Westphall, April 22, 1968, South Vietnam. *WWC*.
———. Letter to Jeanne and Victor Westphall, May 9, 1968, South Vietnam. *WWC*.
———. Letter to Walter Westphall, November 26, 1967, South Vietnam. *WWC*.
———. Letter to Walter Westphall, January 18, 1968, South Vietnam. *WWC*.
———. Letter to Walter Westphall, February 3, 1968, South Vietnam. *WWC*.
———. Letter to Walter Westphall, February 20, 1968, South Vietnam. *WWC*.
———. Letter to Walter Westphall, March 24, 1968, South Vietnam. *WWC*.
———. Letter to Walter Westphall, May 15, 1968, South Vietnam. *WWC*.
Westphall, Victor. Letter to contributors, November 16, 1970, Springer, NM. *WWC*.
———. Letter to Ho Chi Minh, September 3, 1969, Springer, NM. *DWVFC*.
———. Letter to Ted Luna, November 10, 1968, NM. *WWC*.
———. Letter to Ted Luna, November 20, 1968, NM. *WWC*.
———. Letter to Ted Luna, December 5, 1968, Val Verde Ranch, NM. *WWC*.
———. Letter to Ted Luna, January 9, 1969, NM. *WWC*.
———. Letter to Ted Luna, March 28, 1969, NM. *WWC*.
———. Letter to Ted Luna, August 26, 1969, NM. *WWC*.
———. Letter to William P. Rogers, September 3, 1971. Springer, NM. *DWVFC*.
———. Letter to Georg Vedeler, August 11, 1969, Springer, NM. *WWC*.
Westphall, Walter. Letter to board members of the David Westphall Veterans Foundation, February 24, 1999. *DWVF*.

Chapel-Related Documents and Unpublished Essays

Adams, Robert. "Reflections on the Angel Fire Memorial." Unpublished manuscript, last modified March 8, 2016.
Commemorative Program. Vietnam Veterans Peace and Brotherhood Chapel. May 21, 1972. *DWVF*.
"First Memorial Day as a State Park for the Vietnam Veterans Memorial in Angel Fire, Vietnamese-American Group to Present Wreath of Unity; 1.8 million in park improvements planned for 2006-2007." Press Release. New Mexico State Parks. May 22, 2006. *WWC*.
German, Kate. "Self-Guided Tour, Vietnam Veterans Memorial State Park." Vietnam Veterans Memorial State Park, n.d.
Milam, Ron. "Comments Regarding Doc Westphall." Unpublished manuscript, last modified July 2, 2017.
Vietnam Veterans Chapel Announcement. September 15, 1981.
Vietnam Veterans Chapel Bulletin. March 1975.
———. November 1978.
———. December 1979.
———. May 1980.
———. December 1980.
Westphall, David. "Autobiography," University of Montana Teacher Education Application, July 16, 1964. *WWC*.
———. "Autobiography—The Basic School," United States Marine Corps Basic School Application, n.d. *WWC*.

———. "Planning Paper," University of Montana Teacher Education Application, July 16, 1964. WWC.
Westphall, Kimberly. "Grandma Westphall Anecdotes." Unpublished manuscript, last modified March 18, 2016.
Westphall, Victor. "The Chapel Stucco and Aboriginal Tradition: A Sacred Element." N.d. WWC.
———. "Twenty-Fifth Anniversary Address, DAV Vietnam Veterans Memorial." May 22, 1996. DWVFC.
———. "Soil Plaque Dedication, Memorial Day, 1995." May 29, 1995. DWVF.
———. "Summary of Letters." Chapter 4: 1969–1977. WWC.
———. "To My Fellow New Mexicans." Clipping. No publication. N.d. DWVF.
———. "The Vietnam Veterans Peace and Brotherhood Chapel." November 16, 1970. WWC.
Westphall, Walter. "Administrative History." Vietnam Veterans Peace and Brotherhood Chapel information sheets. November 1974. WWC.
———. "Angel Fire State Veterans Cemetery." Unpublished manuscript, last modified October 30, 2018.
———. "Comments Heard at the Chapel by Dr. Westphall." Center for the Advancement of Human Dignity information sheets. N.d. WWC.
———. "Construction History." Vietnam Veterans Peace and Brotherhood Chapel information sheets. November 1974. WWC.
———. "Description," Vietnam Veterans Peace and Brotherhood Chapel information sheets. November 1974. WWC.
———. "Details of the 1st Battalion, 4th Marines Battles near Con Thien, 22 May and 23 May, 1968." Updated June 4, 2015. WWC.
———. "Excerpts from Letters." Center for the Advancement of Human Dignity information sheets. N.d. WWC.
———. "National Memorial Proposal." N.d. WWC.
———. "Recollections about My Mom." Unpublished manuscript, last modified April 8, 2016.

Military Documents

"List of Basic School Courses, United States Marine Corps." N.d. WWC.
"Officer Candidate Assignment to Active Duty for Cpl. Victor D. Westphall" [United States Marine Corps], November 1, 1966. WWC.
"Officer Fitness Report—U.S. Marine Corps" for David Westphall, August 22, 1967. WWC.
"Permanent Change of Station." Issued to David Westphall, July 24, 1967. WWC.

Published Sources, Unpublished Book Manuscripts, and Dissertations

Appy, Christian G. *American Reckoning: The Vietnam War and Our National Identity.* New York: Viking, 2015.

Biesecker, Barbara. "Renovating the National Imaginary: A Prolegomenon on Contemporary Paregoric Rhetoric." In *Framing Public Memory*, edited by Kendall R. Phillips, 212–247. Tuscaloosa: University of Alabama Press, 2004.
Bodnar, John. *The "Good War" in American Memory*. Baltimore, MD: Johns Hopkins University Press, 2010.
———. *Remaking America: Public Memory, Commemoration, and Patriotism in the Twentieth Century*. Princeton, NJ: Princeton University Press, 1992.
Brinkley, Douglas. *Tour of Duty: John Kerry and the Vietnam War*. New York: HarperCollins, 2004.
Brinson, Thomas. "Militarizing Angel Fire." *In the Mind Field*, July 13, 2011. Accessed June 7, 2012. URL no longer exists.
Brown, Jim. *Impact Zone: The Battle of the DMZ in Vietnam, 1967–1968*. Tuscaloosa: University of Alabama Press, 2004.
Browne, Corinne. *Casualty: A Memoir of Love and War*. New York: Norton, 1981.
Caputo, Philip. *A Rumor of War*. New York: Henry Holt, 1996.
Carson, Rachel. *Silent Spring*. Boston: Houghton Mifflin, 1962.
Casey, Edward S. "Public Memory in Place and Time." In *Framing Public Memory*, edited by Kendall R. Phillips, 17–44. Tuscaloosa: University of Alabama Press, 2004.
Cather, Willa. *Death Comes for the Archbishop*. New York: Knopf, 1927.
Coan, James P. *Con Thien: The Hill of Angels*. Tuscaloosa: University of Alabama Press, 2004.
———. *Time in the Barrel: A Marine's Account of the Battle for Con Thien*. Tuscaloosa: University of Alabama Press, 2018.
Cole, Thom. "Hundreds to Brave Rain to Honor New Mexico Vets." *Albuquerque Journal*, May 26, 1992, A1.
Cutler, Thomas J. *The Battle of Leyte Gulf: 23–26 October 1944*. New York: HarperCollins, 1994.
D'Aulaire, Ingri, and Edgar Parin d'Aulaire, *Wings for Per*. Garden City, NY: Doubleday, Doran, 1944.
"The DAV Vietnam Veterans Memorial." [Offprint.] *DAV*, February 1983, N.p. WWC.
"The DAV Vietnam Veterans National Memorial: A Mountain Valley's Place of Destiny . . . And a Nation's Honor." [Offprint.] *DAV*, July 1984, N.p. WWC.
Dubbs, Chris. *America's U-Boats: Terror Trophies of World War I*. Lincoln: University of Nebraska Press, 2014.
Dunaway, Finis. "The 'Crying Indian' Ad that Fooled the Environmental Movement." *Chicago Tribune*, November 21, 2017. Accessed October 16, 2018. http://www.chicagotribune.com/news/opinion/commentary/ct-perspec-indian-crying-environment-ads-pollution-1123-20171113-story.html.
Emerson, Gloria. "Chapel, A Father's Memorial Honors More than Vietnam Dead." *New York Times*, June 15, 1971, 22.
German, Kate. "UH-1D 64-13670 Huey Helicopter." David Westphall Veterans Foundation. Accessed March 9, 2019. https://www.vietnamveteransmemorial.org/memorials-features/huey-helicopter/.
Grabar, Henry. "What the Bombing of Cambodia Tells Us about Obama's Drone Campaign." *Atlantic Monthly*. February 14, 2013.

Hagopian, Patrick. *The Vietnam War in American Memory: Veterans, Memorials, and the Politics of Healing.* Amherst: University of Massachusetts Press, 2009.
Halberstam, David. *Ho.* New York: Knopf, 1971.
Hass, Kristin Ann. *Carried to the Wall: American Memory and the Vietnam Veterans Memorial.* Berkeley: University of California Press, 1998.
Haukebo, Joseph. "Memorial Founder Sues National DAV." *Sangre de Cristo Chronicle,* May 21, 1992.
"He Built It, But What Now?" *Kingsport Times,* May 25, 1971, 17.
Hedges, Chris. "Celebrating Slaughter: War and Collective Amnesia." *Truthdig.com,* October 5, 2009. https://www.truthdig.com/articles/celebrating-slaughter-war-and-collective-amnesia/.
Heller, Joseph. *Catch-22.* New York: Simon & Schuster, 1961.
Jackson, Harold. Obituary for Gloria Emerson. *Guardian,* August 7, 2004. Accessed October 17, 2018. https://www.theguardian.com/news/2004/aug/07/guardianobituaries.haroldjackson.
Jeffreys-Jones, Rhodri. *Peace Now!: American Society and the Ending of the Vietnam War.* New Haven, CT: Yale University Press, 1999.
Kammer, David. "Post-War Suburban Expansion, 1945–1959." Albuquerque, 1945–1959. New Mexico History.org. Accessed July 20, 2015. http://newmexicohistory.org/2014/02/14/albuquerque-1945-1959/.
Kerry, John. *Every Day Is Extra.* New York: Simon & Schuster, 2018.
Khalsa, Shanti K. "Where Eagles Soar." *Retired Officer.* [Offprint.] August 1987. No page. WWC.
Kidwell, Deborah Colene. "Remembering and Forgetting War: Vietnam Memorials and Public Memory." PhD diss., University of Kansas, 2006.
Klay, Phil. "After War: A Failure of Imagination." *New York Times,* February 8, 2014. Accessed March 21, 2019. https://www.nytimes.com/2014/02/09/opinion/sunday/after-war-a-failure-of-the-imagination.html.
Lamb, Patrick. "Viet Veterans Peace Chapel Dedicated in New Mexico." *Albuquerque Journal,* May 23, 1971, 4.
Lehrack, Otto J. *No Shining Armor: The Marines at War in Vietnam, Ar. Oral History.* Lawrence: University Press of Kansas, 1992.
Lembcke, Jerry. *The Spitting Image: Myth, Memory, and the Legacy of Vietnam.* New York: New York University Press, 1998.
Linenthal, Edward. *Sacred Ground: Americans and Their Battlefields.* Urbana: University of Illinois Press, 1993.
Longley, Kyle. *The Morenci Marines: A Tale of Small Town America and the Vietnam War.* Lawrence: University Press of Kansas, 2013.
Mayo, James M. *War Memorials as Political Landscape: The American Experience and Beyond.* New York: Praeger, 1988.
McLean, Jack. *Loon: A Marine Story.* New York: Ballantine, 2009.
Mendoza, Patrick M. *Extraordinary People in Extraordinary Times: Heroes, Sheroes, and Villains.* Englewood, CO: Libraries Unlimited, 1999.
———, and Joe Haukebo, "A Hero's Trail: Dr. Victor Walter Westphall." N.d.
Milam, Ron. *Not a Gentleman's War: An Inside View of Junior Officers in the Vietnam War.* Chapel Hill: University of North Carolina Press, 2009.

Miller, Patrick. "Kerry Had Epiphany at Angel Fire." *Albuquerque Journal*, February 4, 2004, 49.
Nauman, Robert Allen. *On the Wings of Modernism: The United States Air Force Academy.* Urbana: University of Illinois Press, 2004.
Nealson, Christina. *New Mexico's Sanctuaries, Retreats, and Sacred Places.* Englewood, CO: Westcliffe, 2001.
Nguyen, Viet Thanh. *Nothing Ever Dies: Vietnam and the Memory of War.* Cambridge, MA: Harvard University Press, 2016.
Nicosia, Gerald. "Veteran in Conflict." *Los Angeles Times*, May 23, 2004. Accessed October 11, 2018. http://www.latimes.com/style/la-tm-kerry21amay23-story.html.
Ognibene, Andre J., and O'Neill Barrett Jr., eds. *Internal Medicine in Vietnam.* Vol. 2: *Infectious Diseases.* Washington, DC: Office of the Surgeon General and Center of Military History United States Army, 1982.
"A Plea for Eternal Peace: The Vietnam Veterans Peace and Brotherhood Chapel." [Offprint.] *DAV*, July 1977, n.p. WWC.
"Population of Sante Fe." Population.us. Accessed January 1, 2019. https://population.us/nm/santa-fe/.
Prados, John. *Vietnam: The History of an Unwinnable War, 1945–1975.* Lawrence: University Press of Kansas, 2009.
Rottmann, Larry. "Builds Memorial to Vietnam Dead." *Saint Louis Post-Dispatch*, June 8, 1971, 33.
———, Jan Barry, and Basil T. Paquet, eds. *Winning Hearts and Minds: War Poems by Vietnam Veterans.* New York: 1st Casualty, 1972.
Satchell, Michael. "One Man's Shrine to All Who Fell in Vietnam." *Parade*, November 4, 1979, 19–20.
Savage, Kirk. *Monument Wars: Washington, DC, the National Mall, and the Transformation of the Memorial Landscape.* Berkeley: University of California Press, 2009.
Schulzinger, Robert D. *A Time for Peace: The Legacy of the Vietnam War.* New York: Oxford University Press, 2006.
Schwenkel, Christina. *The American War in Contemporary Vietnam: Transnational Remembrance and Representation.* Bloomington: Indiana University Press, 2009.
Stallings, Laurence. *The Doughboys: The Story of the AEF, 1917–1918.* New York: Harper & Row, 1963.
Steinberg, Ted. *Down to Earth: Nature's Role in American History.* 3rd ed. New York: Oxford University Press, 2013.
"*Sun Trails* Home of the Month." *New Mexico Sun Trails*, November 1952, 1–4.
"Tankers at War: Air Refueling in Southeast Asia." National Museum of the US Air Force. May 18, 2015. Accessed September 11, 2018. https://www.nationalmuseum.af.mil/Visit/Museum-Exhibits/Fact-Sheets/Display/Article/196003/tankers-at-war-air-refueling-in-southeast-asia/.
Taylor, Mark. *The Vietnam War in History, Literature and Film.* Tuscaloosa: University of Alabama Press, 2003.
Thorne, Kate Ruland. *Upon this Rock: Marguerite Brunswig Staude and Her Sedona Chapel.* Phoenix, AZ: Amor Deus, 2016.
"A Timeless Message of Dignity." [Offprint.] *DAV.* (June 1985). N.p. WWC.

Trout, Steven. "Forgotten Reminders: Kansas World War I Memorials." *Kansas History* 29 (Autumn 2006): 214.
———. *On the Battlefield of Memory: The First World War and American Remembrance, 1919–1941*. Tuscaloosa: University of Alabama Press, 2010.
Turnbull, Tom. "Response to 'Militarizing Angel Fire' by Thomas Brinson." *In the Mind Field*, August 1, 2011. Accessed June 12, 2012. URL no longer exists.
Turner, Fred. *Echoes of Combat: Trauma, Memory, and the Vietnam War*. Minneapolis: University of Minnesota Press, 2001.
"Veterans find unique way to raise funds for Angel Fire Memorial" [Main title missing from clipping]. *Santa Fe Journal*, April 4, 2002, n.p. *DWVF*.
Vietnam Veterans Against the War. *The Winter Soldier Investigation: An Inquiry into American War Crimes*. Boston: Beacon Press, 1972.
Westphall, David. "The Battle of Glorieta Pass: Its Importance in the Civil War." *New Mexico Historical Review* (April 1969): 137–154.
Westphall, Victor. *David's Story: A Casualty of Vietnam*. Springer, NM: Center for the Advancement of Human Dignity, 1981.
———. *The People's Revolution for Peace*. Angel Fire, NM: Published by the author, 1984.
——— [David White, pseud.]. *Trial by Combat*. [Springer, NM]: Center for the Advancement of Human Dignity, 1978.
———. *Vietnam: The Hinge of Destiny*. Springer, NM: Vietnam Veterans Peace and Brotherhood Chapel, 1972.
———. *What Are They Doing to My World?* New York: Cornwall Books, 1981.
Westphall, Walter. "A Son's Thoughts on His Father's Legacy." [Clipping.] *Sangre de Cristo Chronicle*, n.d., n.p. *DWVF*.
———. "The Vietnam Veterans Memorial at Angel Fire." In *The Vietnam War in Popular Culture*, vol. 2, *After the War*, edited by Ron Milam, 325–343. Santa Barbara, CA: Praeger, 2017.
Winter, Jay. *War Beyond Words: Languages of Remembrance from the Great War to the Present*. Cambridge: Cambridge University Press, 2017.
"Where Eagles Soar . . . A Vietnam Reunion." *DAV* (July 1986). 14–18. *WWC*.
Young, Marilyn B. *The Vietnam Wars, 1945–1990*. New York: Harper Perennial, 1991.

Index

Numbers in italics represent pages with illustrations.

Air Force Academy Cadet Chapel, 97, 98
American Veterans (AmVets), fundraising for Angel Fire Memorial, 182
Angel Fire Memorial
   architect for, 4
   atmosphere of sadness at, 196
   chapel as original structure at, 2
   characteristics vs. Wall in DC, 9–11
   ghosts at, 197–198
   inhospitable natural environment of, 101, 110–111
   as memorial complex, 9, 190
   name changes, 175, 182
   and ongoing debate on Vietnam War, 145–146
   as only national memorial to Vietnam War before Wall in DC, 2
   remoteness of, as obstacle to securing government funding, 159
   as "renegade" memorial, 10
   road from Taos to, 1
   spiritual energy at, 148, 150–152
   as still iconoclastic, 194–195
   three types of memorialization in, 149–150, 153
   transfers of ownership, 12
   as vernacular remembrance, 10, 159–160
   visitors center, gift shop and media room, 192
   wildlife problems at, 101
   See also chapel at Angel Fire Memorial; memorials and artifacts at Angel Fire Memorial; symbolism of Angel Fire Memorial

Appy, Christian, 121
Army of Republic of Vietnam (ARVN) soldiers, on commemorative bricks at Angel Fire Memorial, 195, *196*

Baca, Fidel L., 36–38, 51
Baker, Howard, 165
Battle of New Orleans, commemoration of, 163–164
Berry, Jan, 208–209n29
Biesecker, Barbara, 151
Bilbrey, David, 83
Blake, Henry W., 49, 50
Bodnar, John, 10, 31, 159
Body Shop: Recuperating from Vietnam (Browne), 147
Boyd, Roger, 83–84
Brinkley, Douglas, 124, 129, 130, 131
Brown, Jim, 15, 58, 59, 202n7
Browne, Corinne, 147. *See also Casualty: A Memoir of Love & War*
building of chapel
   completion of outer shell, 109
   cost, actual, 99–100, 124–125
   cost estimates, 99
   delays and disasters in, 96, 100–103
   groundbreaking, 95
   harsh weather and, 101–102, 103
   hiring of second contractor for, 117
   rapid start to, 100
   Victor Westphall's anger at contractor, 101–102, 103
   Victor Westphall's decision to proceed on faith, 112
   Westphall family's labor on, 100–101, 116–117, 129

building of chapel, *continued*
  work remaining after construction of shell, 110, 117–118, 125, 129, 141
  See also funding of Angel Fire Memorial
Burns, Ken, 145

Calley, William, 121
Cambodia, attacks on, during Vietnam War, 120
Caputo, Philip, 31, 51, 82
Carter, Jimmy, 162
Casey, Edward S., 148–149
Casualty: A Memoir of Love & War (Browne), 147–148
  on chapel sound track, 159–160
  metaphors to describe chapel, 2, 148
  Westphall family's views on, 148
Chalmette battlefield park, 163–164
"Chapel, A Father's Memorial Honors More than Vietnam Dead" (Emerson), 140–143
  on chapel's honoring of both US and North Vietnamese dead, 141–143
  on chapel sound track, 159–160
  on vulgarity of chapel visitors, 141
chapel at Angel Fire Memorial
  commemoration ceremony of 1972, 137, 211n5
  comparisons evoked by, 2
  contribution of location to meaning of, 151
  dedication of, 107, 117–118, 129–132
  distinctiveness among memorials, 153
  eerie atmosphere of, 13
  eternal flame, 96, 110, 125, 141
  as expression of grief, 13–14
  as form of raw remembrance, 11
  graves of Victor and Jeanne Westphall at, 93, 184–185
  inscriptions of David's writing in, 13–14, 96–97, 149–150
    Victor Westphall's overestimate of profundity of, 127–128
  as institution with its own rituals and ceremonies, 133
  interior of, 141, *142*, *169*
  nonprofit corporation established for, 100
  and number 13 in chapel design, 141
  open door policy, 133, 183–184
  original name of, 2, 95
  as original structure at site, 2
  origin of idea for, 7, 93–95
  photographs displayed in
    of David, 113, *114*
    DAV's removal of, 175, 177
    of other soldiers, Victor Westphall's inspiration for, 113–115
  as place for Victor Westphall to teach, 94
  stucco exterior, symbolism of, 148, 151–152
  as unique memorial, 95–96
  vandalism at, 133, 183–184
  Victor Westphall as part of experience at, 133
  Westphalls' motives for building, 4, 12
  See also building of chapel; design of chapel; peace message of chapel; symbolism of chapel
chapel, images of
  interior, in late 1970–early 1980s, *142*
  in Nov. 1970, *126*
  in Parade magazine, 167, *168*, *169*
  photograph of David displayed in, 113, *114*
  view of, at dawn, *197*
  view of, from northeast, *7*
  view of, from southeast, *3*
  west wall, *11*
chapel newsletter
  on DAV takeover, 173–174
  first issue of, 124–127
  on legislation to gain federal funding, 147, 165
  on memorialization of veterans' sacrifices, 147
  on *Parade* article, response to, 171
  Victor Westphall's work on, 124–127
  on VVMF funding, 172
  Walter Westphall's work on, 147, 157, 165, 166, 171, 172, 173

Chapel of the Holy Cross (Sedona, Arizona), 97–98
"The Chapel Stucco and Aboriginal Tradition: A Sacred Element" (Victor Westphall), 148, 150–152
commemoration, history's pushback against, 189
Cooper, William J., 91
Currin, Tony, 162

d'Aulaire, Ingri and Edgar Parin. See *Wings for Per*
DAV. *See* Disabled American Veterans
David's Story (Victor Westphall)
  on building of chapel, 115
  on David's depression, 43
  on David's junior-high athletics, 39
  on David's support for Vietnam War, 6
David Westphall Veterans Foundation (DWVF)
  establishment of, 100
  fundraising ideas for, 182
  and Memorial financial problems, 181–182
  as original sole owner of chapel, 100
  and peace-oriented message of Memorial, 195–196
  return of Memorial control to, 178, 179, 181
  statement of purpose, 100
  transfer of Memorial to New Mexico State Parks system, 182, 183
  veterans on board of, 135
  work with New Mexico to manage Memorial, 183–184
Davis, Clyde, 36
dead and wounded, notifying families of
  marines' procedure for, 87–88
  notification of David's parents, 88–90
  See also Morenci, Arizona, marines from
Dear America: Letters Home from Vietnam (documentary), showing in Angel Fire media room, 192, 193–194
Deptula, E. A., 70

design of chapel, 96–99
  architect's statement on, 98–99
  architectural precedents for, 97–98
  blending with environment, 151
  criticisms of, 98–99, 109
  New Mexico's avant-garde tradition and, 151
  Victor Westphall's instructions for, 96
Dewey Canyon III, Operation, 122–124
Dickerson, Dick, 135, 185
Disabled American Veterans (DAV)
  financial support of Memorial, 170, 174
  reasons for interest in Memorial, 170–171
Disabled American Veterans' takeover of Memorial, 5, 108, 175
  agreement with Westphalls, 175
  changes to chapel, 160, 175–176
  and complaints about changes, 176, 177, 214n74
  date of, as thirteen years after David's death, 174
  friction with Westphalls over, 175–176
  introduction of Veterans Day and Memorial Day celebrations, 178–179
  on-site apartment build for Victor Westphall, 108, 175
  purchase of land surrounding chapel, 175, 178
  renaming of, 175
  restoration of original features after complaints, 177
  sale of Memorial to David Westphall Veterans Foundation, 178, 179
  and Victor Westphall as perpetual director, 175
    friction with DAV, 175–176
    marginalization of, 176–177
    Victor's lawsuit to restore contractual status, 177–178
  visitors center construction, 174, 175, 178
  visit to Angel Fire Memorial prior to, 173–174

228 Index

Domenici, Peter, 8-9, 160-163, 165, 172
Dunaway, Finis, 210n64
DWVF. *See* David Westphall Veterans Foundation

Emerson, Gloria, 139-140. *See also* "Chapel, A Father's Memorial Honors More than Vietnam Dead"
environmentalism
  in 1960s and 1970s, 139, 210n64
  Victor Westphall on, 139
Environmental Protection Agency (EPA), establishment of, 139
Every Day Is Extra (Kerry), 131, 209n39

Freedom Pure Water, plan to market, 182
Fuentes, Irene de la Rosa, 7, 49, 51, 52, 53
funding of Angel Fire Memorial, 110-113
  David's insurance and, 5, 100, 110
  Disabled American Veterans and, 5
  financial strain on Westphall family, 5, 100, 110
  and maintenance costs in harsh environment, 110-111
  media coverage and, 117
  veterans' donations, 5
  Westphalls' hope for grants and donations, as mostly unrealized, 111-112
  See also government funding, efforts to obtain; government, obstacles to

German, Kate, 191-192
Goss, Jim, 186
government funding, efforts to obtain, 4, 5, 155, 157
  bills filed in Congress on, 160-161, 165-166
  help from New Mexico's congressional delegations, 160-161, 162, 165, 172
  and Memorial as de facto national memorial, 155, 158
  overshadowing by DC Veterans Memorial plans, 165-166
  rejection by Park Service advisory board, 161-162
  Walter's efforts to refute Park Service's arguments, 162-164
  Walter's leadership role in, 155-156
  and Westphalls' reluctance to relinquish control, 160
government funding, obstacles to
  controversial nature of Vietnam War as, 112, 164-165
  lack of precedents for national war memorial as, 158
  Memorial's lack of national significance as, 162, 163-164
  regional flavor of chapel as, 159, 164
  religious overtones of chapel as, 162-163
  remote location as, 159, 164
  unwillingness to fund war memorials outside DC as, 162, 163
  vernacular style of Memorial as, 159-160, 164

Hackett, Hugh, 39-40, 41, 42
Hagopian, Patrick, 128, 194, 215-216n26
Halberstam, David, 210n74
Harris, Robert E., 66, 80, 82-83, 84
Hart, Gary, 165
Hasford, Chuck, 179, 185
Haukebo, Joe, 189, 190
Hedges, Chris, 13
helicopter at Angel Fire Memorial, *191*
  history of, 191-192
  and meaning of site, 193, 195
  in 2018 documentary, 145
Ho Chi Minh, Victor Westphall's letter requesting photos from, 12-13, 143-144
  Ho's likely response to, 144
  Memorial board's debate on mentioning in 2018 documentary, 145-146
Howe, Chuck, 184

Johnston, Joe, 82–83
Joyner, Dennis A., 177, 178

Kent State University, antiwar protesters shot at, 120, 208n8
Kerry, John
  at dedication of Angel Fire Memorial, 4, 129–132
  FBI file on, 132
  media appearances after DC protests, 129, 209n39
  memoir by, 131
  protests against Vietnam War, 123–124
  See also *Every Day Is Extra* (Kerry)
Kidwell, Deborah, 159, 165, 172, 176
King, Martin Luther, Jr., 137
Kirkland, Charles, 84
Kissinger, Henry, 119

Laos, US attacks on, during Vietnam War, 120
Lehrack, Otto J., 55, 58
Lembcke, Jerry, 119
Lennon, John, 140
Levy, Marv, 42
Lin, Maya, 9, 95, 180
Longley, Kyle, 85, 86, 87–88
Lujan, Manuel, Jr., 160–161
Luna, Ted
  architect's statement on chapel design, 98–99
  at chapel dedication, 130
  design of chapel, 4, 96–99

marines
  notifying parents of David's death, 88–90
  procedure for notifying families of dead and wounded, 87–88
  See also Morenci, Arizona, marines from; Westphall, David, in marines, first tour; Westphall, David, in marines, second tour
Martin, Padre, 106–107
May Day Tribe, 121

Mayo, James M., 196
McKinney, Tom, 60
McLean, Jack, 55, 59
McNamara Line (the Trace), 58, 68–69, 80, 85
McTiernan, Matthew G., 80
media
  coverage of Angel Fire Memorial, 117, 131, 140–143, 154
  coverage of antiwar protesters, 123, 124
  See also "One Man's Shrine to All Who Fell in Vietnam" (Satchell)
memorials and artifacts at Angel Fire Memorial, 2, 190–194
  and changes over time in meaning of site, 12, 14, 129–194
  commemorative bricks, 2, 13, 192
    inclusion of ARVN soldiers on, 195, 196
  conflicting messages of, 14, 190
  Dear America documentary shown in media room, 192, 193–194, 215n24
  Dear Mom and Dad statue (Scott), 192, 193, *193*
  early memorials, 140–141
  gardens, 191, *191*
  Huey helicopter, 145, *191*, 191–192, 193, 195
memorials to Vietnam War dead
  avoidance of larger issues of War in, 194, 215–216n26
  spread of, in 1980s–90s, 194
memorials to war dead, as temples to god of war, 13
Mendoza, Pat, 189, 190
Mexico, David's romance with schoolteacher in, 7, 49, 51, 52, 53
Middleton, Terry, 72
Milam, Ron
  effect of Victor Westphall on, 135–137
  message on Victor Westphall's tombstone, 185
  Not a Gentleman's War by, 55, 136–137
Montoya, Joseph M., 161

monuments
  contribution of location to meaning of, 150–151
  moving of, 150, 211n6
  official vs. vernacular, 159
Morenci, Arizona, marines from
  deaths, 1966–1969, 85–86
  marines' reasons for enlisting, 85
  and Morenci as site of Vietnam War memory, 86
  notification of families of dead, 87–88
music at chapel
  removal by DAV, 160, 175
  sound system for, 116–117, 141, 160
  type of music, 141, 148, 160

National Korean War Veterans Memorial, 158
National Mall, DC
  and contribution of location to meaning of memorials, 150–151
  Vietnam War memorial as first war memorial on, 158
  World War I memorial, plans for, 212–213n32
National Park Service
  rejection of recognition for Angel Fire Memorial, 161–162
  Walter Westphall's effort to refute rejection by, 162–164
National Vietnam Memorial, Washington, DC. *See* Vietnam War Veterans Memorial, Washington, DC (the Wall)
National World War II Memorial, 13, 151, 158
Nauman, Robert Allen, 98
Netsch, Walther, 98
New Mexico
  history of human habitation in Albuquerque region, 35
  postwar growth in Albuquerque, 34–35
  Westphall family move to, 34
New Mexico Department of Veterans Service, takeover of Memorial, 184

New Mexico State Parks (NMSP) system
  acquisition of Angel Fire Memorial, 182–183, *183*
  See also Vietnam Veterans Memorial State Park
New Mexico Sun Trails magazine, article on Westphall family home, 15–18, *16*, *17*
New York Times article on Memorial. *See* "Chapel, A Father's Memorial Honors More than Vietnam Dead" (Emerson)
Nixon, Richard M.
  antiwar protests and, 121
  and EPA, 139
  letter to Victor Westphall, 132–133
  and Vietnam War, 119–120, 127
North Vietnamese
  far left's embrace of, 143, 210n74
  honoring of war dead by, 144
  as unpredictable, intelligent and ruthless, 55
North Vietnamese Army (NVA), fighting near DMZ, 56
North Vietnamese dead, Victor Westphall's plan for chapel tribute to, 12–13, 141–144
  controversy created by, 155, 169–170, 171–173
  Westphalls' failure to grasp importance of, 173
Not a Gentleman's War (Milam), 55, 136–137

"One Man's Shrine to All Who Fell in Vietnam" (Satchell), 154–155, 166–170
  attention garnered by, 171
  exclusive focus on Victor Westphall, 166–167
  negative reactions sparked by chapel's honoring of North Vietnamese dead, 155, 169–170, 171–173, 179
  photographs of Victor Westphall and chapel in, 167–169, *168*, *169*
  on Westphall's financial problems, 167

Ono, Yoko, 140
opening of Angel Fire Memorial, Kerry speech at, 4
Order of the Magi, 94
Ortiz, Louis, 117

Paquet, Basil T., 208-209n29
Parade magazine article on Memorial. *See* "One Man's Shrine to All Who Fell in Vietnam" (Satchell)
Patterson, Harry, 184
peace message of chapel, 4, 10, 12-13
  disappearance after Westphalls' sale, 179-180, 194, 214-215n82
  as minimal component of Luna's architectural design, 99
  as unfulfilled yearning, 197-198
  as unrealistic, 197
  and Victor Westphall's plan for tribute to North Vietnamese dead, 12-13, 141-144
    controversy created by, 155, 169-170, 171-173
    Westphalls' failure to grasp importance of, 173
Peeler, Stan, 173-174
Pentagon Papers, 121, 137
The People's Revolution for Peace (Victor Westphall), 139
Potter, H. W., 117
Prados, John, 121
"The Prophets and Their Times" (David Westphall)
  passage from, on chapel wall, 96-97
  passage read at David's funeral, 91-92
public opinion on Angel Fire Memorial, 153-155
  Victor Westphall's cataloging of, 153, 154

race, David's views on, 44, 45
Reising, Albert, 143
Richardson, Bill, 182
Richardson, Frank, 135, 185
Rogers, William P., 144
Rose, Steven L., 162-163

Rottmann, Larry
  article on Angel Fire Memorial dedication, 130, 131
  friendship with Kerry, 129
  message on Victor Westphall's tombstone, 185
  poems in *Winning Hearts and Minds*, 209n29
  as VVAW member, 129

Sands of Iwo Jima (film), 31
Satchell, Michael, 167. *See also* "One Man's Shrine to All Who Fell in Vietnam"
Schmitt, Harrison H., 172
Schooler, Gerry, 186, 187
Scruggs, Jan, 158, 166, 172-173, 182
Spry, Mary, 20
Stars and Stripes article on Angel Fire Memorial, 154
symbolism of Angel Fire Memorial
  changes over time in, 12, 14, 129-194
  and David Westphall as Christ figure, 128
  and individual grief transformed into larger meaning, 128-129
symbolism of chapel
  mixture of grief and hope in, 10
  original mixed message of honoring veterans and fierce opposition to War, 13
  stucco exterior and, 148, 151-152
  three messages of, 4, 12-13, 95
  See also peace message of chapel

Tafoya, Christy, 183
Taos region, and avant-garde art and literature, 152
Tonning, Lanny, 134-135, 146, 185
the Trace. *See* McNamara Line
Trial by Combat (Victor Westphall), 212n23

"The Ultimate Curse" (David Westphall)
  in father's speech at 1972 commemoration, 211n5
  inscription on chapel wall, 96

Val Verde Ranch property
    David's visits to, 52, 53
    described, 51
    Jeanne Westphall's departure from, 106–107
    Padre's request to build chapel on future sire of Angel Fire Memorial, 106–107
    parallels to *Wings for Per* story, significance for Westphall family, 30, 94–95, 106, 151
    sale of, to fund memorial, 110
    as site of Memorial, 30
    Victor's improvements to, 88
    Victor Westphall's plans to develop, 51, 110
    Westphall family's move to, 51
Vedeler, Georg, 99–100, 102–103, 117
veterans of Vietnam War
    appeal of Angel Fire Memorial for, 4
    opinions on Angel Fire Memorial, 153–155
    poor treatment upon return, 104, 197
    Victor Westphall's effect on, 5, 19, 133–137
Vietnam
    recovery from Vietnam War, 186
    Victor and Walter Westphall's visit to site of David's death, 185–190, 188
Vietnamese Americans, delegations at Angel Fire Memorial, 195, 216n29
Vietnam: The Hinge of Destiny (Victor Westphall)
    and chapel dedication, 131
    on environmental damage, 139
    on need for national secretary of peace, 154
    original speech, 137–139
    preface, on Westphall's letter to Ho Chi Minh, 143–144
Vietnam Veterans Against the War (VVAW)
    antiwar protests, 121–124
    at dedication of Angel Fire Memorial, 4, 129–132
    FBI file on, 132
    war crimes accusations against US, 121–122, 124
Vietnam Veterans Memorial Fund, Inc. (VVMF)
    lobbying to create DC Vietnam Veterans memorial, 166
    promised help in funding Angel Fire Memorial, 166, 170
    withdrawal of support for Memorial, over plan to commemorate North Vietnamese dead, 171–173, 179
Vietnam Veterans Memorial State Park
    admission fee for, as issue, 183–184
    DWVF work with State Parks system to manage, 183–184
    establishment of veterans cemetery at, 184
    plans for PTSD facility in, 184
    takeover by New Mexico Department of Veterans Service, 184
Vietnam War
    attacks on Cambodia and Laos under Nixon, 120
    challenges of dense jungle, 61, 62
    changes over time in views on, 194
    Con Then, bombardment of, 56, 58
    controversy surrounding, and difficulty of funding memorial, 112, 164–165
    David Westphall's support for, 6, 69, 128
    challenges to, while in Vietnam, 32
    childhood experiences shaping, 28–32
    lessons of World War II and, 31–32
    deaths of Morenci Nine, 85–86
    fall of Saigon, 165
    as first war lost by US, 165
    halts in bombing on North Vietnam, 77
    harsh climate, 55
    increased bombing of North under Nixon, 120

Khe Sanh, siege of, 56, 58
large number of wounded *vs.* earlier
    wars, 170–171
Leatherneck Square, 58, 79, *81*
literary and cinematic treatments of,
    216n26
media's extensive coverage of protests
    against, 123, 124
as mismanaged, 58
Nixon's strategy for, 119–120, 127
patriotic portrayals of World War II
    and, 31
peace negotiations, 77, 119
protests against, 120, 121–124
and PTSD, 72
snakebite injuries and deaths in, 66
spread of memorials to, in 1980s–90s,
    194
Tet Offensive, 67
turn of public opinion against, 121
as US overwhelming firepower vs.
    North Vietnamese stealth, 61
Vietnamization and, 120, 165,
    207–208n2
Vietnam War, David Westphall in
  application for aerial observer position,
      70
  arrival and assignment to 4th Marine
      Regiment, 59–60
  awareness of risk, 59
  on battle at Con Thien, 73
  death of, 4
    damage to parents' marriage from, 5,
        106–108
    destruction of NVA unit responsible
        for, 84–85
    fatal wounds, conflicting reports on,
        84, 90
    father and brother's visit to site of,
        185–190, *188*
    father's psychological damage from,
        5, 6, 90–91
    final fatal battle, 79–85
    fog of war surrounding, 90, 189
    Mother's psychological damage
        from, 91, 104–109
    notification of parents, 88–90
    parents' obsession with, 90–91
    psychological damage to father from,
        5, 6, 90–91
  duty extension, reasons for agreeing to,
      71–72
  excellent fitness reports received by, 70
  final fatal battle, 79–85
  first unit casualties, 63
  and friendly fire incidents, 76
  friendship with Captain Wirsching, 59
  frustrations with leadership, 69
  and "gook" as term, 75–76
  harsh climate, 61–62
  last known photograph of, 78
  letters home, 73–79
    on civilian casualties, 75–76
    discussions of reading in, 75
    final letter, 77–79
    on financial matters, 75
    interest expressed in life at home, 76
    number of, 73
    requests for equipment and supplies,
        73–75
  and media presence, 62
  missions and patrols, 60–65, 67–68,
      70
  near misses by artillery shells, 71
  periods of boredom, 72
  pleasant moments of relaxation, 64
  promotion to First Lieutenant, 70–71
  prospects for advancement at mid-
      point of tour, 77
  replacement of commanding officer,
      66
  respect earned from fellow soldiers, 63,
      64, 72
  on "satisfactions and fascinating
      aspects" of job, 69–70, 71–72
  snakebite, hospitalization from, 65–66,
      75–76
  views on US strategy, 68–69
Vietnam War, Demilitarized Zone (DMZ)
    in
  booby traps as less common in, 56
  danger of areas near, 58–59, 202n7

Vietnam War, Demilitarized Zone (DMZ) in, *continued*
   and McNamara Line (the Trace), 58, 68–69, 80, 85
   military circumstances near, 56–59, 57
   penetration by North Vietnamese, 58
   regular NVA units fighting near, 56
   removal of civilians from area, 56
   US defenses along, 57, 57–58
The Vietnam War (Burns documentary), 145
The Vietnam War in American Memory (Hagopian), 215–216n26
Vietnam War Veterans Memorial, Washington, DC (the Wall)
   attention attracted by, 9
   characteristics vs. Angel Fire Memorial, 9–11
   and contribution of location to meaning of memorials, 151
   design of, 9
   as first war memorial on National Mall, 158
   influence on other memorial designs, 9, 194
   overshadowing of Angel Fire Memorial, 14, 165–166, 180
visitors to Angel Fire Memorial
   decline of, after building of Wall memorial in DC, 14
   decline of, by late 1970s, 8
   effect of Victor Westphall on, 5, 19, 133–137
   emotional effects on, 2
   media coverage and, 117
   number of, in first decade, 4, 8
VVAW. *See* Vietnam Veterans Against the War

Wall, the. *See* Vietnam War Veterans Memorial, Washington, DC
war memorials and museums, as temples to god of war, 13
Warner, John, 165
water, bottled, plan to market, 182
Wayne, John, 31
Westmoreland, William, 58, 179, 214n81
Westphall, David
   appearance, morbid self-consciousness about, 28, 45, 46, 49
   birth of (1940), 21
   burial of, 92, 92–93
   and father, similar minds of, 70
   final hike with father, 53–54, 95
   funeral of, 91–92
   intellectual interests of, and isolation from peers, 43, 44
   intellectual promise of, 92
   life insurance, 5, 100, 110
   memorial options considered by parents, 93
   and pacifism, father's claim of David's support for, 127, 128
   relationship with father, 6–7, 45
   religious background of, 94
   romance with Mexican schoolteacher, 7, 49, 51, 52, 53
   talent as writer, 44, 92
   and Vietnam War, support for, 6, 69, 128
      challenges to, while in Vietnam, 31–32
      childhood experiences shaping, 28–32
      lessons of World War II and, 31–32
   and West Point, failure to gain entrance to, 41
   and women, difficult relations with, 7
   See also "The Prophets and Their Times"; "The Ultimate Curse"; Vietnam War, David Westphall in
Westphall, David, and athletics, 40
   Father's excessive pressure to excel in, 6–7, 38, 39, 41–42, 45
   junior high school successes, 38–39
   success at Oklahoma Military Academy, 41
   tensions over, at Highland High School, 39–41, 42
   tensions over, at University of New Mexico, 41–42

Westphall, David, childhood and
adolescence
  experiences shaping patriotism of,
    28-32, 51
  foreshadowings of later psychological
    problems, 28
  in New Mexico, 35, 36-38, 37, 105
    death of neighbor child in
      swimming pool, 104
    transfer to Oklahoma Military
      Academy, 40-41
  in Wisconsin, 22, 26-28, 27
  See also Westphall, David, and
    athletics
Westphall, David, in marines, first tour
  enlistment, 42
  isolation from peers, 44
  return to school following, 47
  and strains on marriage, 47
Westphall, David, in marines, second
    tour
  application for Officer Candidate
    School (OCS), 50-51
  career success, 52
  decision to reenlist, 50-51
  Officer Candidate School and Basic
    School, 50, 52
  pre-deployment visit to parents,
    53-54
  reconnaissance training, 52, 59
  unit served in, as same as first-tour
    unit, 60
  See also Vietnam War, David Westphall
    in
Westphall, David, marriage of, 7, 45-48
  divorce, 7, 49
  honeymoon, 47
  nervous breakdown before wedding, 7,
    46
  and strain of military life, 47
  as troubled, 46-49
Westphall, David, personality of, 43-45
  as child, 28
  contradictions in, 44-45
  impatience with incompetence, 69
  leadership ability, 51

Westphall, David, psychological problems
    of, 6-7
  and application to Marine OCS, 50
  childhood incidents foreshadowing, 28
  emergence in high school, 43
  marriage and, 46, 48-49
  relief from, in marines, 72
  treatment for, 49
Westphall, David, at University of
    Montana, 47-48, 48
  application essays, 43-45
  as happy period of his life, 7, 49
  subjects studied at, 7, 43, 48
  success as student, 7, 47-48
Westphall, David, at University of New
    Mexico, 41-42
Westphall, David (son of Walter), 109,
    186, 187
Westphall, Dorothy Wilson (wife of
    Walter), 186, 187
Westphall, Jeanne, 23, 37
  birth of children, 21
  and building of chapel, 4, 7
  burial site at Angel Fire Memorial, 93,
    184-185
  as casualty of Vietnam War, 104-106,
    105
  and chapel clerical work, 125
  collapse of marriage after David's
    death, 5, 106-108
  courtship and marriage, 21
  on David as child, 28
  and David's death
    notification of, 89-90
    obsession with, 90-91
    severe psychological damage from,
      91, 104-109
  David's divorce and, 49
  at David's funeral, 91
  death of, 184
  departure from Val Verde Ranch,
    106-107
  employment in New Mexico, 35-36
  grandchildren, enjoyment of, 109
  grave at Memorial, 93, 184-185
  happiness in Albuquerque, 104

Westphall, Jeanne, *continued*
  later life of, 108–109, 184–185
  and origin of idea for building chapel, 7, 93, 94–95
  personality of, before David's death, 104
  prediction of Tet Offensive, 67
  religious background of, 94
  superstitiousness of, 30
  tuberculosis of, 34
  Victor in military and, 23
  work in family business, 104
Westphall, Kimberly (daughter of Walter), 109, 184–185, 186, *187*
Westphall, Victor, *17*, *22*, *35*, *37*
  and athletics, pressure on David to excel in, 6–7, 38, 39–40, 41–42, 45
  on Browne's *Casualty*, 148
  and building of chapel, 100–102, 103, 117, 129
  burial site at Angel Fire Memorial, 93, 184–185
  career
    as builder in New Mexico, 4–5, 36
    collapse after David's death, 110
    early jobs in Wisconsin, 21, 33
    wealth accumulated in, 4–5, 18, 35–36
  and chapel, as distraction from crippling grief, 100, 106
  and chapel newsletter, 124–127
  on chapel's honoring of both US and North Vietnamese dead, 12–13, 141–144
    controversy created by, 155, 169–170, 171–173
    Westphalls' failure to grasp importance of, 173
  childhood and adolescence, 19–20
  collapse of marriage after David's death, 5, 106–108
  courtship and marriage, 21
  David's divorce and, 49
  at David's funeral, 91
  David's relationship with, 6–7, 45
  death of, 5, 184, 185
  and dedication of chapel
    invitation to Kerry to speak at, 130
    speech at, 130–131
  education, 20, 21, 35–36
  effect on visiting veterans, 5, 19, 133–137, 185
  exchange of soil between David's death site and Angel Fire Memorial, 189
  and fading of peace message at Memorial, 194
  family home designed by, 15–18, *16*, *17*
  final hike with David, 53–54, 95
  grave at Memorial, 93, 184–185
  greeting of all visitors to Memorial, 4, 117, 185
  Jeanne's mental illness and, 106, 107
  Mother's death, 26
  motives for building chapel, 4, 12
  mystical/superstitious bent of, 26, 30, 90–91, 94, 113–114, 189
    and special significance of number "13," 113–115, 141
    and views on spiritual energy at Angel Fire Memorial, 148, 150–152
  nickname of "Doc," 133–134
  and Nixon, letter about chapel from, 132–133
  opposition to Vietnam War, 12
  Parade magazine article on, 154–155, 167–170, *168*, *169*
  as part of chapel experience, 133
  peace scholarship, 8, 156, 179
    motives for pursuing, 140
    separation from Memorial after sale, 179–180, 214–215n82
  personality of, 19–20
  public's comments on Memorial, cataloging and distribution of, 153, 154
  return to work, 156
  sale of Memorial, and loss of control, 179
  as scholar, 6, 94, 137, 145–146, 156

thanks from veterans inscribed on
    headstone of, 185
turnover of some duties to Walter,
    155–156
visions and dreams featuring David,
    90–91, 112–113
on war, 137–138, 139
weightlifting and physical fitness,
    lifelong devotion to, 4–5, 17,
    20–21, 25
and World War I, influence on,
    200n27
See also "The Chapel Stucco and
    Aboriginal Tradition: A Sacred
    Element"; *David's Story*; *The
    People's Revolution for Peace*; *Trial
    by Combat*; *Vietnam: The Hinge of
    Destiny*
Westphall, Victor, and David's death
    and collapse of construction business,
        110
    and collapse of life, 18
    notification of, 88–90
    obsession with, 90–91
    psychological damage from, 5, 6,
        90–91
    visit to site of, 185–190, *188*
Westphall, Victor, and devotion of life
    to Angel Fire Memorial, 18–19,
    107–108, 134
    move to apartment on chapel site, 5,
        108
    move to cabin built on site, 107–108,
        108
    as possible atonement for pressure on
        David, 134
Westphall, Victor, and funding of Angel
    Fire Memorial, 4–5
    determination to proceed on faith,
        112, 113
    financial strain of, 5, 110
    search for outside grants and
        donations, 111–112
Westphall, Victor, pacifism of
    claimed support of David for, 127, 128
    death of David and, 91–92

dormancy before David's death, 34
early indications of, 33, 200n27
fear of nuclear war and, 12, 126, 138–
    139, 150, 212n23
peace scholarship, 8, 156, 179
    motives for pursuing, 140
    separation from Memorial after sale,
        179–180, 214–215n82
    statement on, in first chapel newsletter,
        125–127
as unformed, in early stages of chapel
    design, 99
World War II service and, 33–34, 99,
    125–126
Westphall, Victor, as perpetual director
    of DAV-owned chapel, 175
DAV's marginalization of, 176–177
friction with DAV, 175–176
Victor's lawsuit to restore contractual
    status, 177–178
Westphall, Victor, on Vietnam War,
    137–139
complexity of views, 145–146
as irrational and wasteful, 138–139
and US as arrogant and offensive,
    127
Westphall, Victor, World War II service,
    23–26, *24*, *27*, 32
and ephemeral nature of alliances, 34
as fulfilling experience, 33
and later radical pacifism, 33–34
letters home from, 23
return to family, 32
suffering and death witnessed in,
    25–26, 32, 99, 125–126
Westphall, Walter, *35*, *37*, *187*
Air Force career, 115–116, 156
continuation with, despite David's
    death, 99, 115
on attention garnered by *Parade* article,
    171
birth of, 21–23
on Browne's *Casualty*, 148
and building of chapel, 100, 116–117
and chapel newsletter, writing of, 147,
    157, 165, 166, 171, 172, 173

Westphall, Walter, *continued*
  and damage from father's honoring of North Vietnamese war dead, 171, 179–180
  David's closeness with, 76–77
  at David's funeral, 91
  on David's leadership ability, 51
  and David's letters for Vietnam discussing books, 75
  on David's potential, 92
  on DAV takeover, 173–174
  on early publicity for Memorial, 117
  efforts to reconstruct David's fatal battle, 79
  effort to refute rejection by National Park Service, 162–164
  on father's death, 185
  on father's pacifism, 33, 34
  on father's *People's Revolution for Peace*, 139
  on father's request for photos from Ho Chi Minh, in 2018 documentary, 145
  final trip with David, 52–53
  and government funding, spearheading of effort for, 155–156
  maintenance of peace-oriented message of Memorial, 195
  marriage and children, 186
  marriage plans (1968), 76–77
  on Memorial financial problems, 181
  on mother's later life, 108–109
  on mother's personality before David's death, 104
  notification of David's death, 89
  on Padre proposing chapel at Val Verde, 106–107
  personality of, 156
  on psychological damage of David's death, 104
  religious background of, 94
  search for direction after Air Force, 156
  and Vietnam War
    criticisms of, 99, 116, 156–157
    service in, 4
  visit to site of David's death, 185–190, 188
  and VVMF, disavowal of, 172–173
  work at Federal Home Loan Bank Board, 156, 186
  on work with State Parks system to manage Memorial, 183
  writing talent of, 157
Westphall family
  death of neighbor child in swimming pool, 104
  move to Albuquerque, New Mexico, 34
  move to Moreno Valley, New Mexico, 51
  religious background of, 93–94
Westphall home in Albuquerque (Juan Tabo house)
  construction of, 36
  move to, 36–37
  New Mexico Sun Trails magazine article on, 15–18, *16*, *17*
  property surrounding, 37, 38
Willmarth, Mary Lynne (David's wife)
  divorce, 49
  honeymoon, 47
  marriage, 7, 45–48
  and strain of military life, 47
Wilson, Richard M., 171
Wings for Per (d'Aulaire and d'Aulaire), 28–32, *29*
  as David's favorite childhood book, 28
  David's request for mother to save, 30, 94
  influence on David's patriotism, 30–32
  parallels to Val Verde Ranch property, significance for Westphall family, 30, 94–95, 106, 151
  story of, 28–30
Winning Hearts and Minds: War Poems by Vietnam Veterans (Berry and Paquet), 208–209n29
Winter Soldier Investigation, 122
Wirsching, Rocky
  arrival in Vietnam, 59–60
  career of, 59
  friendship with David Westphall, 59

injury and reassignment to Saigon, 66
missions and patrols, 62
World War I
  influence on Victor Westphall, 200n27
  potential National Mall memorial for, 212–213n32
World War II
  influence of patriotic portrayals on baby boomers, 31, 51
  National Memorial to, 13, 151, 158
  See also Westphall, Victor, World War II service

www.ingramcontent.com/pod-product-compliance
Lightning Source LLC
Chambersburg PA
CBHW050858160426
43194CB00011B/2208